IMAGES
of America

WARRINGTON

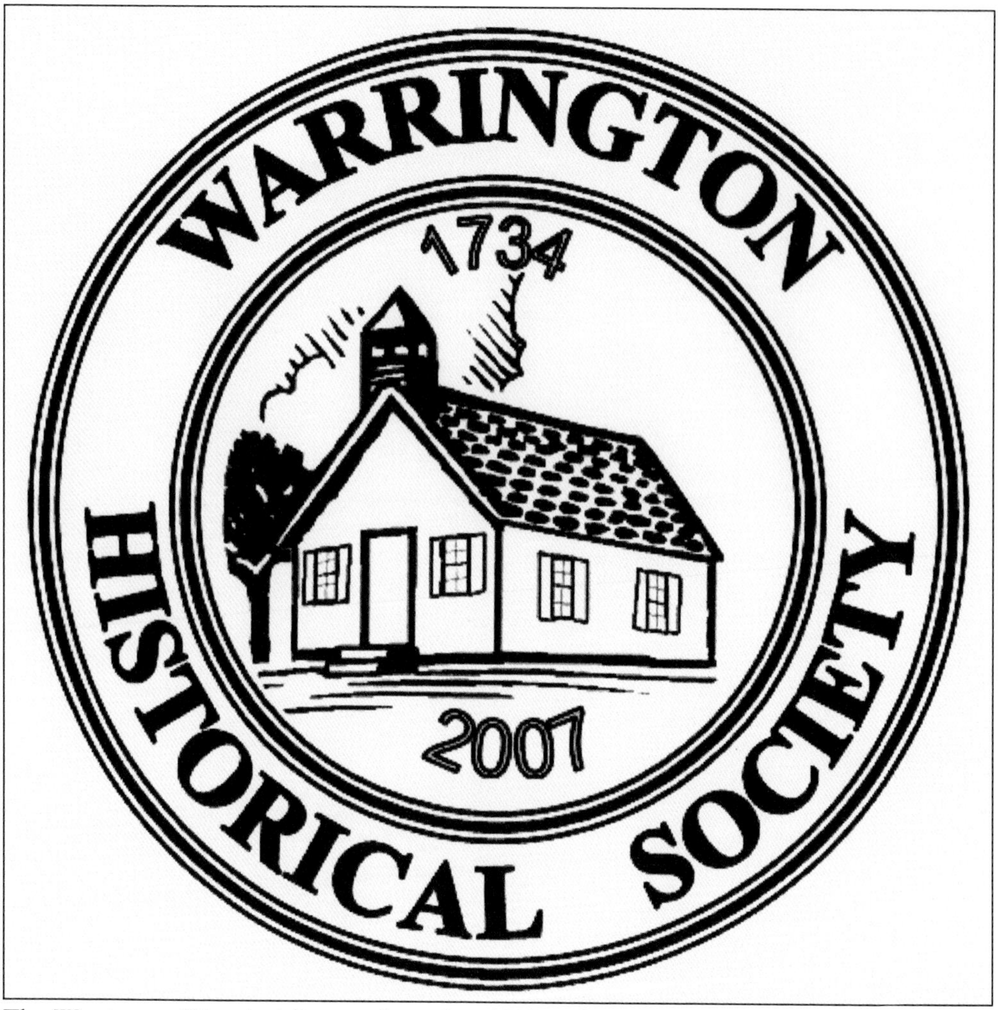

The Warrington Historical Society formed in 2007 and is a 501(C)(3) nonprofit corporation. The seal of the society consists of a rendering of the County Line Schoolhouse located at 10 Folly Road; the year 1734, which represents the founding of the township; and the year 2007, which represents the founding of the society.

On the cover: Warrington Lions Club members pose in the spring of 1942 with their newly erected sign located where the shopping center at 1111 Easton Road is now located. These members are, from left to right, (first row) Erv Mayer, Roland Waterfield, and Bill Lueckel ; (second row) Ernest Clark, Al Breinig, John Wiley, Tom Clark, and Doug Clark; (third row) Pete Crouthamel, Al Clarance, John Waterfield, and Forrest Kline. (Courtesy of the Lueckel family.)

IMAGES
of America

WARRINGTON

Mary Doyle Roth and Kenneth Samen
for the Warrington Historical Society

ARCADIA
PUBLISHING

ISBN 978-0-7385-6292-6

Published by Arcadia Publishing
Charleston SC, Chicago IL, Portsmouth NH, San Francisco CA

Printed in the United States of America

Library of Congress Catalog Card Number: 2008930814

For all general information contact Arcadia Publishing at:
Telephone 843-853-2070
Fax 843-853-0044
E-mail sales@arcadiapublishing.com
For customer service and orders:
Toll-Free 1-888-313-2665

Visit us on the Internet at www.arcadiapublishing.com

Dedicated to Bill Lueckel, whose hobby of photography helped us preserve history, and Dolores Deabler Capone, whose dedication to detail produced a written history to build on.

Contents

ACKNOWLEDGMENTS

On behalf of the Warrington Historical Society, I wish to extend our sincere thanks and appreciation to all the contributors and lenders of photographic and historical memorabilia; without this effort the book would not have been possible. The following are some who went through their attics, opened up their family albums, and entrusted us with their memories of early Warrington: Frank Ace, Jeanne DeLong, Janet Doyle, Betty Feriod, Bill Grun, Bob and Jane Henderson, Ronald and Viola Lewis, Steve and Diane Lueckel, Edna Mae "Mich" Michener, Bob and Sarah Murphy, Laurie Garges Myers, Judy Holbert Paterson, Joe and Marjorie Simons, and Henry and Shirley Strawn. There were many others who helped contribute to this book even if their pictures were not published. Countless stories and memories were also shared with us.

Current and past members of the Warrington Historic Commission are recognized for their participation on this project. Current members include Doris Dillingham, Scott Yates, Jane Henderson, Stuart Cohen, Joe Wright, vice chairman Ken Samen, chairman Mary Doyle Roth, township supervisor liaison Glenn McKay, and secretary Dorothy Smith. Past members whose work we built on include chairman from 1998 to 2004 Tom Mackin, Raymond Bloemker, Jayne Lester, Sarah Murphy, Don Riley, Maryann Scarpill, James Dyer, Susan Bachman, Susan Sowden, Pennsylvania representative Katharine Watson, township liaison Sue Kolodziejski, township supervisor liaison Becky Kiefer, and secretary Vivian Bell.

Special recognition goes to Ken Samen, without whom this book would not have been possible. Ken copied all the images and insured they met the guidelines. His energy and dedication was the driving force that kept us on track to meet our deadlines. His wife, Melissa Samen, also needs to be acknowledged, since she spent a lot of time reviewing and editing our work. I would also like to thank my husband, Ron Roth, for his patience and understanding. Throughout this project our dining room was the collection point for the albums, files, and pictures.

—Mary Doyle Roth
President, Warrington Historical Society

INTRODUCTION

It was during the late Woodland period, starting around AD 1550, when Europeans began to explore and eventually settle in North America. During this time, the area was populated by groups of Native Americans called the Unami ("people down the river") of the Lenni-Lenape tribe ("original people" or "men among men"). Their villages were located along the Delaware River, which the Lenni-Lenape called the Lenapewihittuk ("river of the Lenape"), and along the Neshaminy Creek ("the double drinking place" or "where we drink twice"). One of these villages was located at the western boundary of Warrington Township on the slopes above the Neshaminy Creek, at the meeting of Park Creek and Little Neshaminy Creek. Another was located on the eastern boundary of the township close to Little Neshaminy Creek, where the Palomino Farms Development is today.

In England during the mid-1600s, the British government became indebted to William Penn's father for services rendered and money loaned, about £16,000. Seeking a haven in the New World for persecuted Friends, Penn asked the king to grant him land in the territory between Lord Baltimore's province of Maryland and the Duke of York's province of New York. With the duke's support, Penn's petition was granted. The king signed the Charter of Pennsylvania announcing the grant of 40,000 acres and letters patent on March 4, 1681; it was officially proclaimed on April 2. When it was necessary to name to the country covered by the grant, Penn chose New Wales, but the king objected. Penn then suggested Sylvania, to which the king prefixed the word *Penn*, in honor of William's father, and thus the country was given the name it bears—Pennsylvania, or Penn's Woods. One of the first counties of Pennsylvania was called Bucks County, named after Buckinghamshire (Bucks) in England. Penn and his heirs were constituted absolute proprietary of the country; and they were empowered to establish laws, appoint officers, and do other acts necessary to govern the country. Later the proprietor arrived in Pennsylvania on the ship *Welcome*. *Welcome* sailed from Deal, England, departing on August 31, 1682, and arrived at the mouth of the Delaware River (New Castle) on October 28, 1682. Penn visited Philadelphia, which was just laid out as the capital city, and created the three original counties. While in this country, Penn himself acquired additional land. On June 23, 1683, the chiefs Essepenaike, Swampoes, Okettarickon, and Wessapoak, for themselves and their heirs, conveyed to William Penn and his heirs a portion of their land. The location of the land was "lying between Pennypack and Neshaminy creeks, and backwards of the same, and to run two days journey with a horse up into the country." That same day, chiefs Tamanen (his name appears on the document as Tamanen, although the Native American form of the name was usually spelled Tamanend) and Metamequan released to Penn and his heirs the same territory, omitting the two-day journey. On July 5, 1697, this grant and the "two days journey was confirmed." This land included the future townships of Bensalem, Southampton, Warminster, and Warrington.

Thomas Holmes's (surveyor of Penn) map of Bucks County from the mid-1680s shows that there was a limited amount of landowners in the area, including Charles Jones Jr., Richard Ingelo, Samuel Carpenter, R. Sneed, and R. Vickers; none of these landowners resided on the land they owned. On February 14, 1686, Penn granted 600 acres to Richard Ingelo. Ingelo, son of English Church clergyman Nathaniel Ingelo, was among the passengers on the ship *Welcome*. "600 a. to R'd Ingles of Philad'a, Gent. was laid out within the Welch Tract, patent dated February 14, 1686." This land was located "on the county line below the lower state rd." In 1682, Samuel Carpenter joined Penn in Philadelphia, where in addition to many responsible official duties, he engaged largely in foreign commerce. He was one of the trustees of public schools (established in 1689 by Friends in Philadelphia) and also a member of the provincial assembly. In 1701, Penn appointed him a member of the council of state. He appears to have been constantly involved with public affairs, either as member of the general assembly, council of state, or treasurer of the province. Much of the property controlled by Carpenter was transferred to William Fishbourne, who was married to Carpenter's daughter Hannah. Later the will of Penn gave 10,000 acres in the county to his grandson William Penn Jr., of which 1,417 acres lay in Warrington. On August 25, 1728, the whole of the 10,000 acres was conveyed to William Allen. Allen, a leading merchant of Philadelphia, played an important part in the settlement of Bucks County and was one of its largest landowners. Allen was one of the three gentlemen of the province who kept his own carriage. His was a Landau, drawn by four black horses and driven by a driver imported from England.

Warrington Township, located in Bucks County, was officially established in October 1734. While information is scarce and the exact day has not been found, the anniversary is celebrated on October 7. The court record stated, "Ordered that the land above and adjoining Warminster shall be a township and shall be called Warrington." It was named after a town in Lancashire, England. In the early years, there seemed to be no definitive borders, and the population was not recorded. Information regarding the formation of Warrington Township is scarce as well. Per W. W. H. Davis, "Our knowledge of the organization of the township is very limited, and the little that we know not very satisfactory. The records of our courts are almost silent on the subject. It is interesting to know the preliminary steps taken by a new community toward municipal government, and the trials they encounter before their wish is gratified. But in the case of Warrington we know nothing of the movement of her citizens to be clothed with township duties and responsibilities." At the October 7, 1734, session, the following was entered of record, "Ordered that the land above and adjoining to Warminster Township shall be a township, and shall be called Warrington." J. D. Battles states that, "In 1734 Warrington was laid out without the usual novitiate experience." The original borders of the township contained the area between just above Lower State Road, Bristol Road, Valley Road, and County Line Road and consisted of 5,397 acres or 8.43 square miles. On February 8, 1850, the northwest boundary was extended from Lower State Road to Upper State Road, adding 1,500 acres or 2.34 square miles to the township. On September 11, 1850, the boundary was expanded again. As a result, the Warrington Township line left Bristol Road and followed Turk Road to the north, forming an elbow up into Doylestown ending at the Neshaminy Creek. On September 20, 1852, some of this newly acquired land was reevaluated for the township of Doylestown to govern. With these additions and deletions, the boundaries of the township were as they are today. Warrington Township is rectangular in shape except for an elbow of land north of Bristol Road; this section cuts into Doylestown Township. The current size of the township is 8,812.8 acres or 13.77 square miles.

Warrington Township started to have supervisors' meetings in 1906. The original three supervisors were John T. Detweiler, Benjamin Hough, and Levi M. Garner. At first, they met solely in members' homes, and later at Worthington's general store. From 1914 through 1941, the supervisors held the township meetings at the Neshaminy Inn. Between 1944 and 1958, meetings were held at the old firehouse on Maple Avenue. In 1958, the supervisors' meetings were held in the old township building located at the old Mill Creek School on Pickertown Road. Since 1993, township meetings have been held at the new township building located on Easton Road. Warrington was one of the first townships in the area to establish the position of a township manager. On December 28, 1954, Leonard H. Point was appointed to the position by the township supervisors. He assumed his duties on January 3, 1955. An official township office was set up in the basement of Point's home on Bristol Road.

Early on there was little use for roads, as inhabitants lived along rivers and creeks and traveled by water. With the English came the need for land transportation. Penn projected highways on northwest lines parallel to each other, running back from the Delaware River into the interior and then intersected by other roads as close to right angles as circumstances would permit. Street, Bristol, and County Line Roads were all part of this plan. His strategy was interfered with when the early settlers enclosed their lands with fences before the roads could be laid out. Road and bridge building was primarily a local affair well into the 20th century, with petitioning by residents for construction and the county governments playing the dominant role. Street Road's (Route 132) formation can be traced to the year 1696. Bristol Road was laid between 1722 and 1752. Pickertown Road was opened from Bristol Road prior to 1722. Easton Road (Route 611, previously known as Governors Road/Dyer's Mill Road/Doylestown-Willow Grove Turnpike) began its formation in 1723. County Line Road was opened by piecemeal between 1722 and 1752. From the Easton Road to four miles above, it was opened in 1722, apparently to accommodate Gov. William Keith. The opening was objected to because it was not needed, as there was a road on either side about a mile distant. Bradford Avenue was opened in 1737. At the time, it was named Barefoot Alley, after a Native American family who lived in the grove of trees west of the area at the end of Tohickon Lane, where it meets Bradford Avenue. Lower State Road was created in 1756. Valley Road (Muddy Lane) was created in 1785, opened by the Long family so their mill would have a means to transport goods. Limekiln Pike, Route 152 (Whitehall Pike, Old Turnpike Road, Butler Pike) was created in 1785 and redirected to its current route in 1855. Upper State Road was created in 1830. As roads formed, so did the villages of Warrington, Neshaminy, Tradesville, and Eureka. The borders of the villages were not well defined but were centered on crossroads. Each of the villages had its own post office and school. For the purpose of this book, properties that had not been defined in the past with a particular village have been listed within the nearest village center.

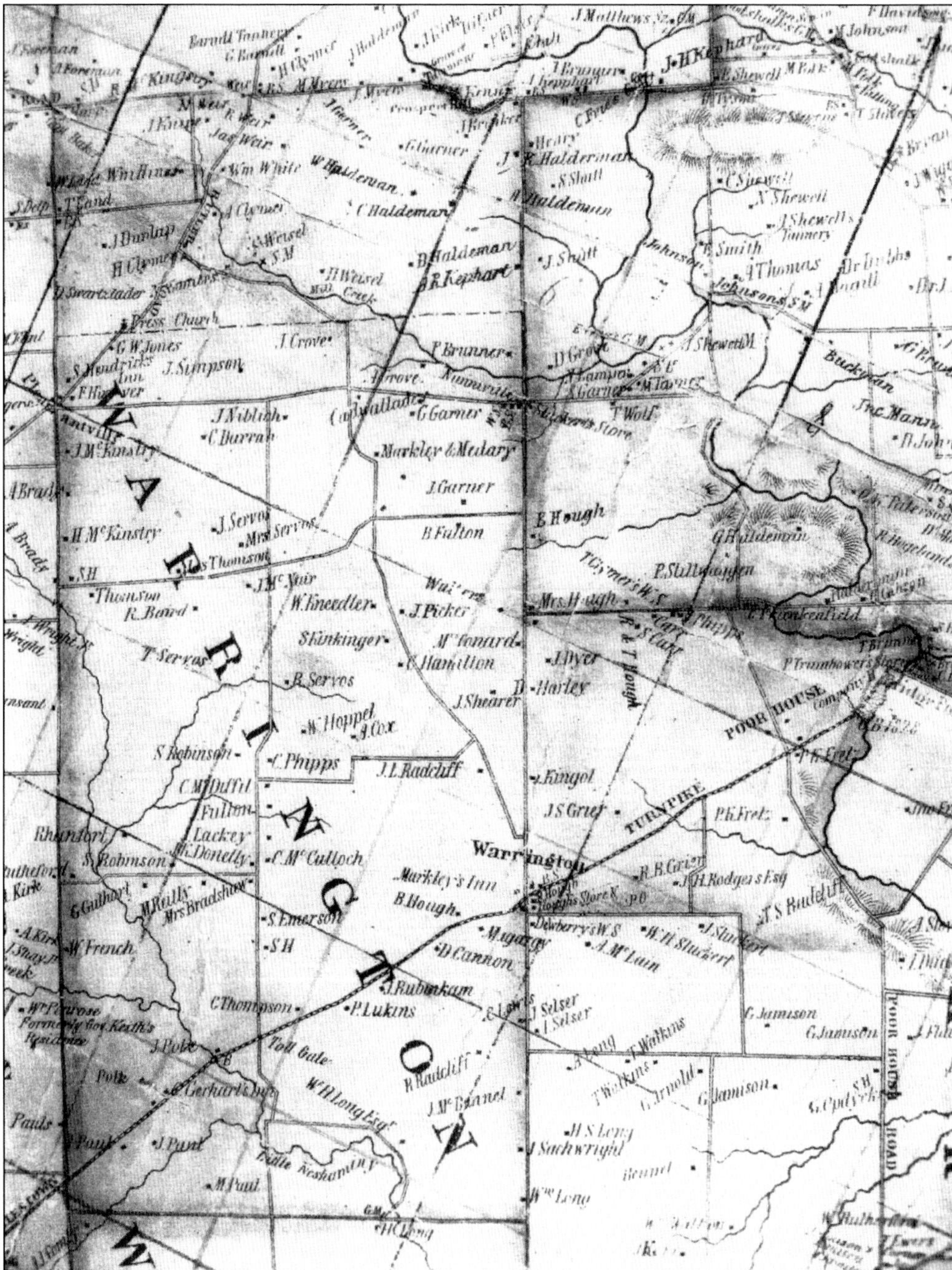

Shown here is a map of Warrington Township from 1850, produced by W. E. Morris, which shows the township at its largest size. This map illustrates the township borders after the February and September 1850 expansions had taken place and prior to the September 1852 reevaluation (which gave some of the September 1850 added land to Doylestown to govern).

One

Village of Warrington

Warrington Village is located at the intersection of Bristol and Easton Roads. Prior to being called Warrington, the area was known as Newville, from as early as 1805 until as late as 1839, when the Warrington Post Office opened. In the 1820s, Francis Gurney Lukens was the hotel proprietor; thus the area was named Lukens Corner. The names Lukens Corner and Newville were probably used interchangeably for many years. In the early 1830s, Newville was described as a small village on the line of Warrington and Warwick Townships. There was a store, a tavern, and six or eight houses. Later the area would be known as Warringtonville. The *ville* was dropped from the name of the village, and the area became known as Warrington when Warrington Square was renamed Neshaminy in 1864 with the opening of its own post office.

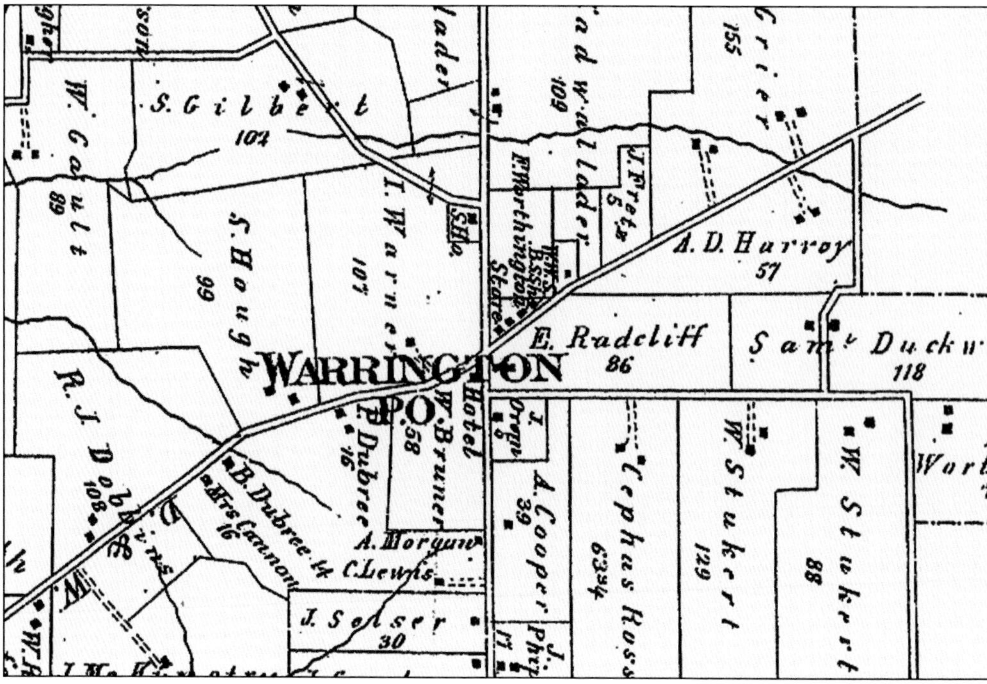

Pictured here is a village of Warrington map from the 1876 atlas of Bucks County by J. D. Scott.

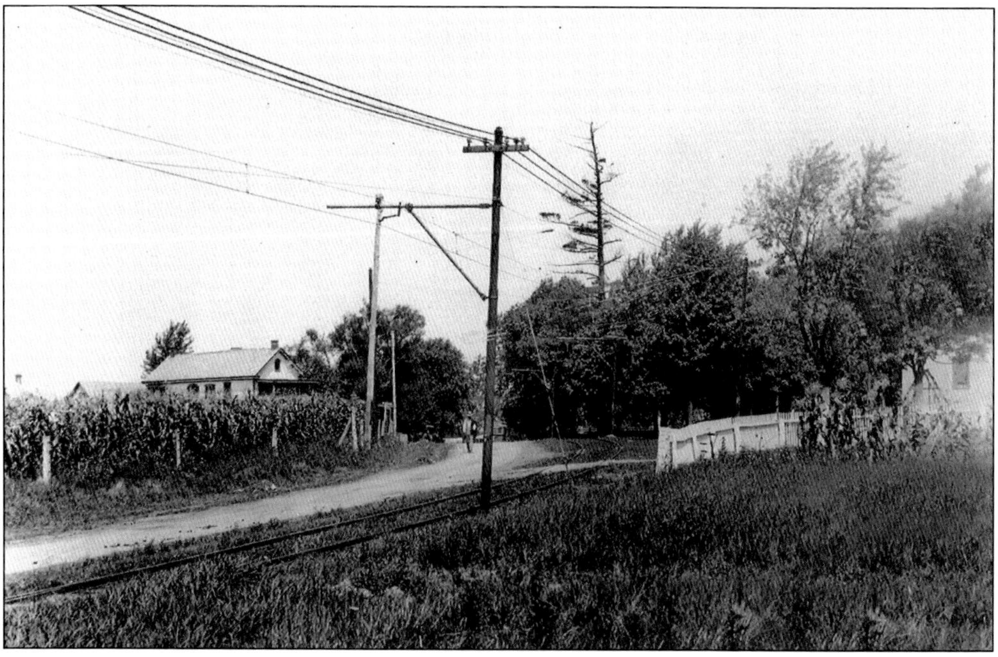

Above is a 1909 view of the Easton and Bristol Roads intersection looking north toward Doylestown. From left to right are the general store, trolley tracks, and a tall white pine in front of the Barclay House. Barely viewable on the right is the Warrington Inn. Even longtime residents would have a hard time recognizing this due to the busy intersection it became over time.

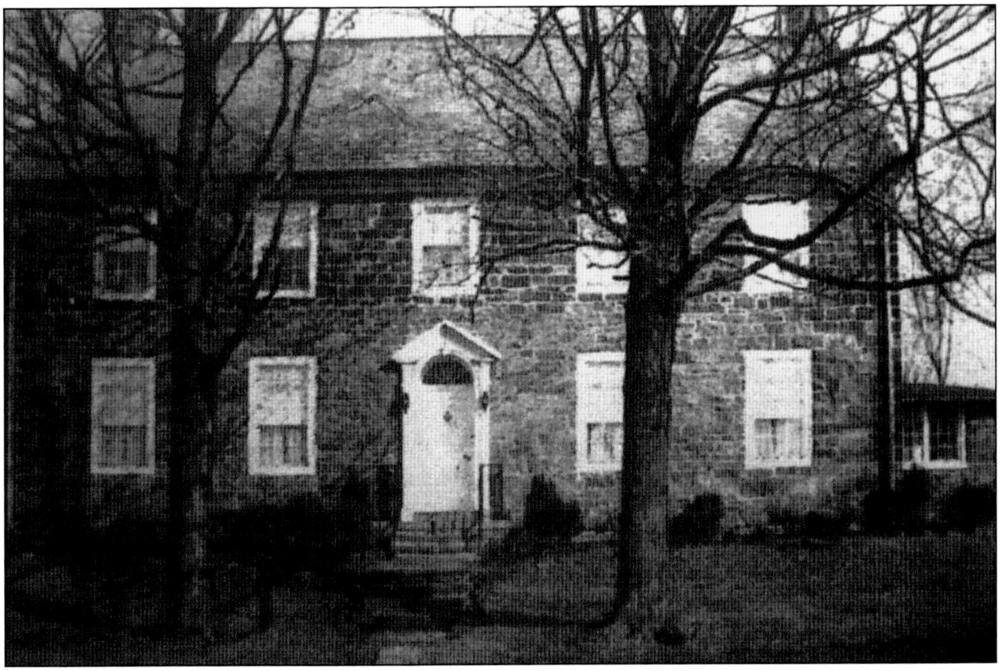

In 1790, John Barclay bought property located at the corner of Easton and Bristol Roads from Gideon and Elizabeth Pryor. There was a tall white pine tree on the lawn of the Barclay House. It was nearly three times as tall as the mansion and a conspicuous landmark. The tree was damaged by lighting in 1910 and was taken down five years later. Benjamin Hough bought the house in 1833.

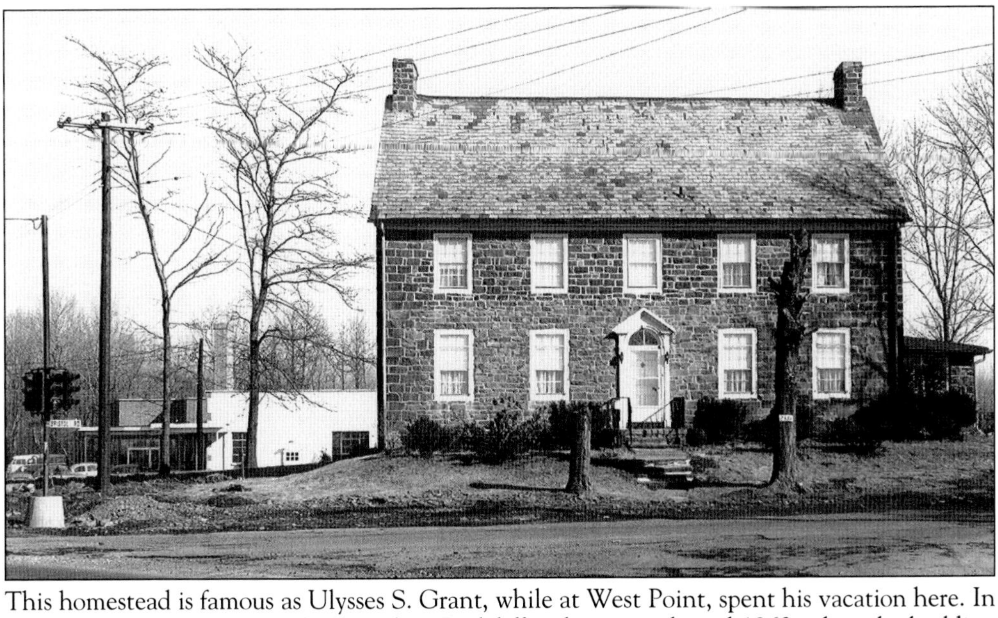

This homestead is famous as Ulysses S. Grant, while at West Point, spent his vacation here. In 1855, the property was bought by Robert Radcliff and remained until 1963, when the building became the Warrington branch of Hatboro Federal Savings Bank. The home was touted as being part of the Underground Railroad, as a tunnel emptied from the home into a structure that was at one time a sandwich shop.

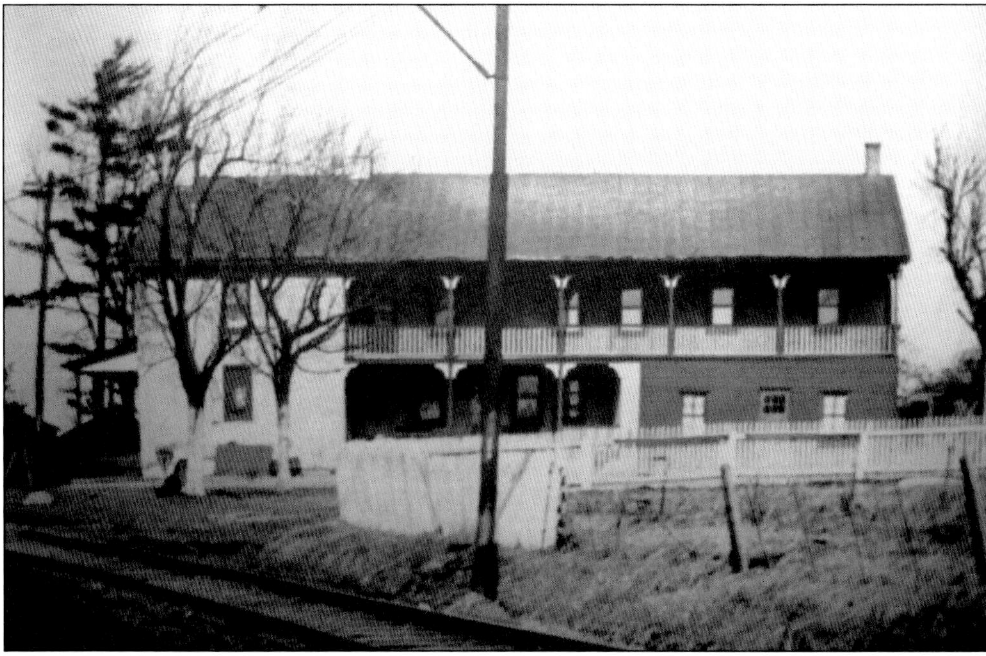

John Craig, son of Daniel and Margaret Craig, opened a public house in 1757. The tavern was known for many years as Craig's Tavern and was the first tavern opened in the township. In 1765, the property was described as "a good two story stone house, four rooms on a floor, a stone kitchen, suitable for public business, it being an old accustomed tavern for many years."

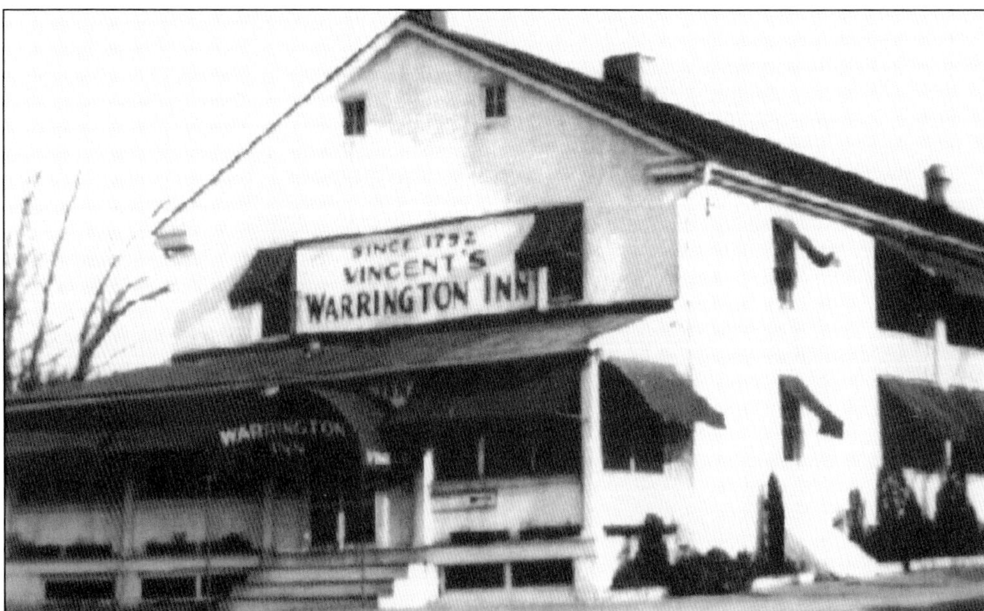

In 1792, under the new ownership of John Jones, the inn's name was changed to Warrington Inn. For a short time, while under ownership of Francis Gurney Lukens, the inn was called the Plow Tavern. During Lukens's ownership it was a great stopping place for the heavy teams that passed up and down the road, and as many as 30 wagons were known to have stayed there overnight.

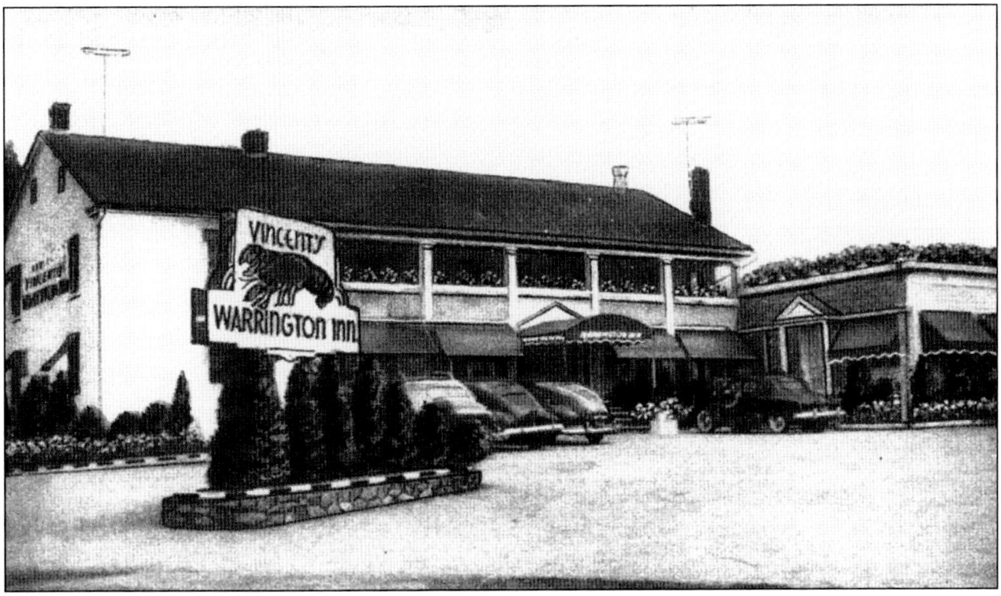

In 1916, Innocenzo Fererro bought the Warrington Inn. Frank Conti leased it from 1932 until he bought the Cross Keys Inn in Doylestown. In 1941, Fererro's nephew Vincent Coggiola purchased the inn, adding *Vincent's* to its name. It was expanded and remodeled. Coggiola's sons took over this popular meeting place until the property was sold in 1996. The danger of it being demolished provoked the township to form a historic commission.

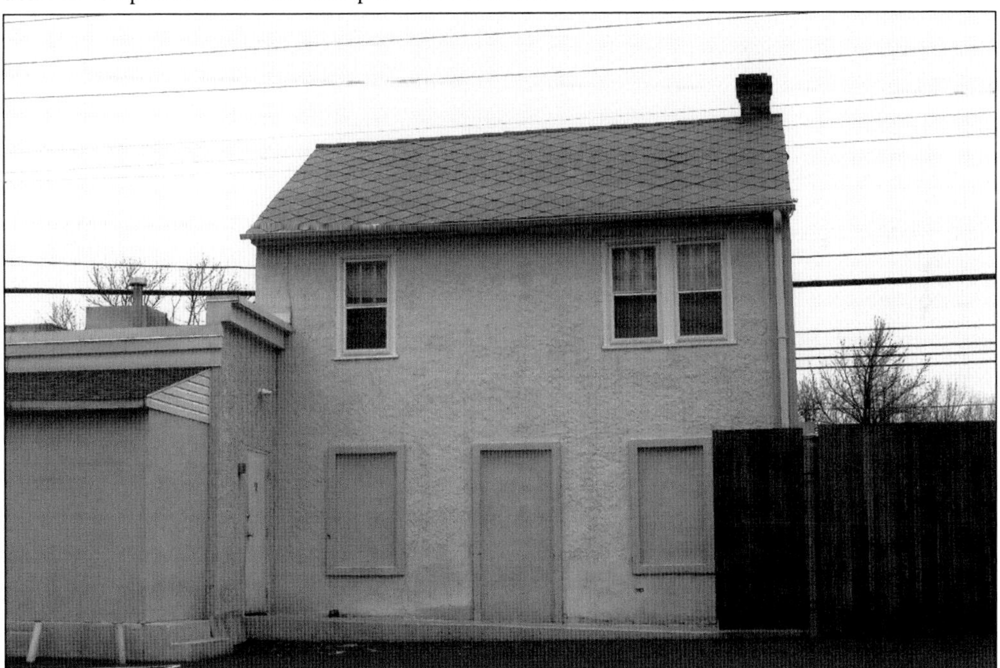

This two-story stone dwelling next to the inn was termed Odd Fellow's Hall prior to 1860, when the property was placed for sale (the Warrington Lodge of the Independent Order of Oddfellows group formed in 1851). The structure was also used for public meetings, spring and fall elections, select balls, and parties. The structure is now connected to the inn.

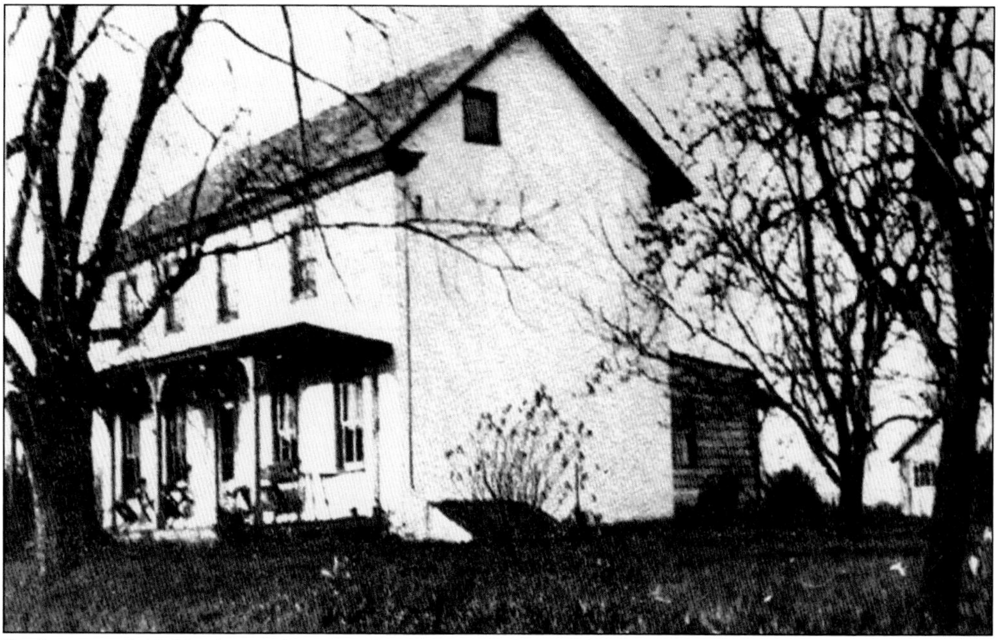

Built around 1850, shown here is the structure that today houses Amelia's Flowers on Bristol Road. This picture shows the structure before the stucco was removed to expose the area fieldstone and an enclosed porch was added. Past owners of the house were the Dewberrys in 1850, C. Cooper in 1860, J. Orem in 1876, and M. Morgan in 1891.

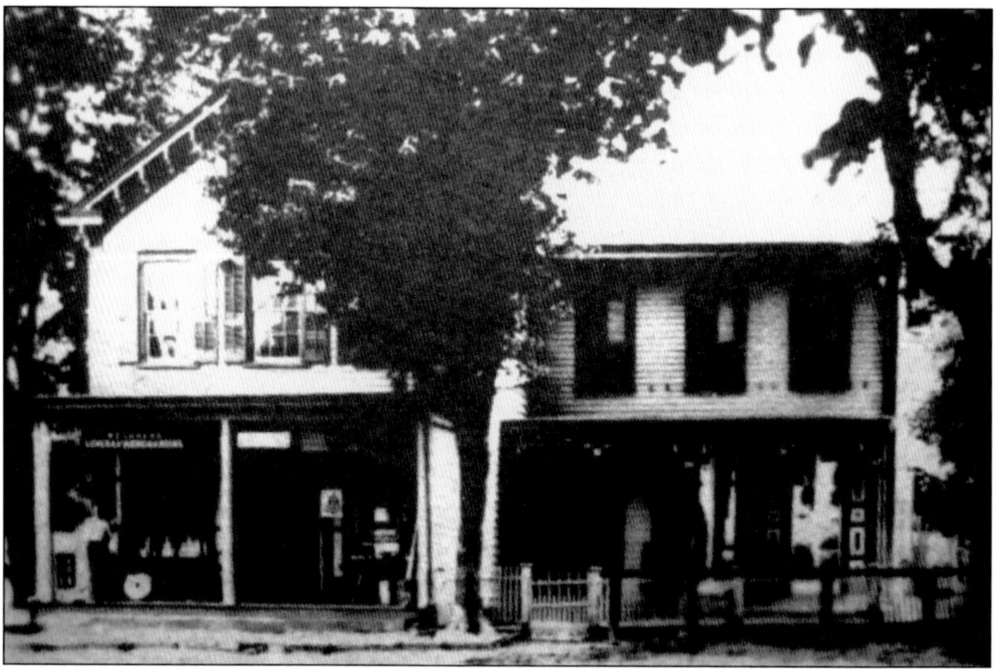

The post office and general store in Warrington Village were located at the corner of Bristol and Easton Roads. The site of the first post office was possibly located in Benjamin Hough's home (the Barclay House) when it was established on December 30, 1839. The post office was operated by Francis Gurney Lukens in the mid-1800s when this general store location was built.

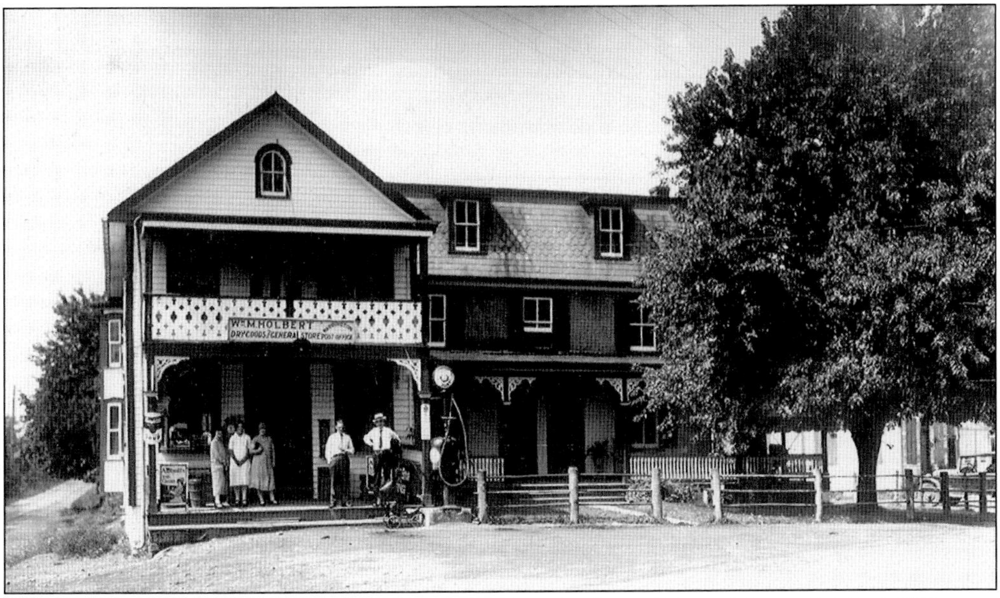

Lukens, William Holbert, Norman Cornell (1929–1944), and Ervin Mayer (1944–1959) were all past keepers of the store and post office. Walt Burger purchased the store a year before the building was taken by the state for the widening of Bristol and Easton Roads. Howard Holbert ran the hardware store located next to the general store. Today this location houses a gas station.

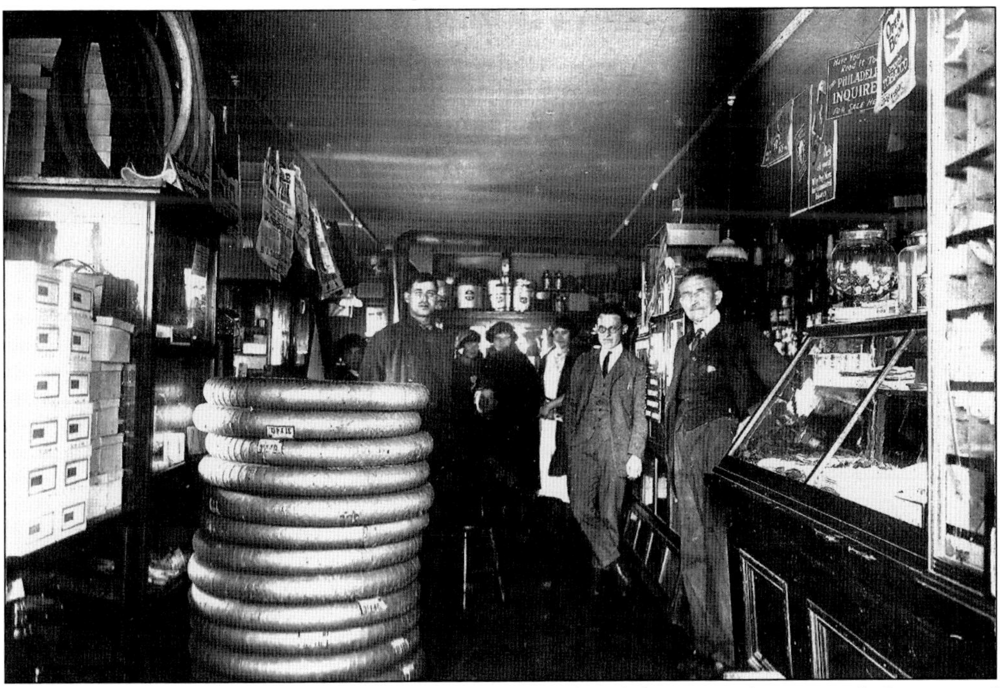

This photograph, taken about 1900, shows the inside of the general store and the type of merchandise that was available when owned by the Holberts. From left to right are C. Leroy Murry, Howard Holbert Sr., and William Holbert. General merchandise was located on the main floor, while linens and clothing were displayed on the second floor. Mailboxes can be seen on the far right. (Courtesy of Judy Holbert Paterson.)

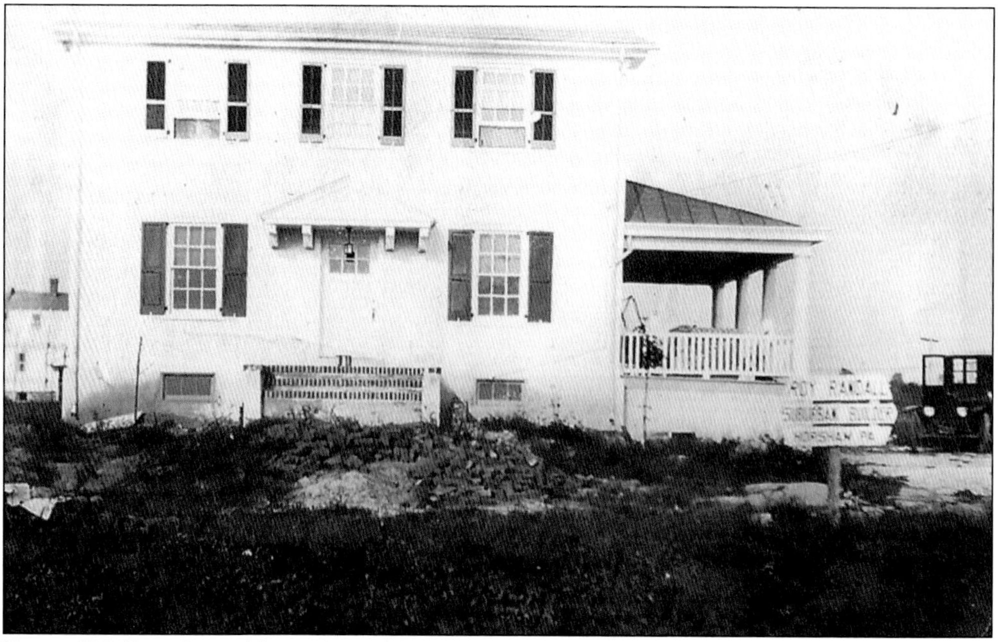

Howard Holbert Sr. and his wife, Mildred, built their dream house on Bristol Road in the early 1920s behind the family store. Their oldest son, Howard "Chick" Holbert Jr. and his wife, Evelyn "City," lived in half the house next door (the home closest to the store). Their daughter Virginia and her husband, Vince Turner, built a house on the other side. (Courtesy of Judy Holbert Paterson.)

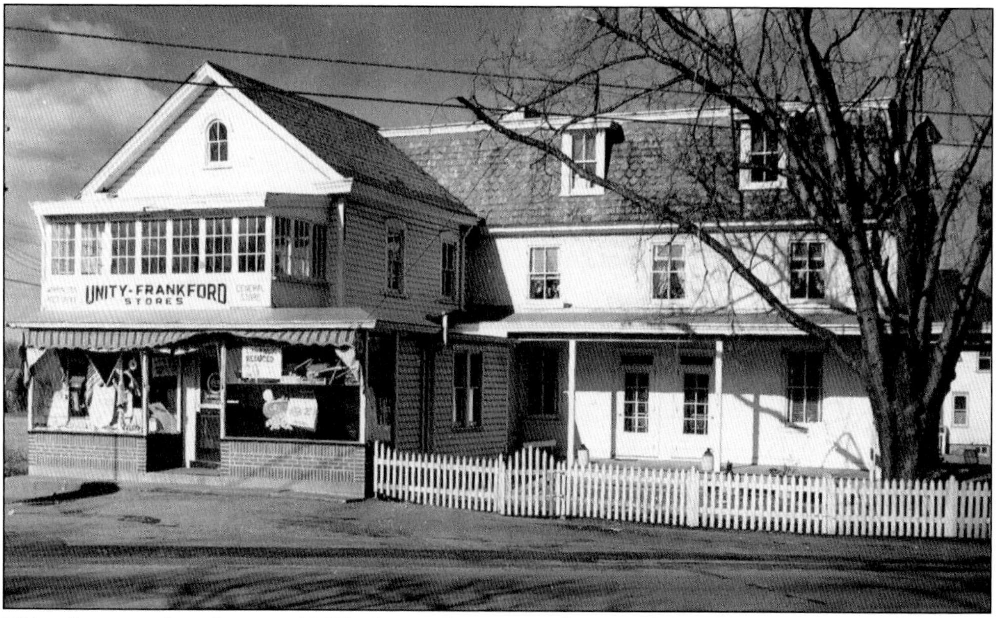

This photograph, taken in 1957, shows the store, along with gas pumps, when owned and operated by Ervin Mayer and part of the Unity-Frankford Store chain. This was the hub of the village. The post office was removed from this location when the Warrington Post Office merged with the Neshaminy Post Office on April 15, 1960. Warrington Hardware, which was located next door also eventually moved to the new shopping center.

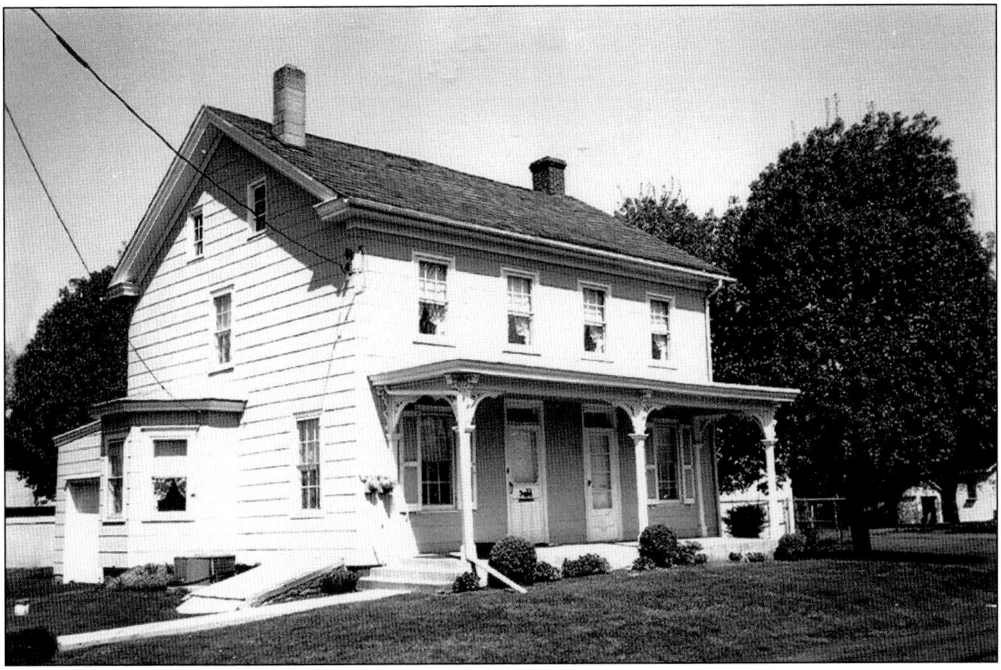

This house was built around 1850 and still stands on Easton Road. John Pross, the original owner, was a justice of the peace. When Wilmer Fox married Martha Pross in 1921, they moved into this house. They raised three children there, Donald, Mary and Russell. Martha was elected to fill the justice of the peace position after her father passed away. Criminals would be brought in the house for hearings.

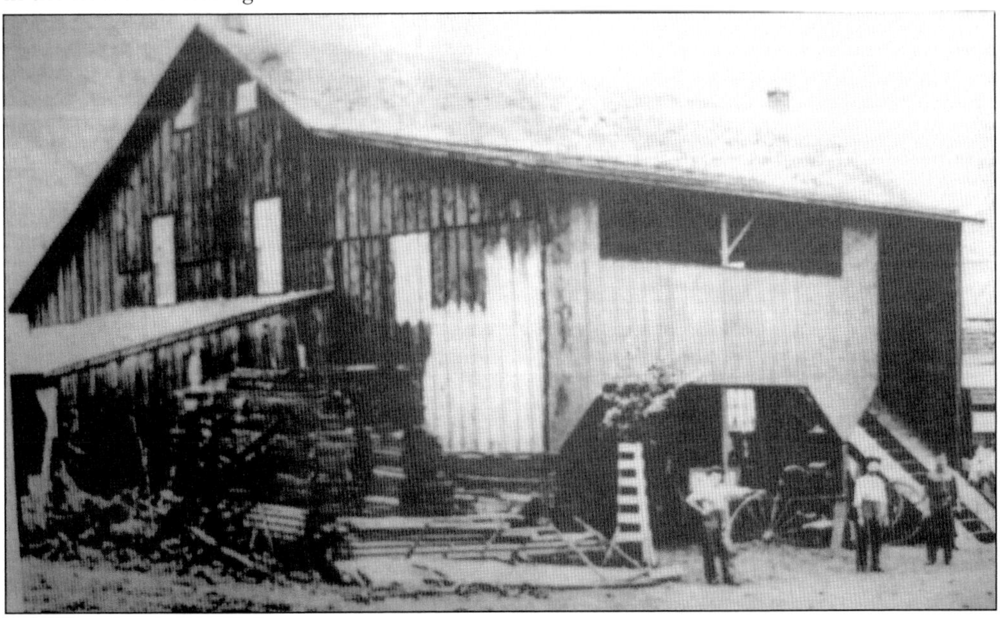

One of Warrington Village's earliest businesses, established in 1886, was a wagon-making/ blacksmith shop that was located at the northwest corner of Bristol and Easton Roads, behind where Henry's Gems is today. The owner of the business was John Pross; he was deeded the property in 1869. Pross died in 1931.

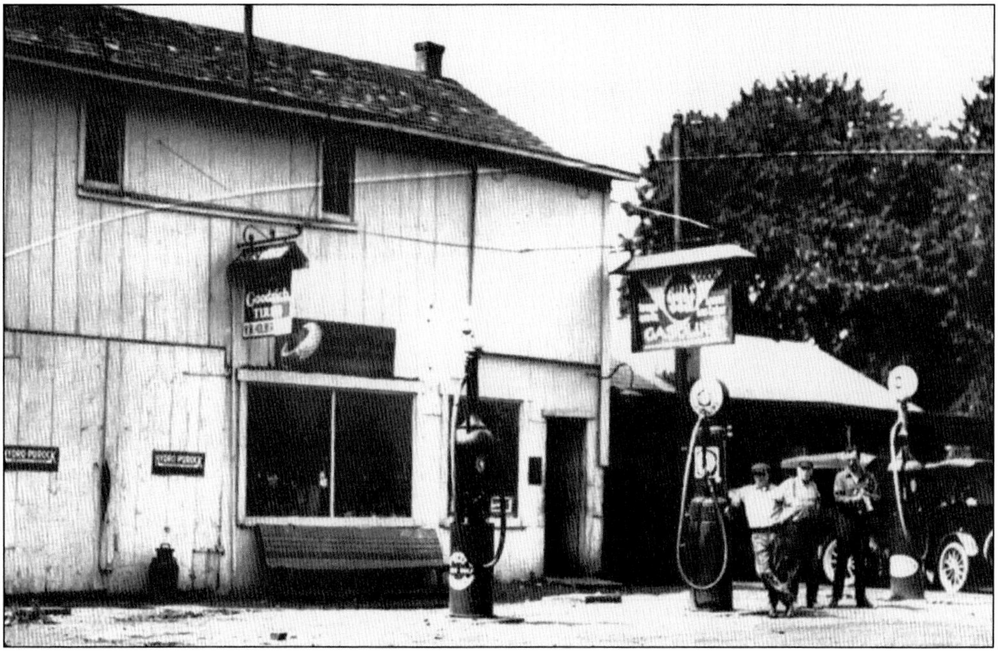

Bob Holbert was born in Warrington in 1923. After World War II, he took a job at a service station owned by his brother-in-law Vince Turner that was located next to his father's hardware store. He eventually bought this business, which was located in the old Pross wagon-making/blacksmith shop.

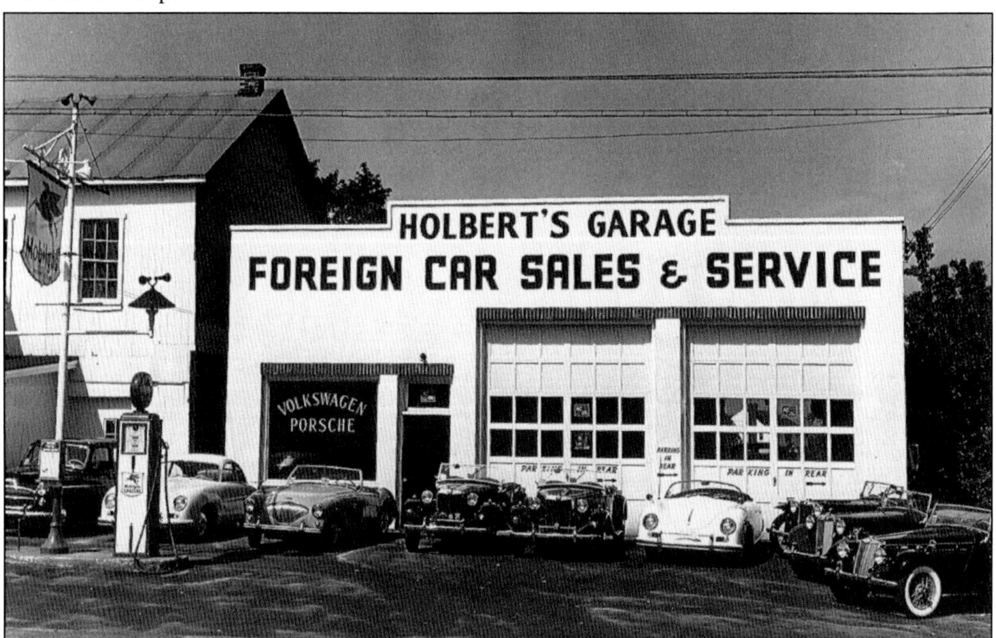

In 1951, Holbert opened Holbert's Mobil Gas and Foreign Car Service Station in the frame building next to the family business, specializing in foreign and sports cars. In 1954, Holbert's Mobil Gas and Foreign Car Service Station became one of the first authorized Porsche dealers in the country.

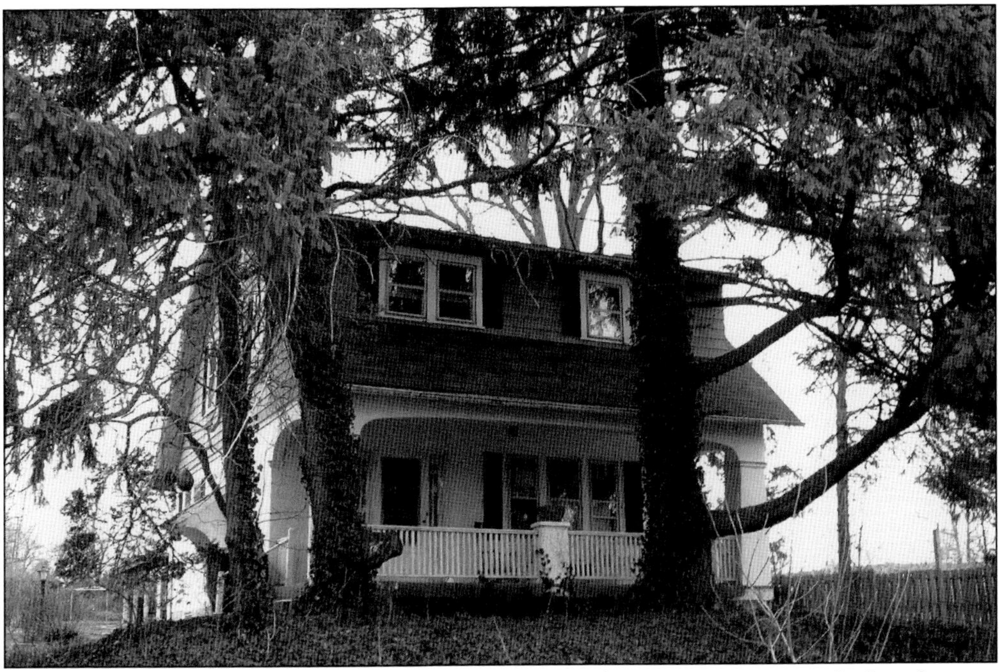

In the early 1920s, Joseph Barness and his wife, Mary, who were at one time chicken farmers, purchased 80 acres of land to build homes. In 1925, he formed the Barness Organization. George and Ethel Klein were the first to buy a Barness home in the late 1920s. The house located on Bristol Road near Winding Brook Farm still stands, pretty much in its original condition.

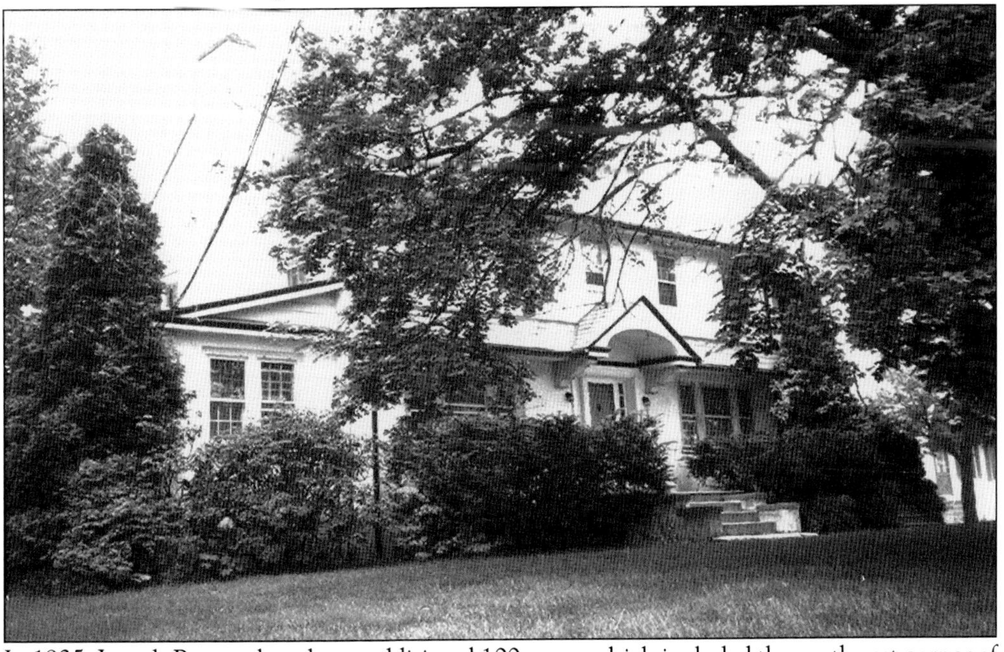

In 1935, Joseph Barness bought an additional 100 acres, which included the southwest corner of Easton and Bristol Roads where his residence and office would be located for many years. Now the home of several businesses, it still stands at 1334 Easton Road (pictured above). Up until the 1960s, the corner was home to a baseball field.

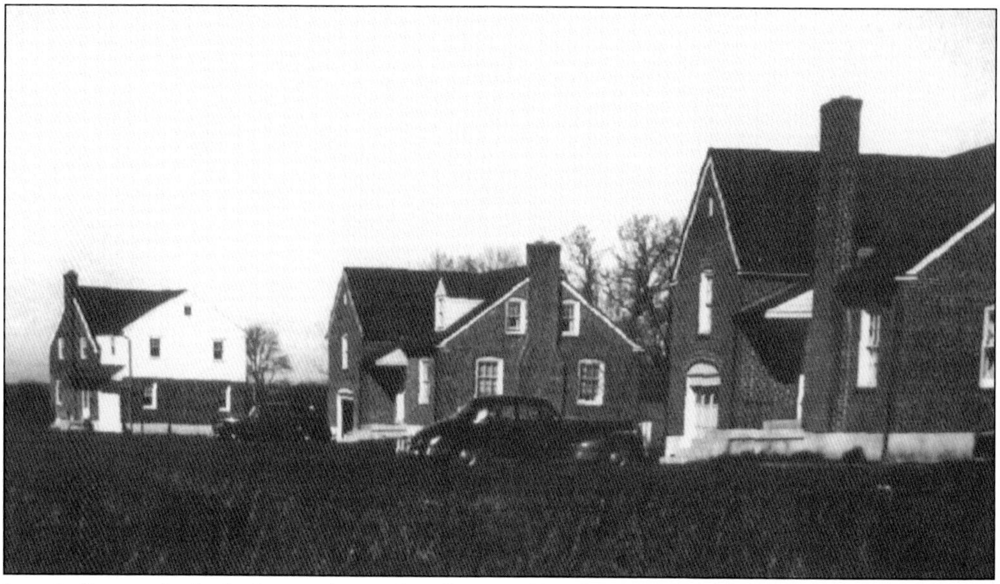

Joseph Barness built the homes located on Barness Road during World War II. Since there were wartime restrictions on building homes, Barness obtained permission to build 30–32 homes on the Richard J. Dobbins farm off Easton Road, with the stipulation that they be rental properties for defense workers. Most of the original occupants worked for Brewster Aircraft, which later became NADC in Warminster. (Courtesy of the Barness family.)

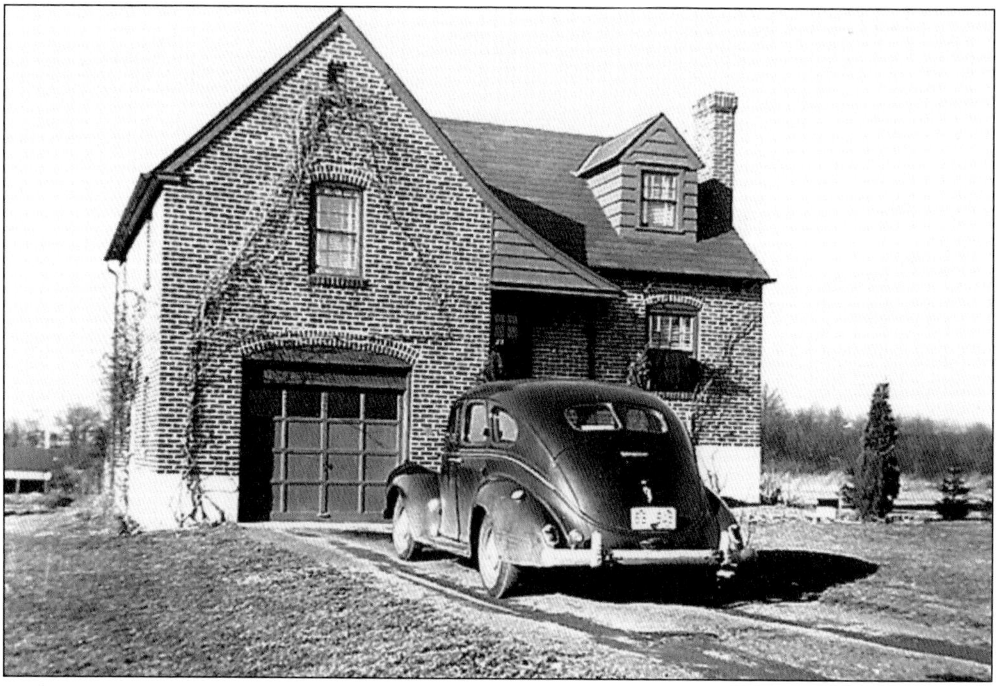

Each house on Barness Road was situated on one acre of land; most were constructed of brick and had slate roofs. No two houses were exactly alike due to the materials that were available for use at that time. Pictured here is the Doyle family residence from 1949 to 2004. (Courtesy of Janet Doyle.)

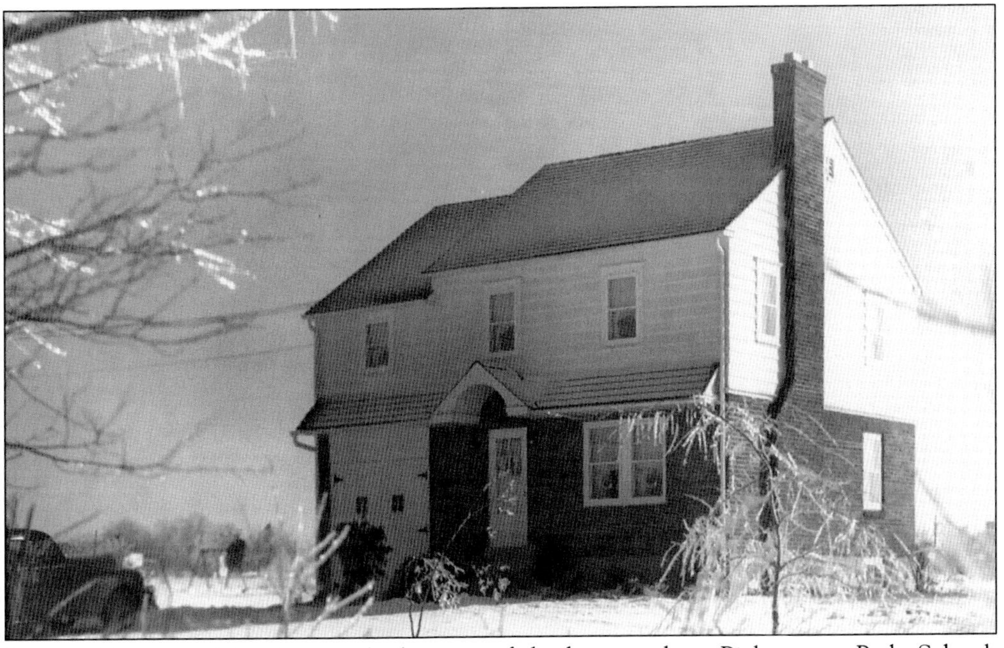

In the 1940s and 1950s, Barness built many of the houses where Pickertown, Park, School, and Bristol Roads meet. He also built most of the houses where County Line and Stump Roads meet, as well as those along Stuckert, Longview, and Herblew Roads. The house shown here was the home the Lueckel family owned from 1940 to 2000. The original heater lasted until 1980. (Courtesy of the Lueckel family.)

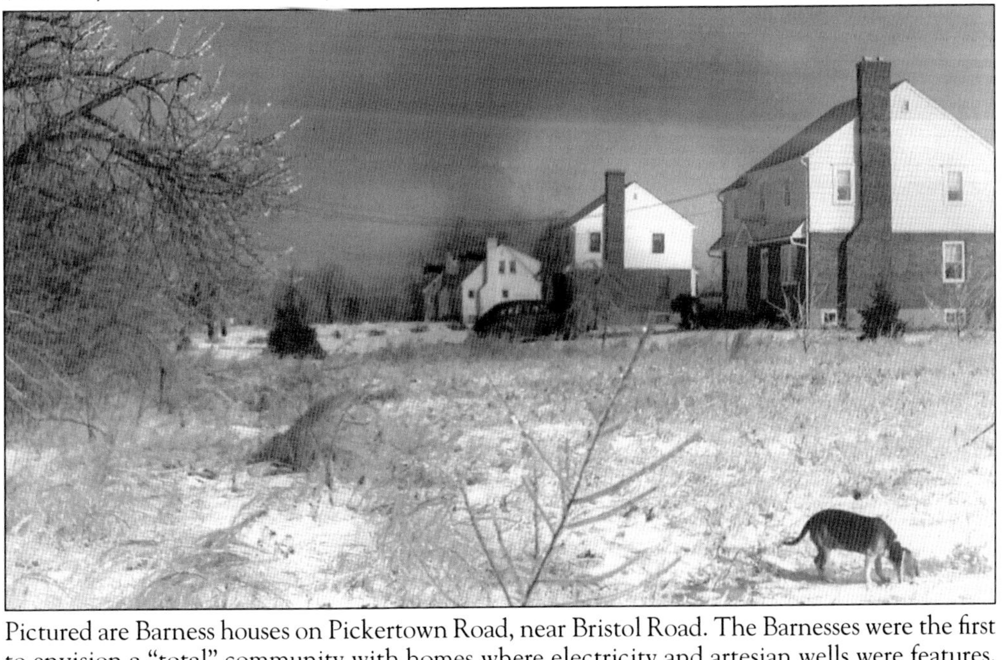

Pictured are Barness houses on Pickertown Road, near Bristol Road. The Barnesses were the first to envision a "total" community with homes where electricity and artesian wells were features. Most of the houses included a chicken coop. A few of the originals are still standing. It was documented in 1962 that 60 to 65 percent of the homes in Warrington were built by Barness. (Courtesy of the Lueckel family.)

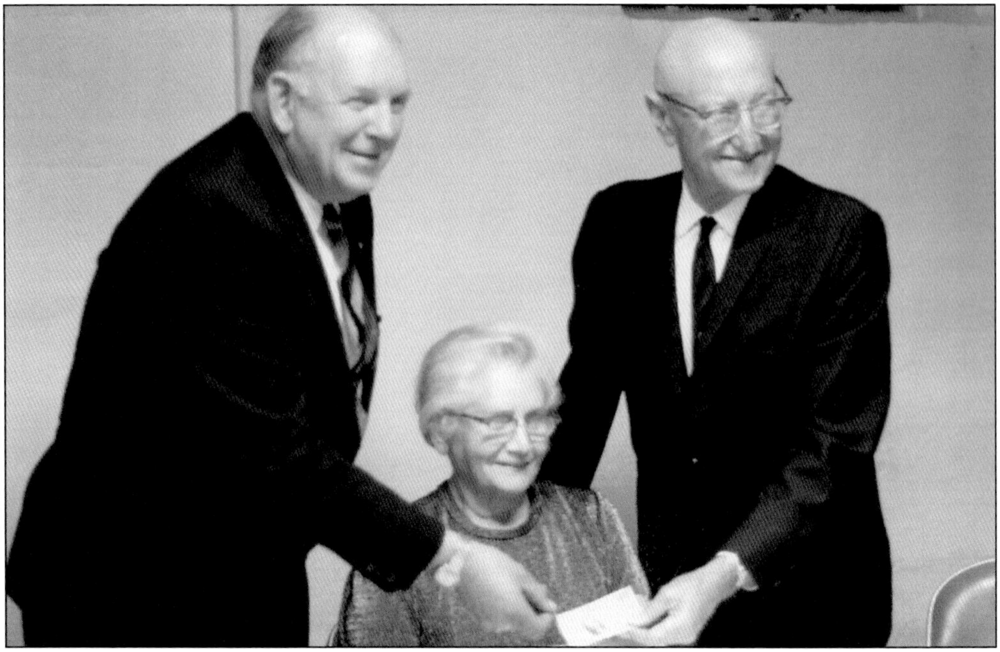

Pictured here is the ceremony in which Joseph and Mary Barness sold 22.8 acres of land on Bristol Road to Warrington Township for $1 on January 1, 1962. This would become Barness Park, home of the Warrington Warwick Athletic Association. This was an important gift to the community since the informal ball field located at Easton and Bristol Roads was developed into the Warrington Shopping Center.

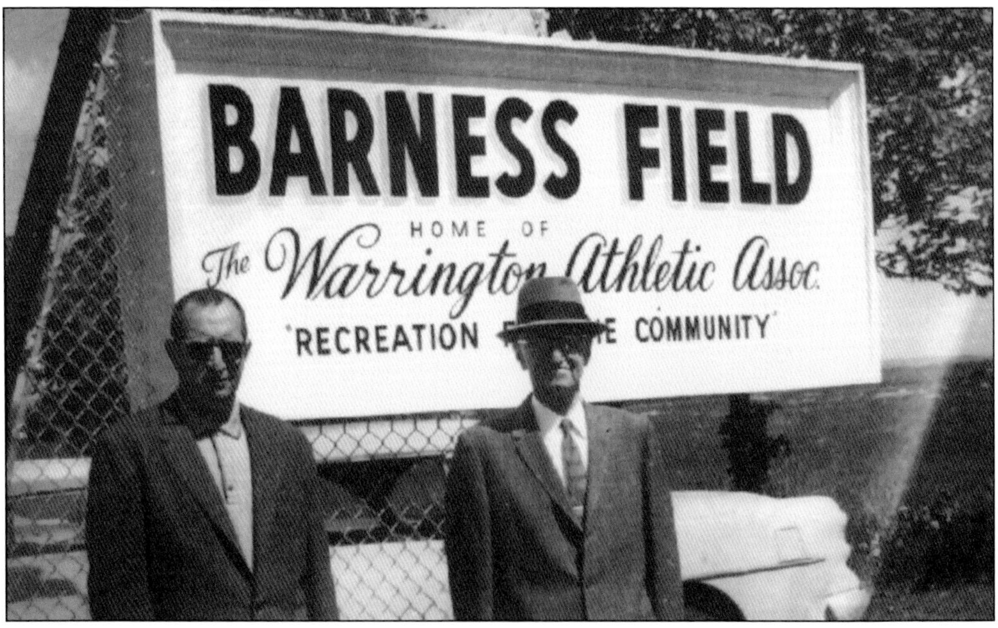

Herbert Barness and his father, Joseph, pose in front of the then new Barness Field on Bristol Road. Several local fathers persuaded the Barness organization to set aside the land for a baseball field. At that time, it was one of the few in the area and some parents had been driving their sons to Southampton to play in an organized league. (Courtesy of the Barness family.)

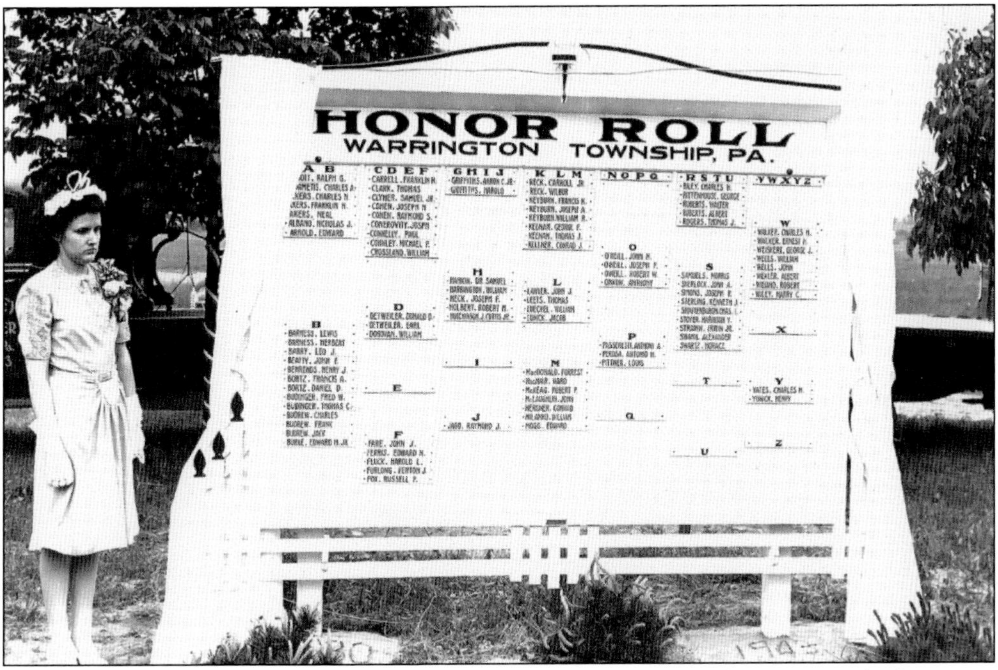

In the mid-1940s, a World War II memorial was erected at Bristol and Easton Roads, the corner where the Warrington Shopping Center is today located. Pictured here with the monument is one of the Wiley children. It was constructed of wood. In the 1960s, when Easton Road was widened, the memorial was removed with the plan to erect it somewhere else in the township. In time, it was destroyed.

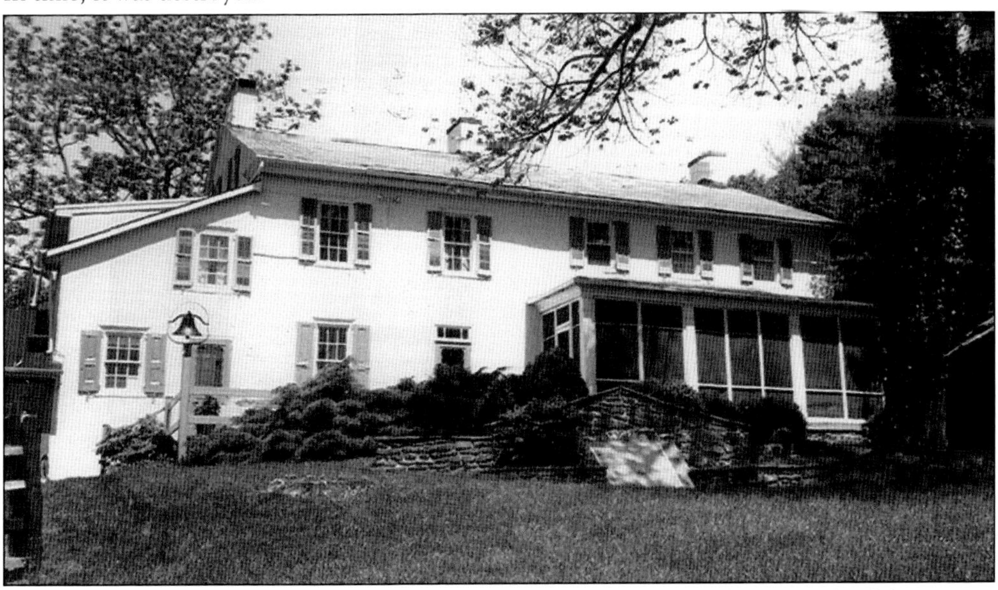

In 1735, Andrew Long owned 400 acres. In 1760, a log house was built just south of the present dwelling, located at what today is the corner of Bristol and Valley Roads. A room in the house was used as a hospital during the Revolutionary War, probably when Gen. George Washington's army was camped in the Neshaminy Hills. This home received a certificate and plaque from the Bucks County Heritage Conservancy in 1978.

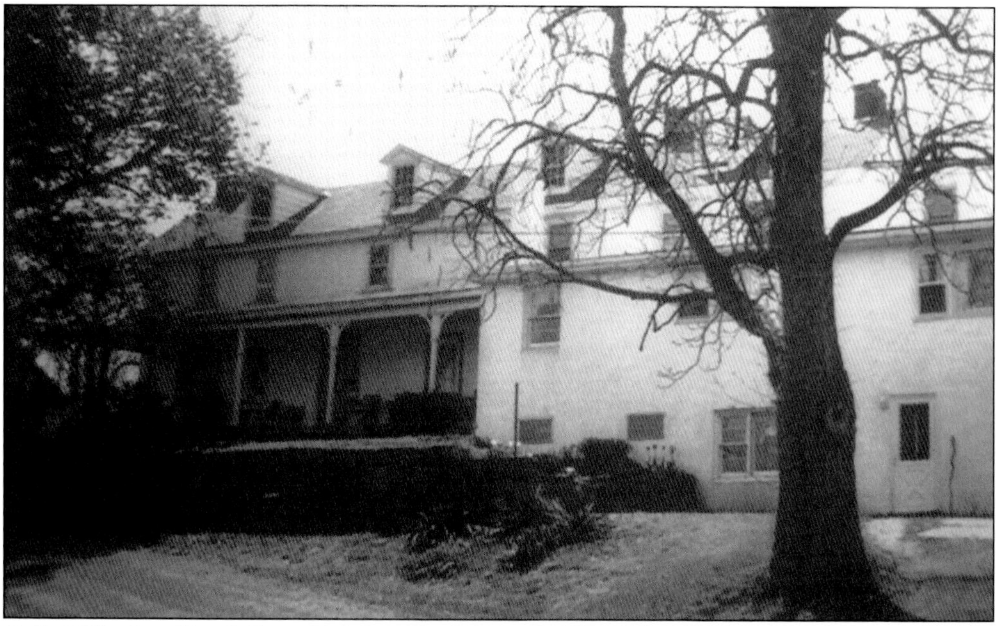

Called Winding Brook Farm, it has remained in the Walter/Garges family for over 200 years. It is still an integral part of the township with active farm functions, including dairy cows and crops of both corn and wheat. The farm is well known for its hayrides and corn maze created for the Halloween season. In 1999, the farm became part of the Bucks County Agricultural Preservation Program.

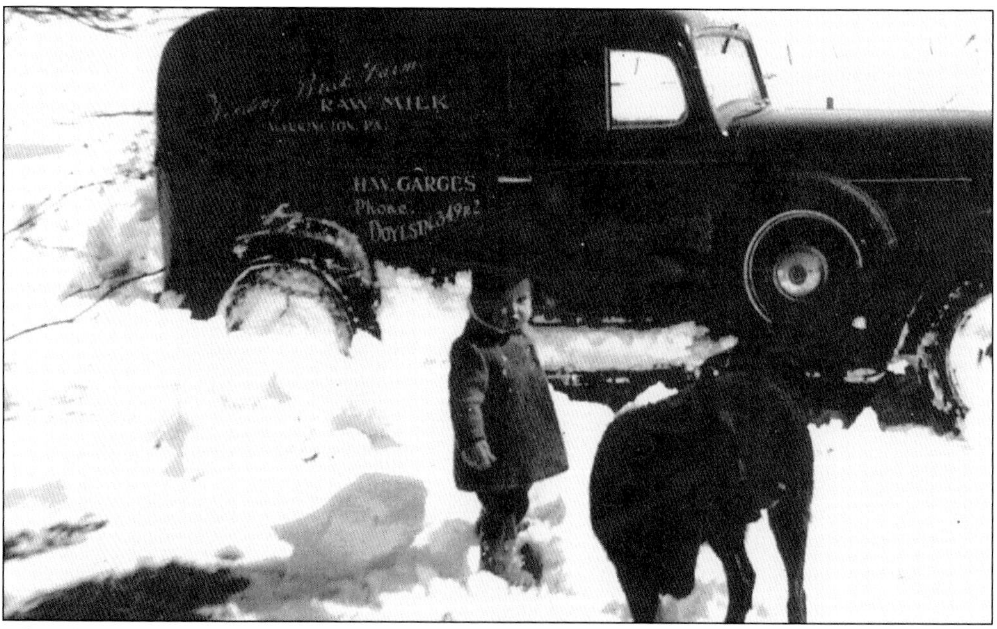

Edward Garges purchased the property of his father-in-law, John B. Walter, for $7,500 in 1902. He gave his undivided attention to the cultivation of field and garden and to the sale of his products at the markets. He raised stock for the support of his farm. He also conducted his blacksmith shop on the farm. Pictured here is Ryda Garges with a Henry Garges Milk Truck. (Courtesy of the Garges family.)

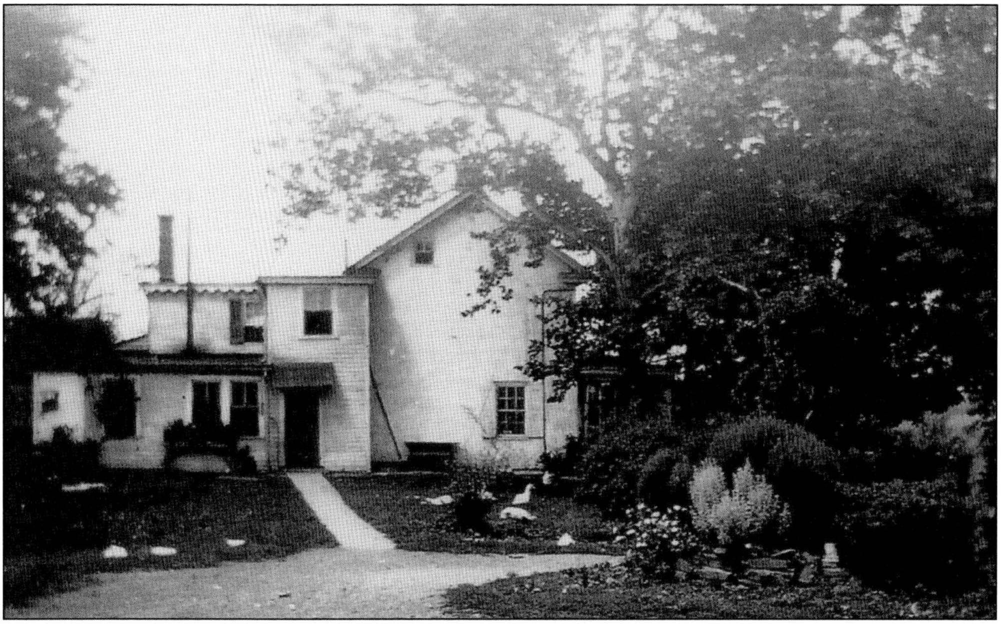

Pictured is the Garges Farm house in the early 1900s. The homestead has a long lane with a branch of the Neshaminy Creek running through it. It was one of the first homes in the township to have indoor plumbing and a bathroom installed. (Courtesy of the Garges family.)

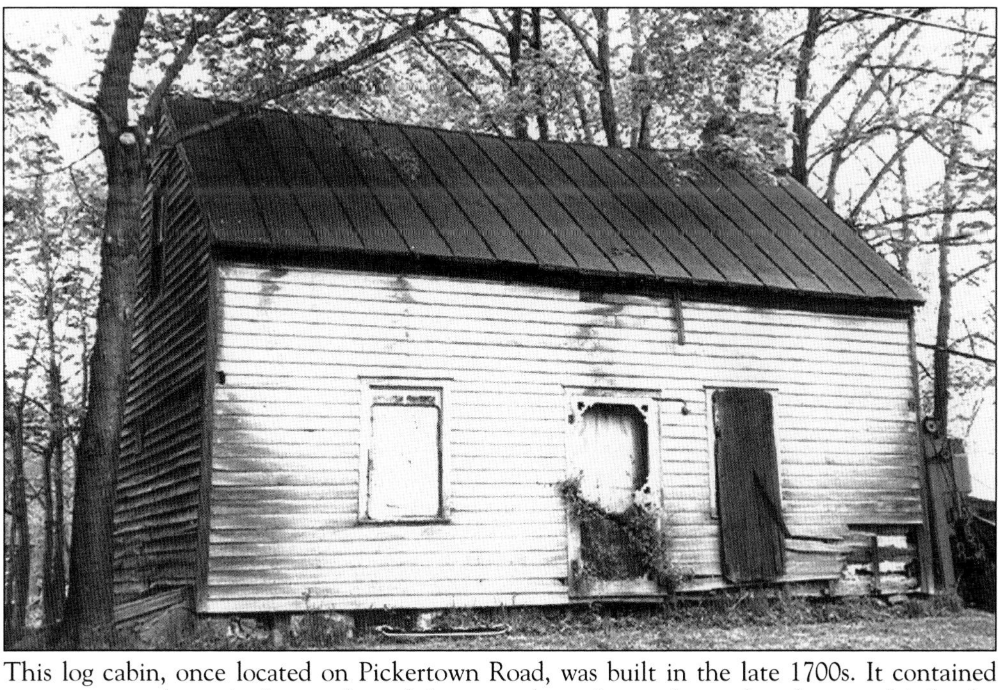

This log cabin, once located on Pickertown Road, was built in the late 1700s. It contained two rooms on the main floor and two loft rooms above. It was donated to the township by the Kentopp family in 1975. It was to be moved and become the centerpiece of the township's bicentennial festivities. Due to the high cost, the project ended. After further deterioration, it was razed in the 1980s.

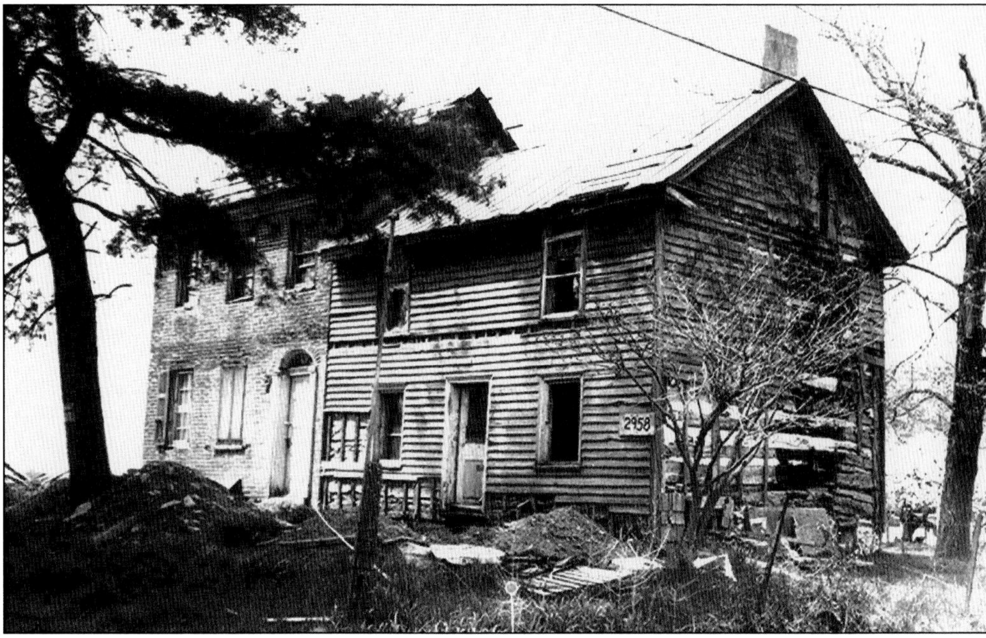

This home was built by John Kerr around 1810, after he bought the property from John Barclay. The log-and-frame portion of the home was built first. The more ornate brick section was probably added in the mid-1800s. Unoccupied for many years, the house once located at 2958 Pickertown Road was razed around 2000 for a housing development.

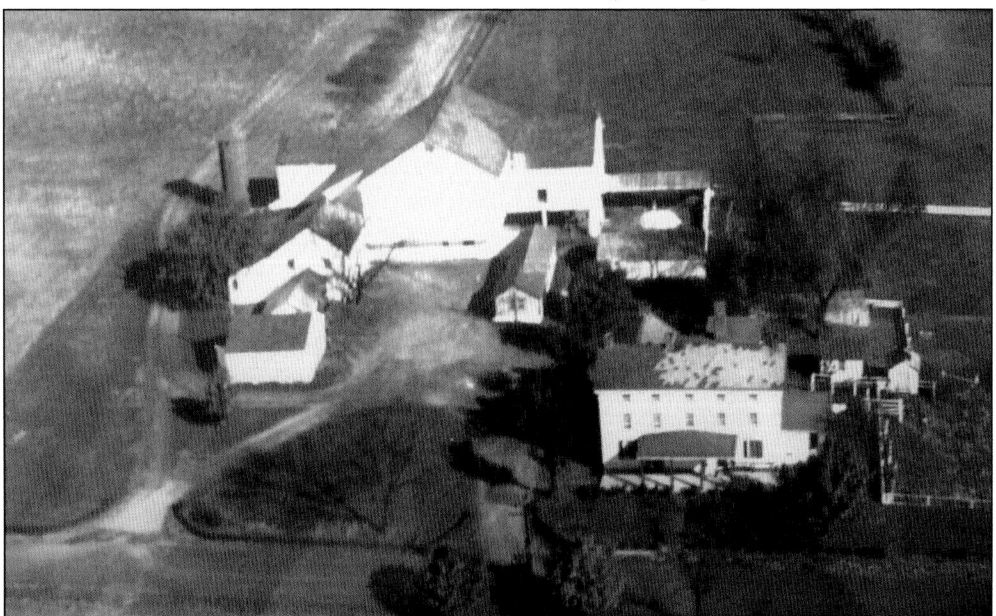

The Cornell family bought a large tract of land from the Cadwalladers in the mid-1940s. The Warrington Airfield began operation shortly after World War II when Norman Cornell provided part of his property to his son Ernest Cornell, who had returned from World War II and wanted to continue his love of flight. (Courtesy of Alby Cornell.)

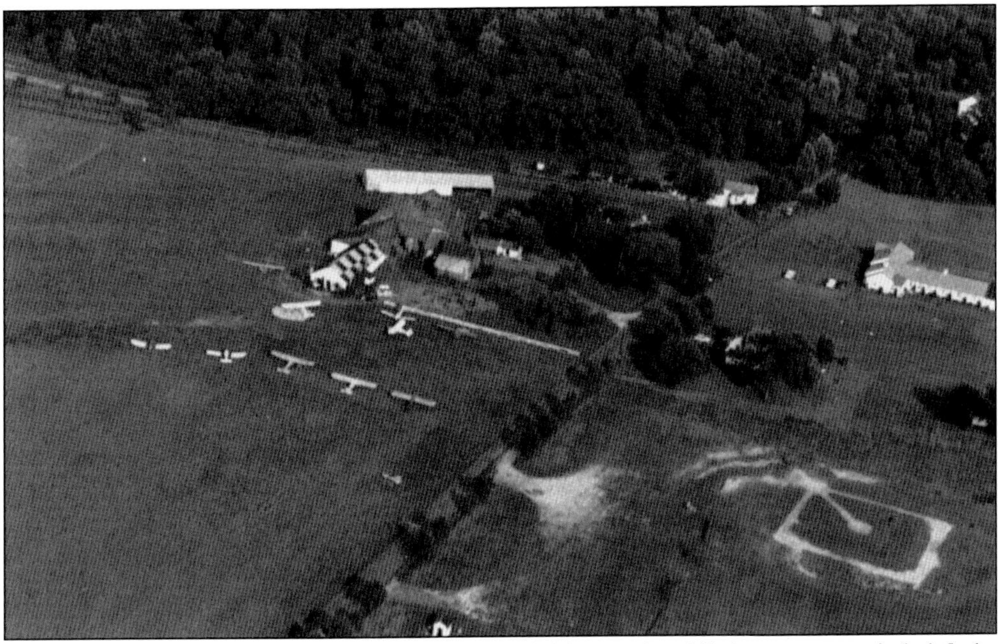

Ernest's brother, Alby Cornell, took over the airfield in 1951. Alby's services included flight lessons, transportation, and plane storage. Later it would become a common place for providing shuttle services to the Philadelphia Airport. The main runway at Warrington was paved in 1973. The airport closed in 1991. (Courtesy of Alby Cornell.)

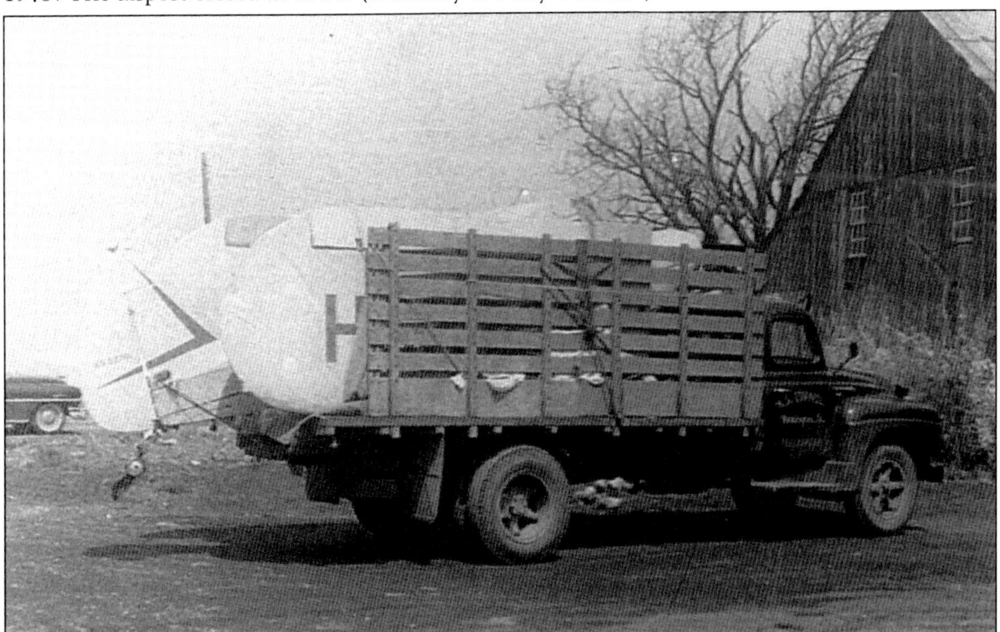

When planes were forced to land on a farmer's field of crops, unable to land on a designated airfield, the plane would need to be disassembled and brought back to the airport. Seen here is a Cornell truck transporting a disassembled plane back to the Warrington airfield. The plane would quickly be reassembled and take to the air once again. (Courtesy of Jeanne DeLong and Frank Ace.)

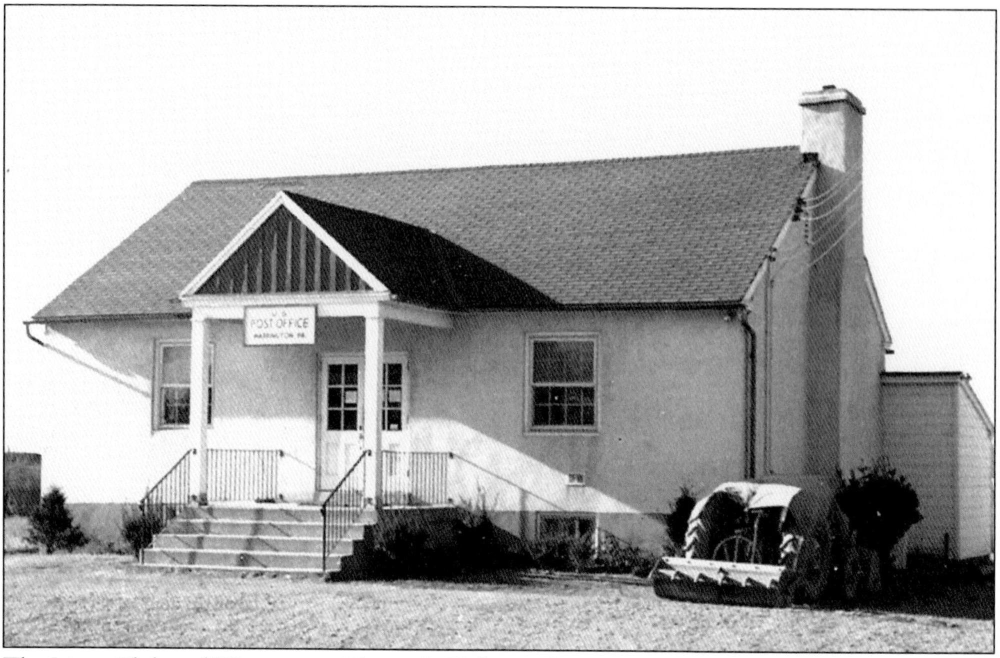

The Lions Club and Warrington Woman's Club members were instrumental in raising funds and constructing a community center building, located on Easton Road in 1952. On April 15, 1960, when the Warrington and Neshaminy Post Offices merged, the new post office was temporarily relocated to the community center building. Because there was no official township building at the time, many township functions took place here.

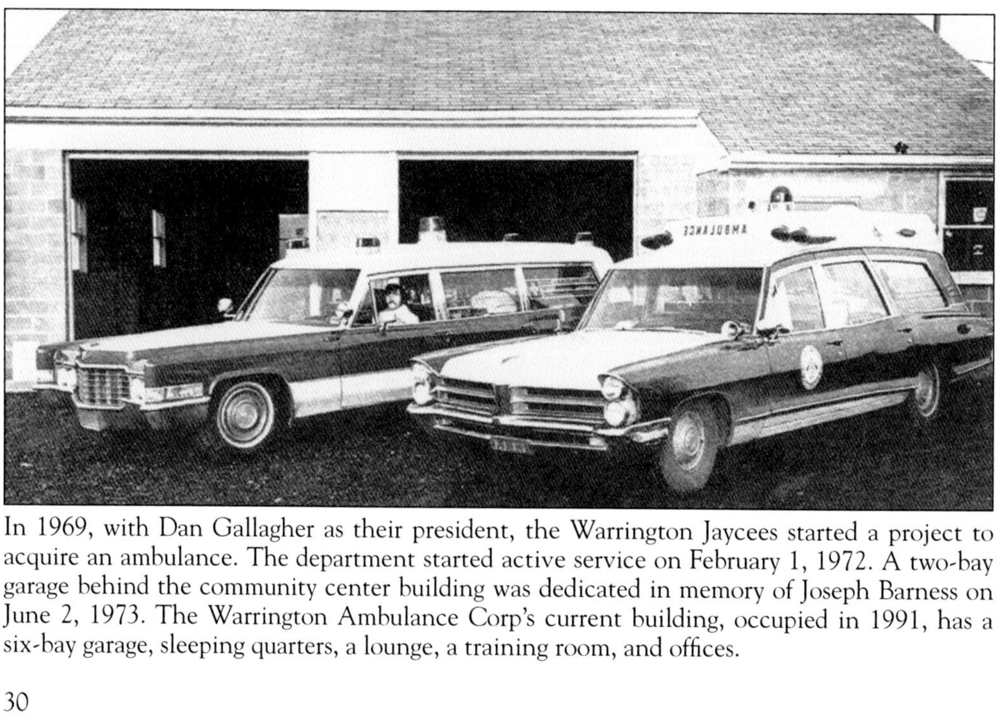

In 1969, with Dan Gallagher as their president, the Warrington Jaycees started a project to acquire an ambulance. The department started active service on February 1, 1972. A two-bay garage behind the community center building was dedicated in memory of Joseph Barness on June 2, 1973. The Warrington Ambulance Corp's current building, occupied in 1991, has a six-bay garage, sleeping quarters, a lounge, a training room, and offices.

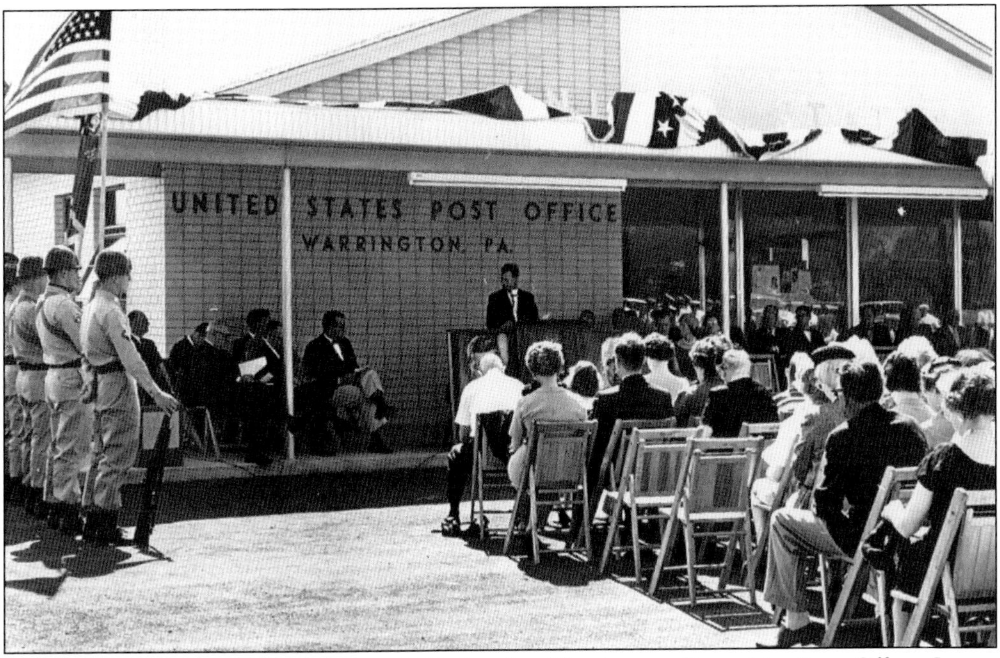

Opening ceremonies were held in 1962 for the Warrington Township Post Office. Lester Gordon was the first postmaster of this new location. Today this building continues its use as a post office, but the newer facade allows it to blend in with the remainder of the Warrington Shopping Center, located at the corner of Bristol and Easton Roads.

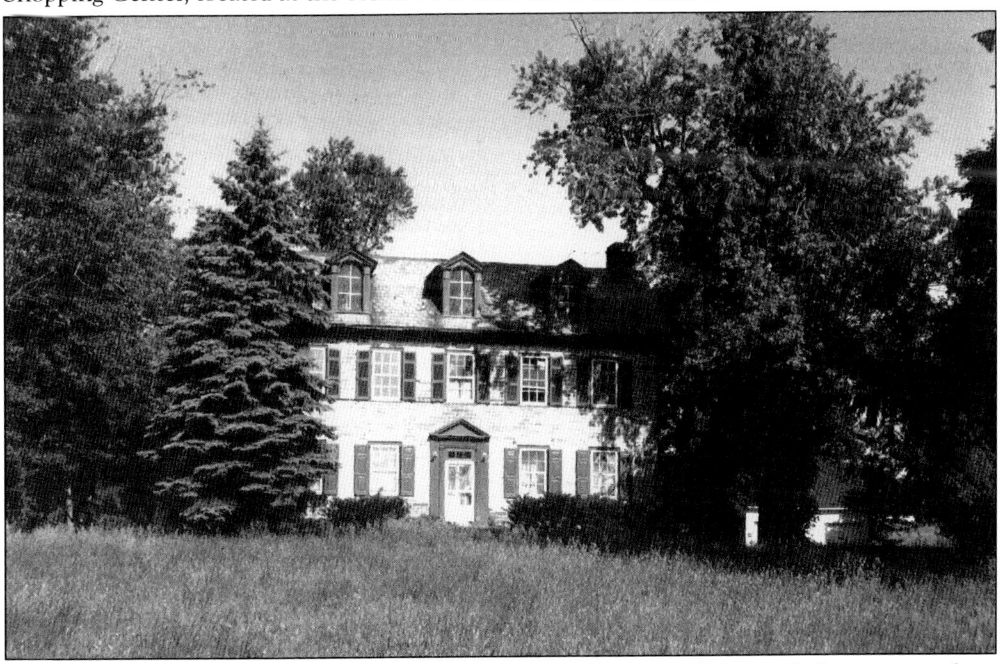

The manor at 850 Easton Road was built by Nathaniel Irwin, who owned the property from 1785 to 1812. The foundation of the house dates back to 1734. In 1980, Randolph A. Scott, Esq., bought the building. He restored the home to use as offices for his law firm. This home received a certificate and plaque from the Bucks County Heritage Conservancy in 1981.

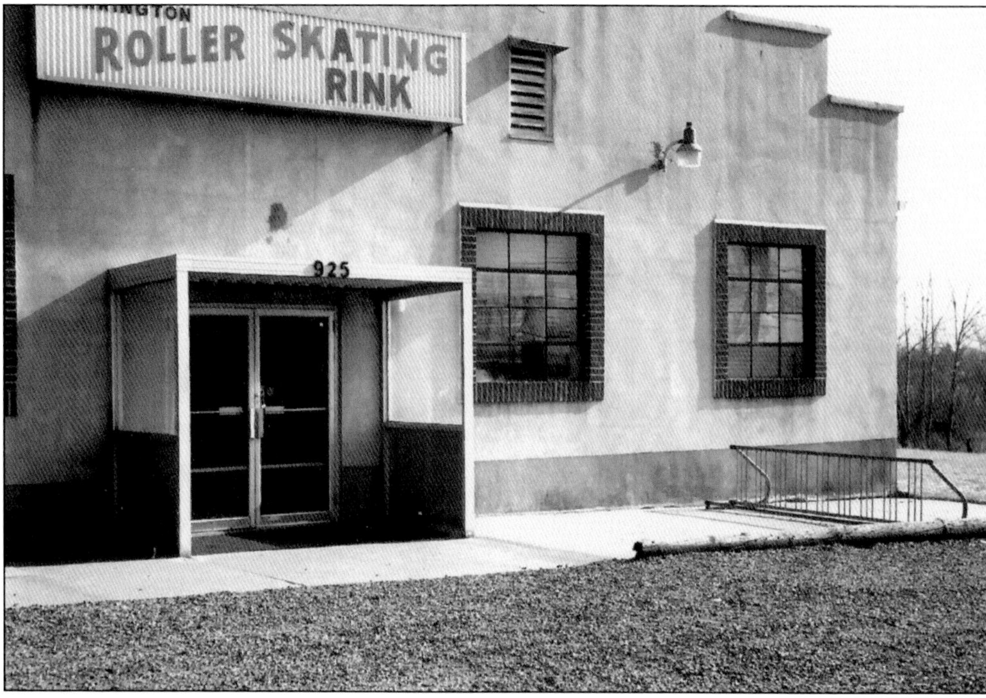

The Warrington Skating Rink, located at 925 Easton Road, was owned and operated by George and Ann Mekosh as of 1955. Built in 1948, the prior use of the building was as an industrial building. As a rink, it was a popular gathering site for all age groups.

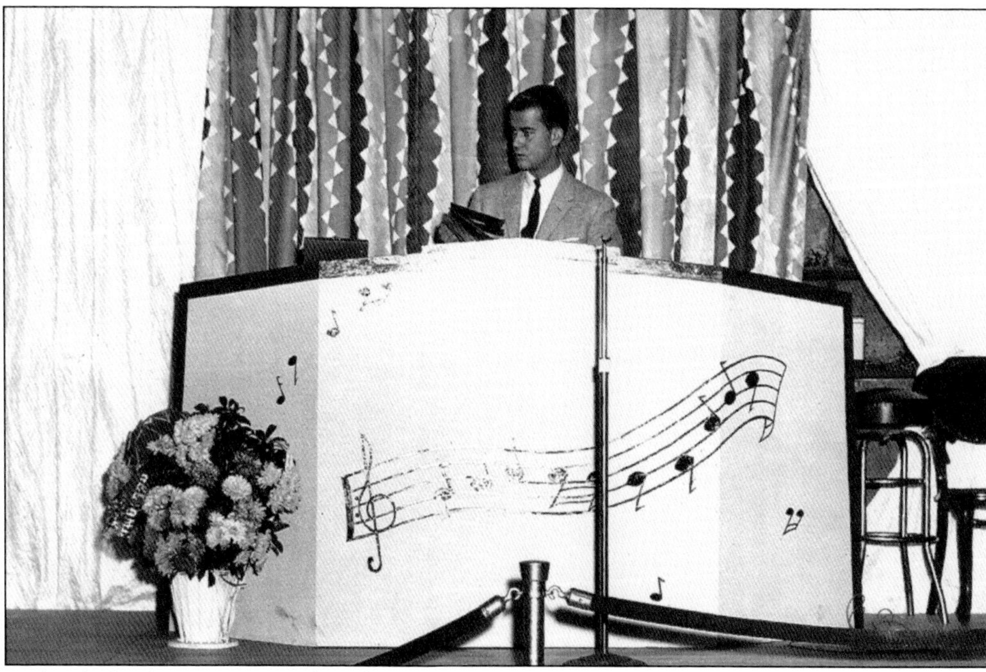

Dick Clark of *American Bandstand* was at the rink several times from 1958 to 1959 holding dances. Youth and adult hockey leagues, public skating sessions, rink rental, and party packages were available. Ownership changed, but the rink remained open until the late 1990s.

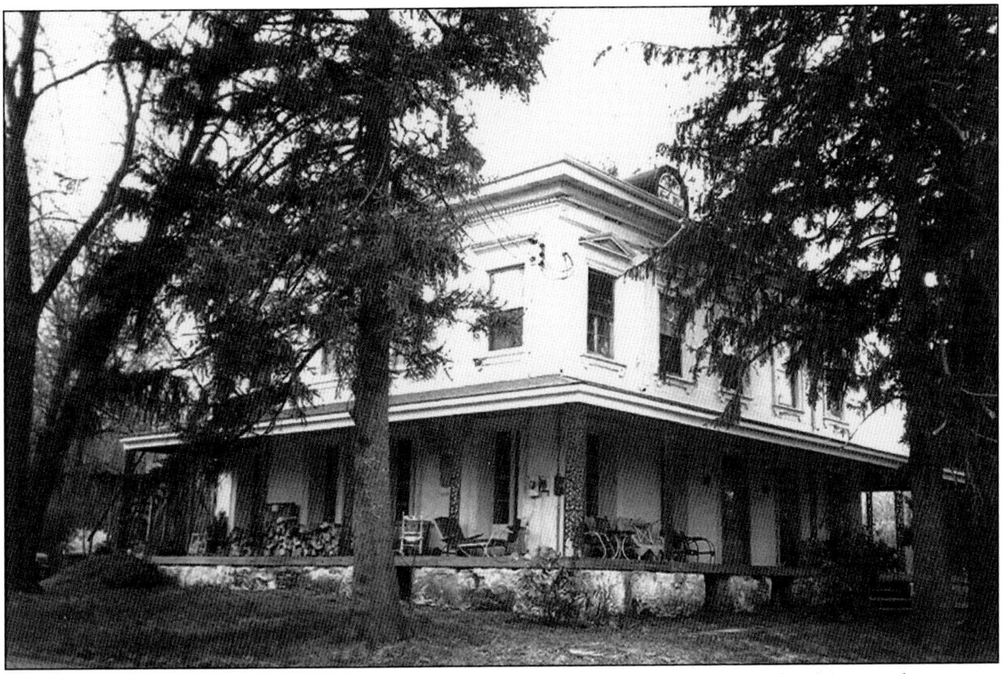

Folly Road was given its name because of the property located on it, which was once known as Brown's Folly. Picnics, dances, and other social gatherings were sometimes held there, and at times, the owner took in summer boarders. On January 8, 1945, agents of the Alcohol Tax Unit of the FBI raided the property. They seized moonshine whiskey and liquor-making equipment.

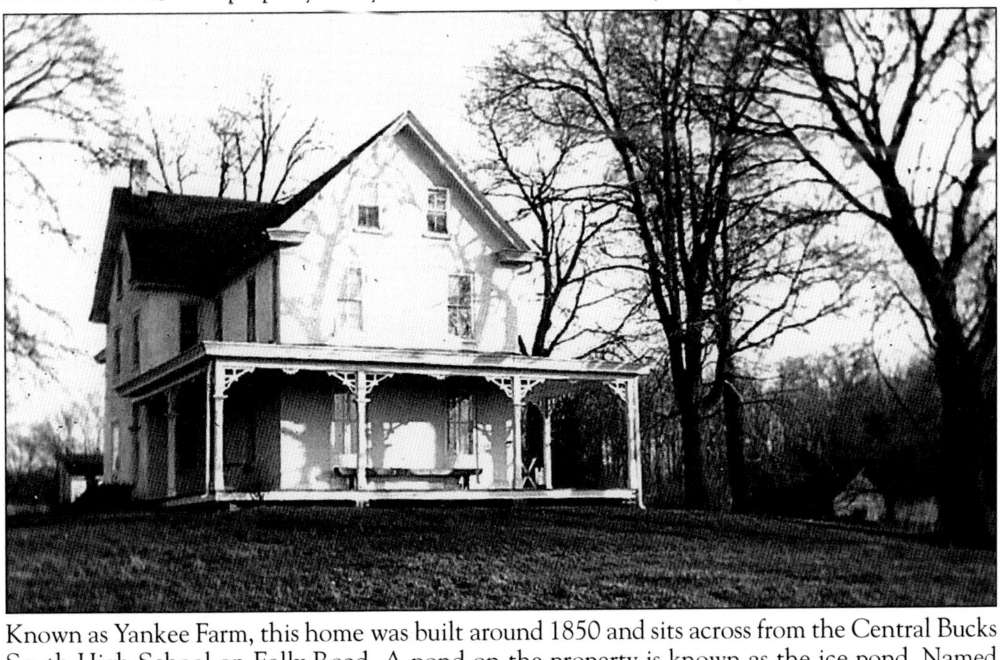

Known as Yankee Farm, this home was built around 1850 and sits across from the Central Bucks South High School on Folly Road. A pond on the property is known as the ice pond. Named appropriately, ice was harvested from the pond and sold to the public. This home received a certificate and plaque from the Bucks County Heritage Conservancy in 2000. (Courtesy of Jeanne DeLong and Frank Ace.)

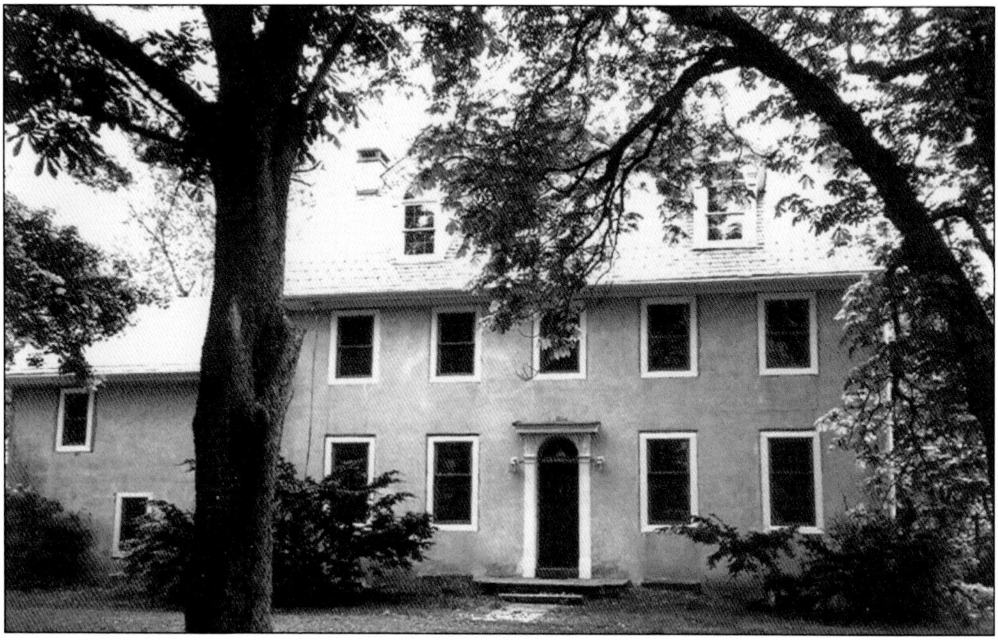

Henry Stuckert, a prominent farmer, was born and reared in Germany where he learned the trade of a baker. In 1811, he purchased 213 acres in Warrington, now located on Stuckert Road. William, son of Henry, was born in Warrington Township. In March 1903, William was taken into partnership by his uncle, William Stuckert, under the law firm name of William and William R. Stuckert.

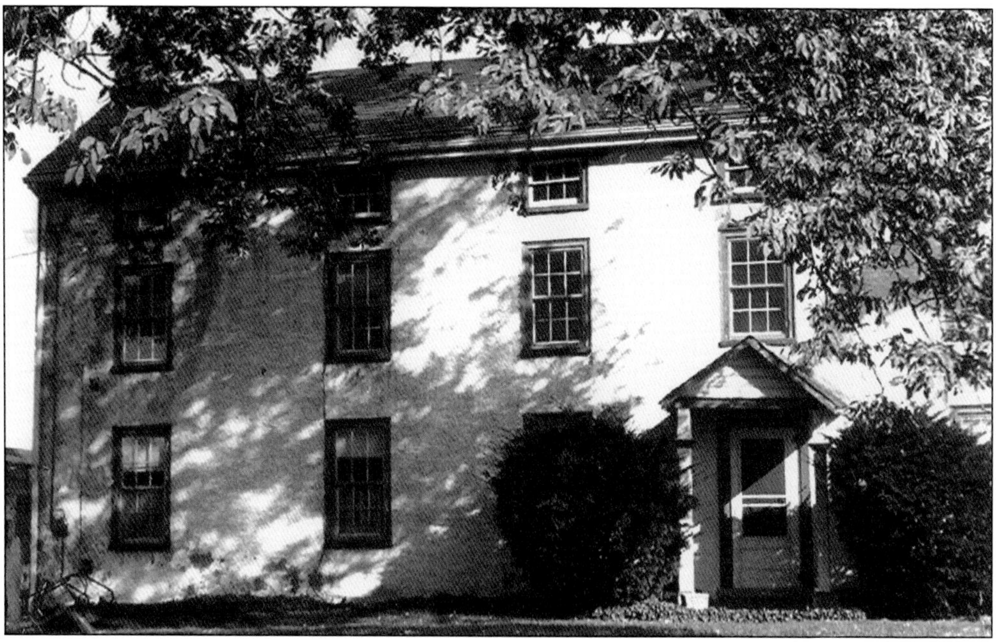

Love Farm, on Stuckert Road (where Wheat Sheaf Lane is today), was removed to make way for the Hidden Meadows Subdivision. During World War II, a Civil Air Defense post was set up in the area. Supplied by Joseph Barness, it was a 20-by-10-foot white building. The purpose of the post was to monitor the air space above Warrington in case of an invasion.

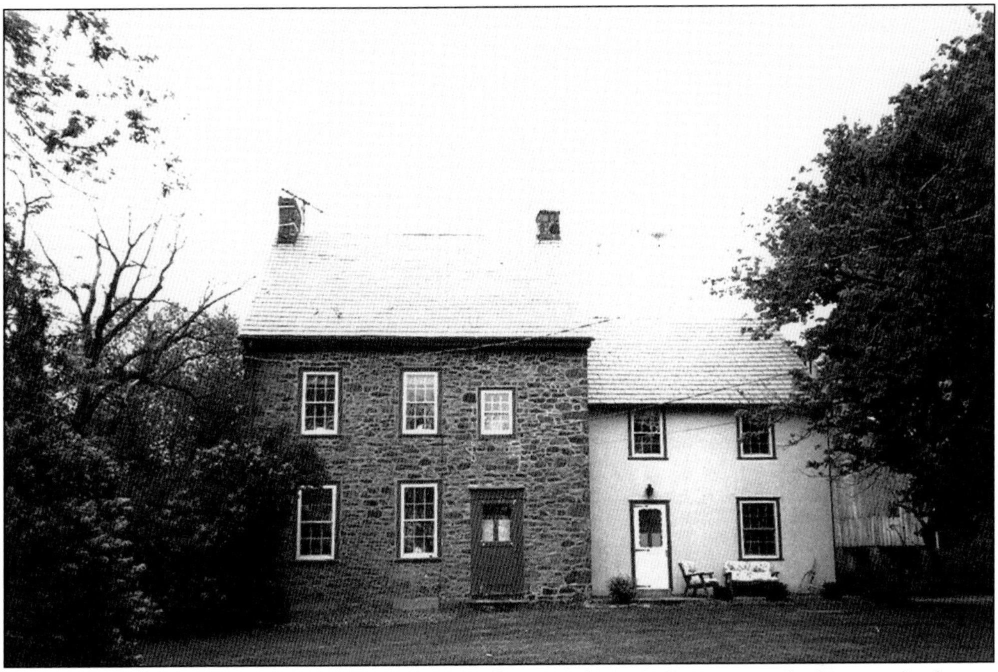

This house, located on Warwick Road, was built around 1840. Constructed of stone, the house has two interior chimneys, one brick and the other stone. A framed bank barn built on a stone foundation, still on the property, was built in 1856 and has a date stone that shows the initials of the owner Thomas Radcliffe.

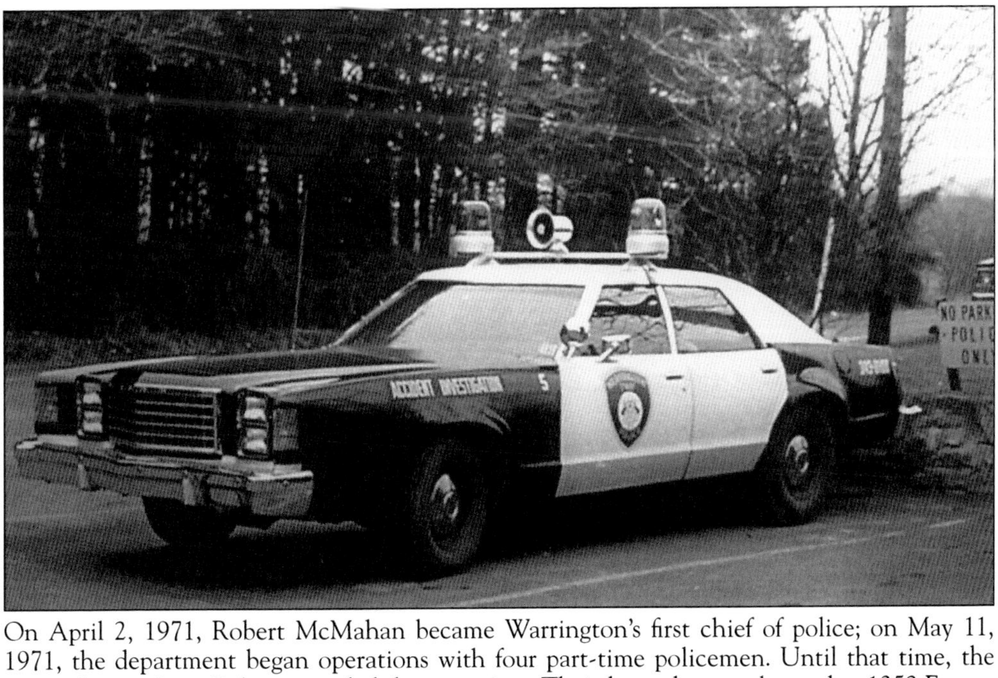

On April 2, 1971, Robert McMahan became Warrington's first chief of police; on May 11, 1971, the department began operations with four part-time policemen. Until that time, the Pennsylvania State Police provided these services. Their barracks were located at 1352 Easton Road. The police station was located at the old Mill Creek School until 1993 when it was relocated to the township building on Easton Road.

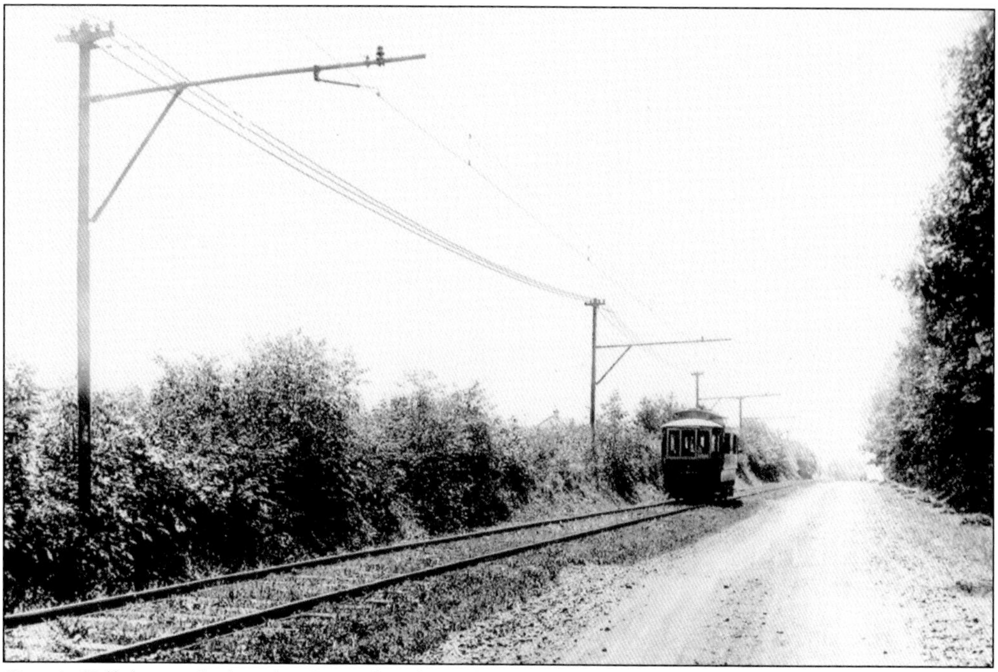

Grier's Hill (named after the Grier family and later called Warrington Hill) was a long descent on Easton Road, north of the village of Warrington. In the early days of the Bucks County Railway, the hill gained a reputation as the "Toboggan Slide" from the practice of motormen allowing the trolley cars to coast down the hill at a speed of 60 miles an hour or more.

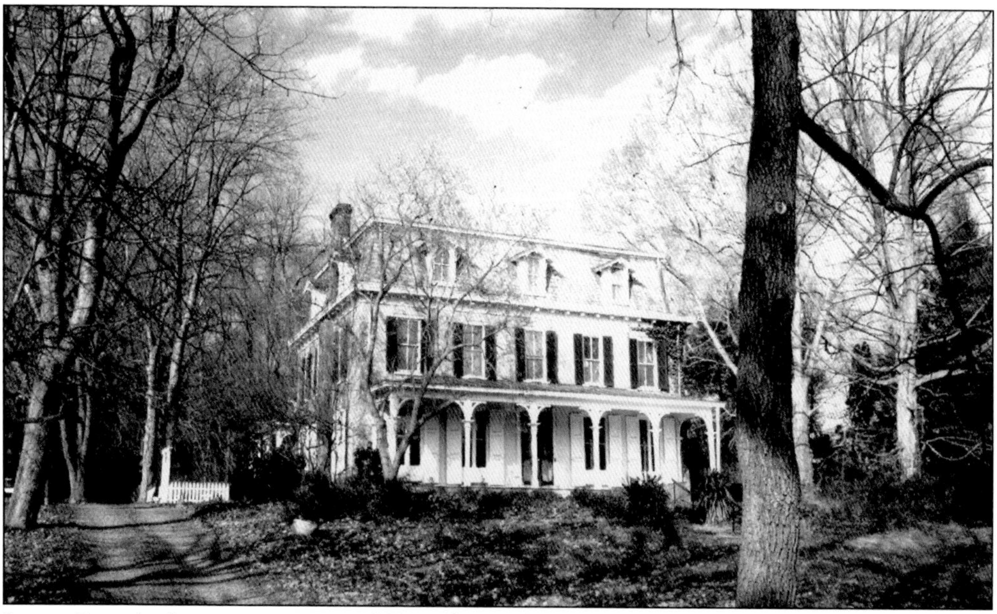

James Grier built a mansion named Broadlawns, located at 1574 Easton Road, in 1872. The building is a Victorian mansion designed in the French Colonial architecture with a mansard roof. The nine-bedroom house and barn were constructed of sandstone quarried on the property. It included 31 acres at the foot of Grier's Hill. James Grier's later years were spent at the Warrington farm.

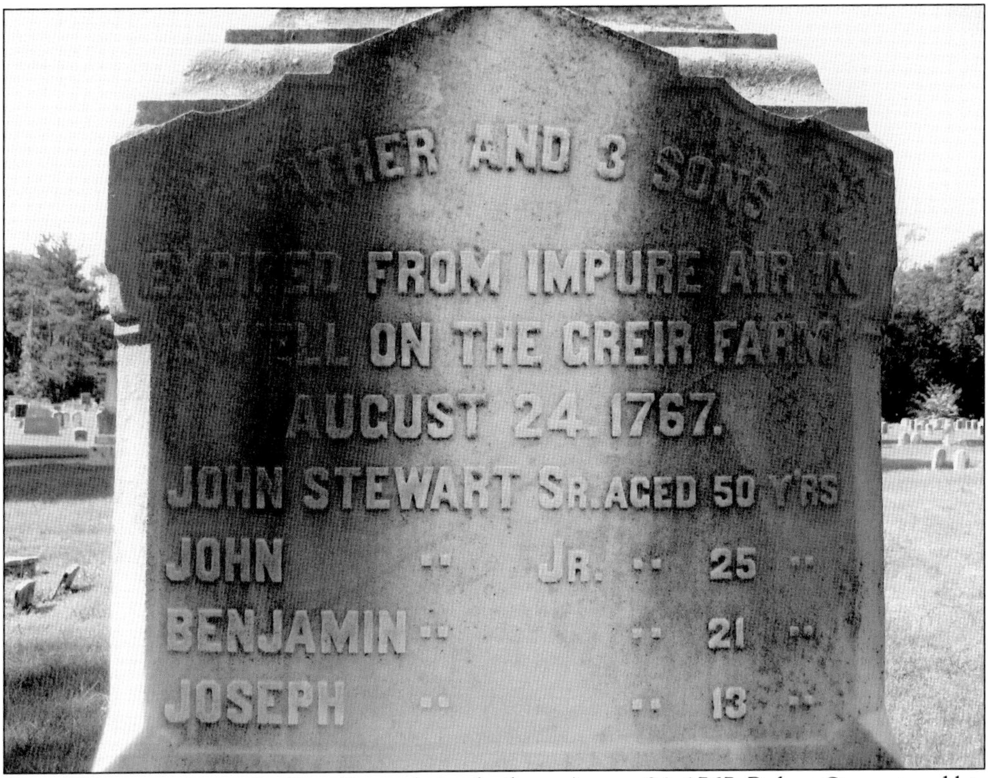

Over 100 years prior to the Broadlawns being built on August 24, 1767, Robert Stewart and his three sons all died in a well on the property; after the father was trapped by impure air, his sons, ages 25, 21, and 13, each attempted to save the other. After the death of Robert Stewart, the farm came into the possession of John and Jane Stewart Grier.

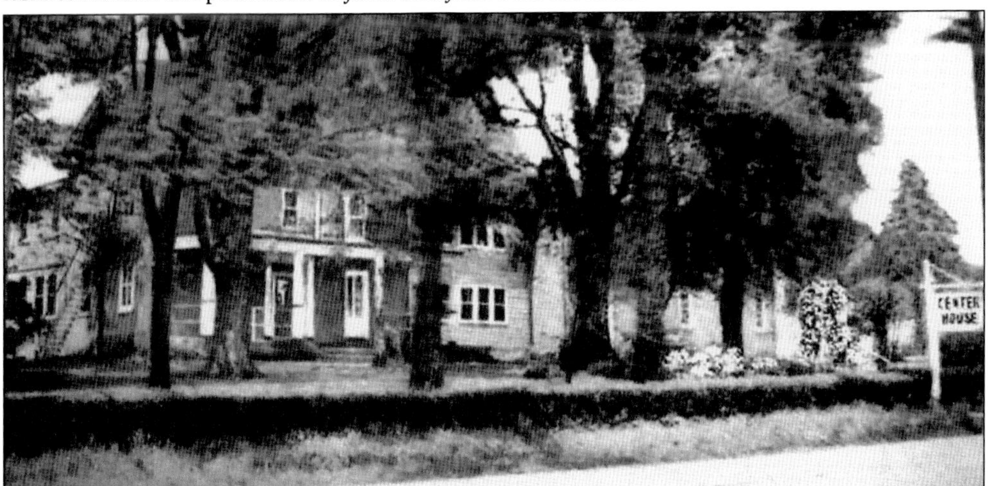

Center House, located on Easton Road next to what is now Freedoms Way, was owned by the German Club, which also owned all the property behind it that comprised the Warrington Swim Club. In the 1960s, this building was a boardinghouse with rooms for rent. There were fields between Center House and the pool that were planted with rotating crops of corn and soybeans.

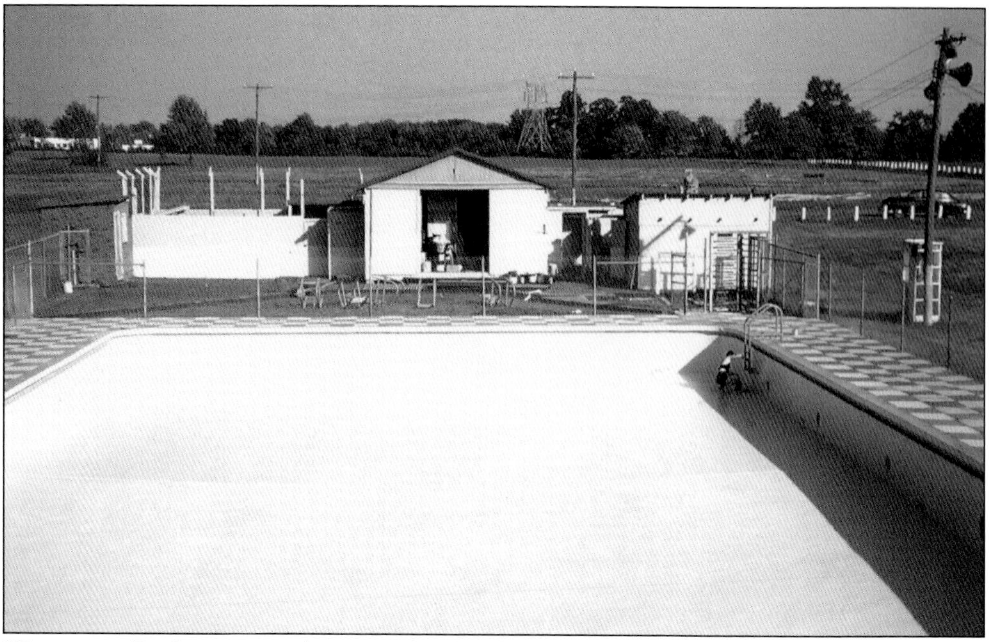

Warrington Pool was opened in 1939 by the Philadelphia District of the Workman's Benefit Fund. The Department of the Navy took over the pool during World War II. The German Club then retained ownership up until the 1970s. This photograph shows the original pool with the changing rooms that did not have a roof, locker room, snack bar, and office in the background. (Courtesy of Edna Mae "Mich" Michener.)

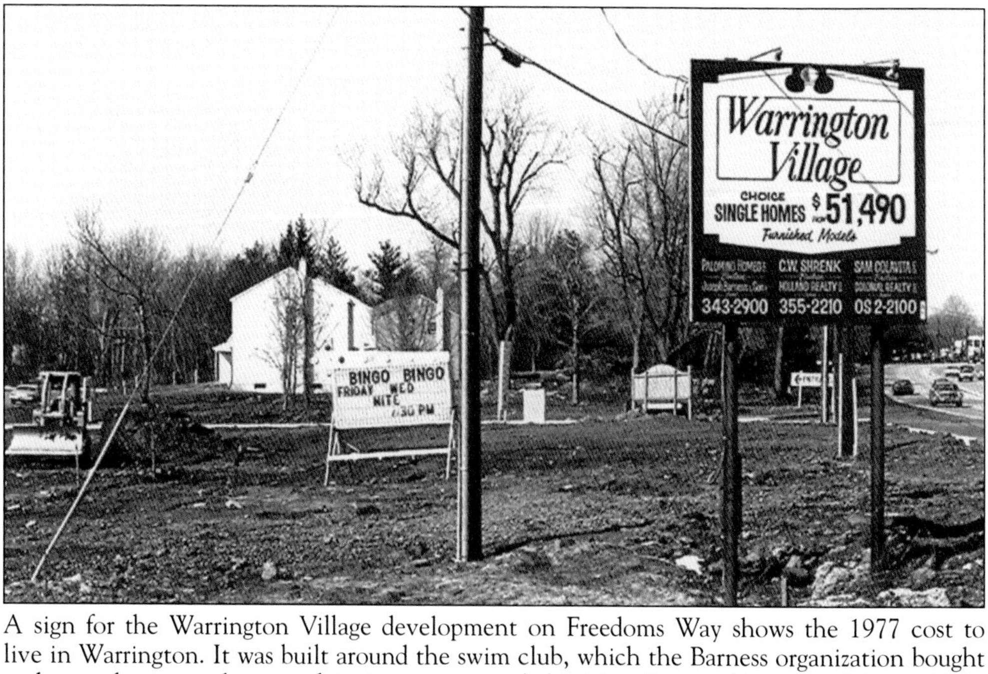

A sign for the Warrington Village development on Freedoms Way shows the 1977 cost to live in Warrington. It was built around the swim club, which the Barness organization bought and turned over to the township; it was renamed the Mary Barness Tennis and Swim Club. The dance hall and outhouses behind the picnic groves were torn down to make room for the development.

Two

VILLAGE OF NESHAMINY

Neshaminy Village is located at the intersection of Easton and Street Roads. The village was named after the Neshaminy Creek, which flows along the southerly side. The village underwent a name change from Warrington Square to Neshaminy on February 10, 1864, when the post office was organized. Frog Hollow was the name given to a portion of Little Neshaminy Valley in the southwestern portion of Warrington Township. Paul Valley is another area of Neshaminy Village that was named after the Paul family.

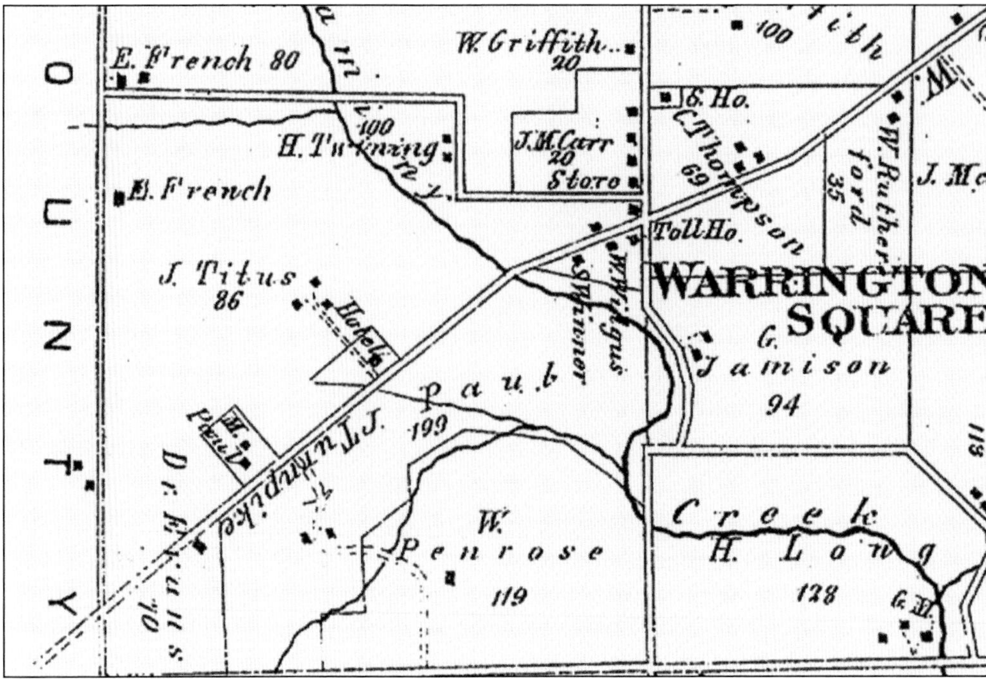

Pictured here is a village of Neshaminy map from the 1876 atlas of Bucks County by J. D. Scott.

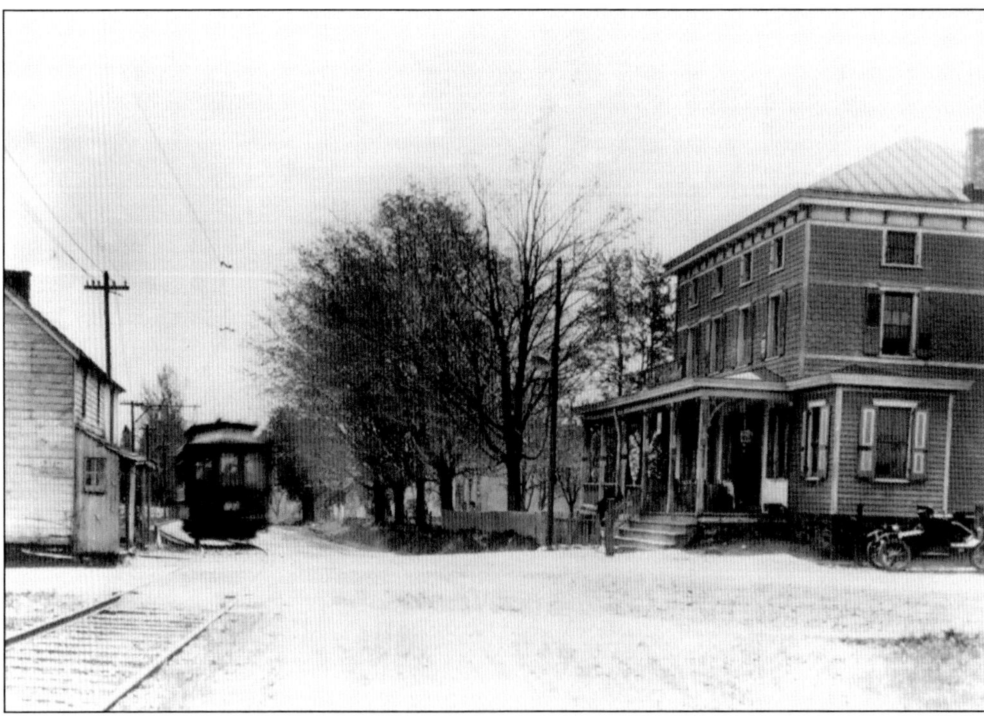

A 1909 view shows the Neshaminy Village (Easton Road and Street Road) looking south toward Willow Grove. Pictured are, from left to right, the old tollhouse, the Philadelphia Rapid Transit Company Trolley Tracks, and Worthington's General Store/Post Office.

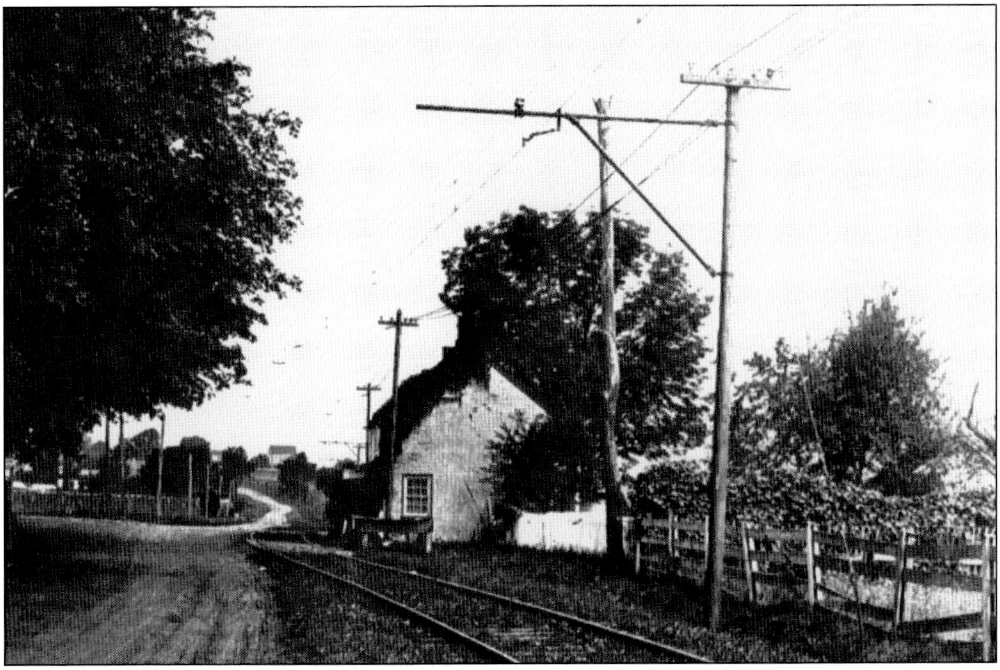

A 1909 view shows Neshaminy Village (Easton Road and Street Road) looking north toward Doylestown. Seen here, from left to right, are the Philadelphia Rapid Transit Company trolley tracks and the old tollhouse where John Williams collected the 5¢ toll from the horse-drawn wagons and buggies, cars, and trucks. At this time, Easton Road was not paved and took a winding path up toward Warrington Village.

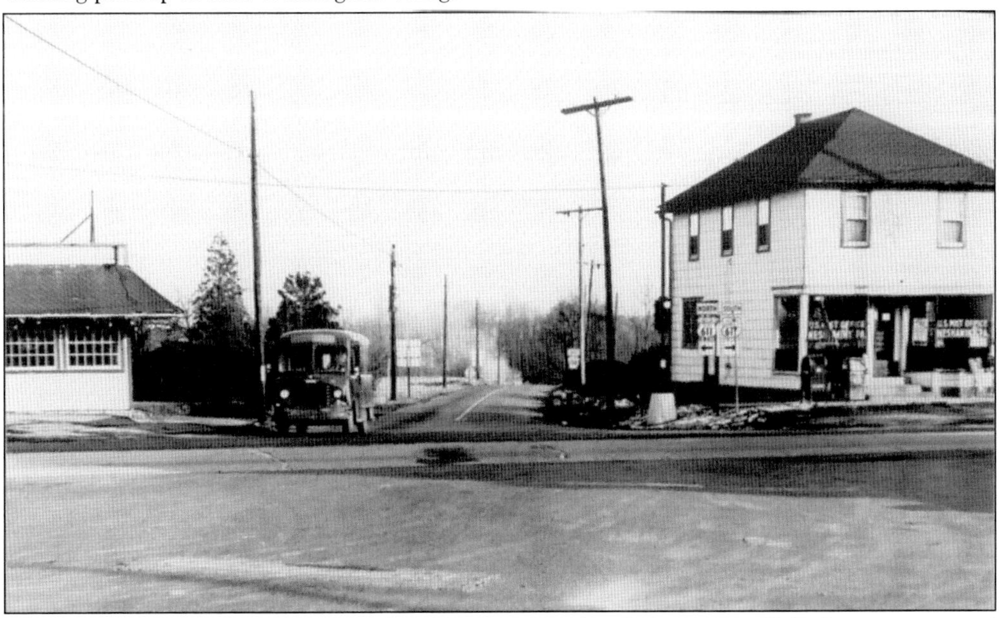

A 1960s view shows Neshaminy Village (Easton Road and Street Road) looking east toward Southampton. Pictured are, from left to right, Speakman's Store, a milk delivery van, and the Neshaminy Post Office. Street Road was two lanes at that time, and the trolley tracks had been removed years ago.

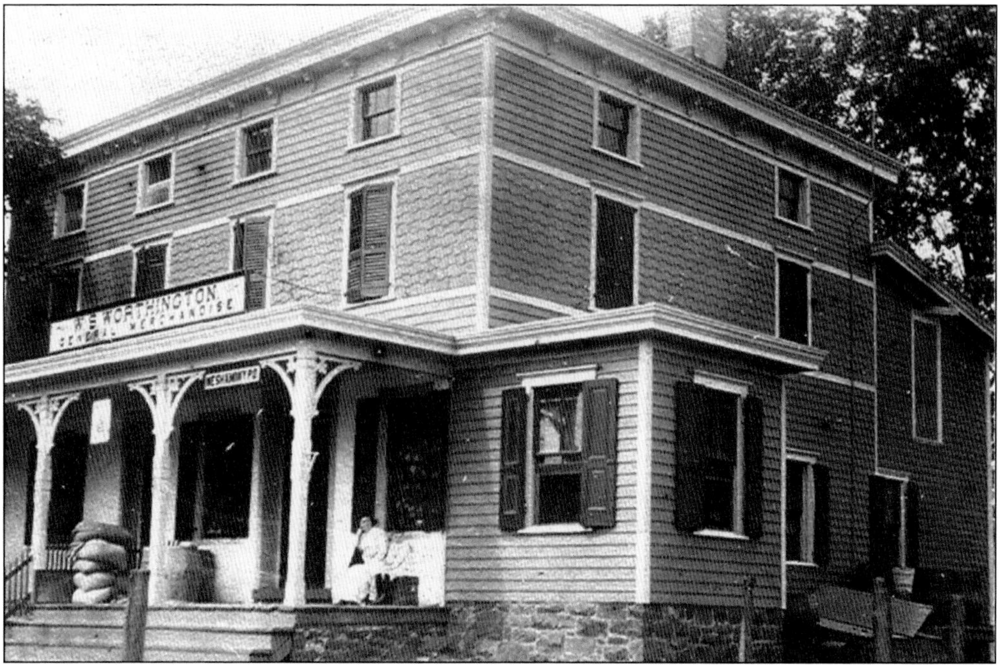

On July 26, 1867, John H. Worthington was appointed postmaster at Neshaminy in place of Daniel S. DuBree. The post office was located in the general store, which was known as the Worthington General Store from 1869, when F. L. Worthington ran the business. This building was razed in 1960 when Easton Road was widened. (Courtesy of Jane Henderson.)

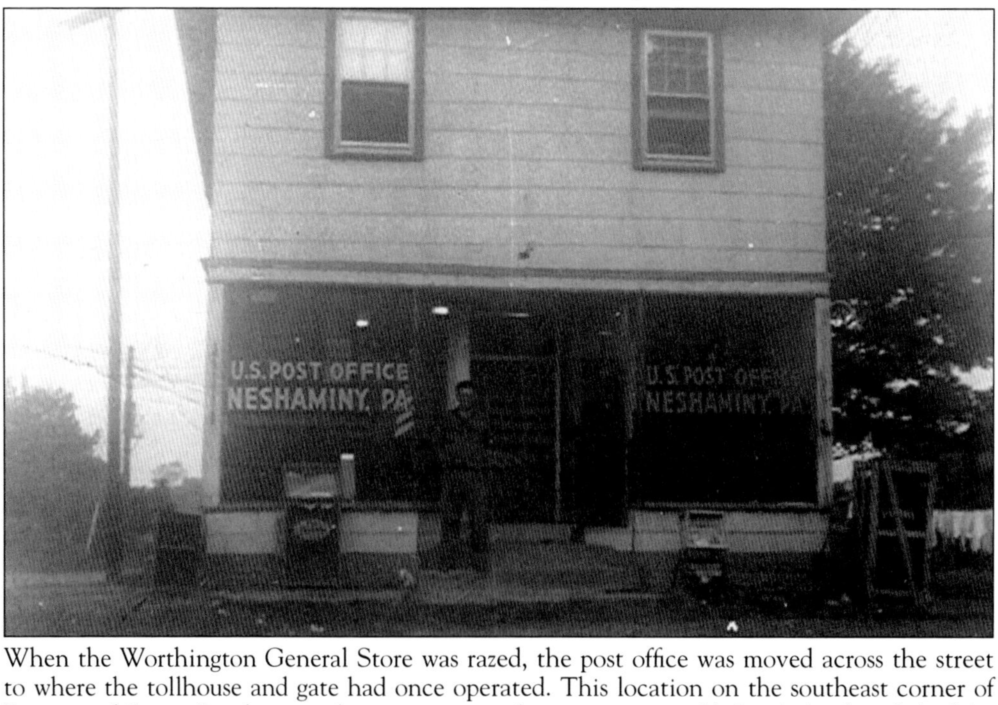

When the Worthington General Store was razed, the post office was moved across the street to where the tollhouse and gate had once operated. This location on the southeast corner of Easton and Street Roads was only temporary, as this structure would shortly be demolished for Easton Road's widening too.

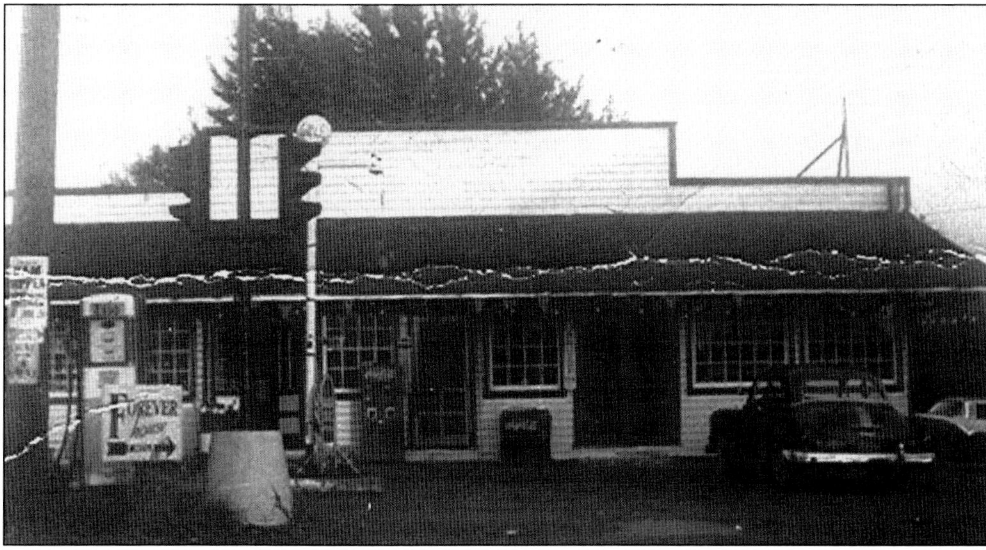

Jim Speakman's store was located on the northeast corner of Street and Easton Roads. After the store was razed, the corner became the location of a gas station. Soon, as part of the Valley Square shopping center, the corner will include a restaurant with a monument-type sign stating "Warrington Township." Speakman also ran an establishment that sold beer. It was located on the southeast corner of Street and Easton Roads.

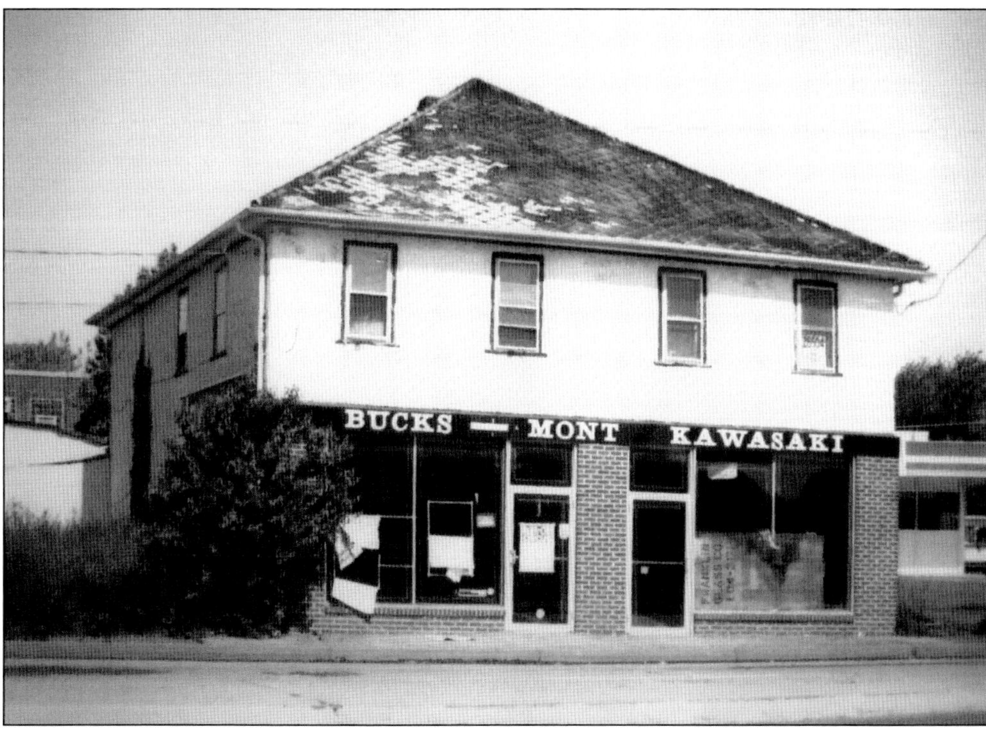

Joseph Penrose Sr. built one of the first structures containing multiple stores and apartments in the township in the 1920s. At one time, it housed a taxidermist and later a motorcycle dealership. Up until the early 1960s, this structure sat next to Worthington's General Store. Today vacant, it is located at 566 Easton Road.

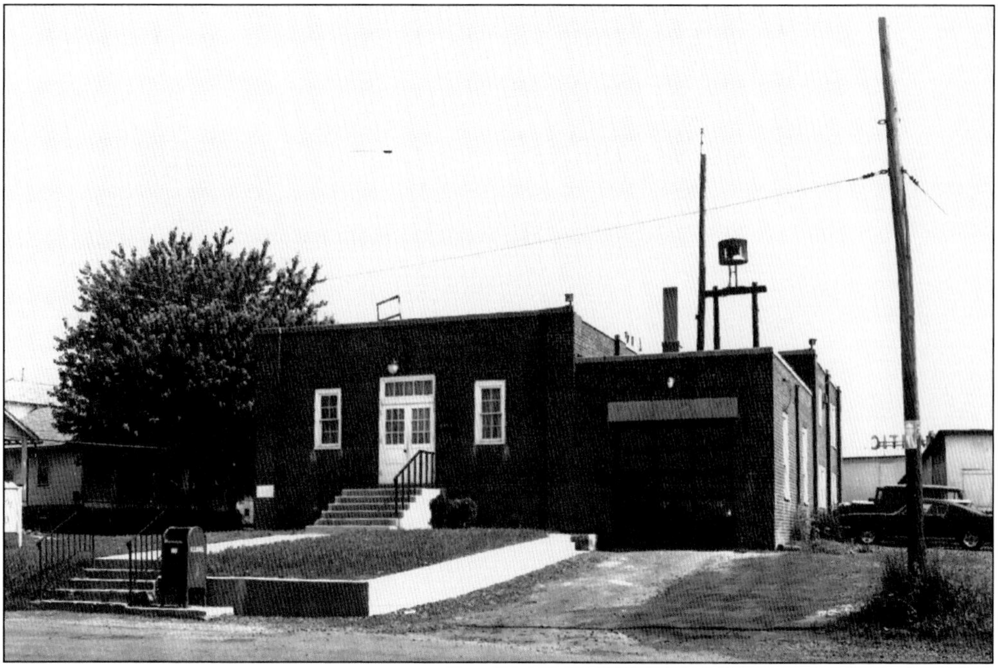

On April 3, 1934, the fire department trustees reported a bill of sale to purchase ground from Anna Penrose to build the new firehouse. A. Oscar Martin drew up plans. Ground was broken shortly after this, and the dedication of the firehouse took place on March 2, 1935. In 1939, an addition was made to the building at a cost of $3,760.99. (Courtesy of Warrington Fire Department.)

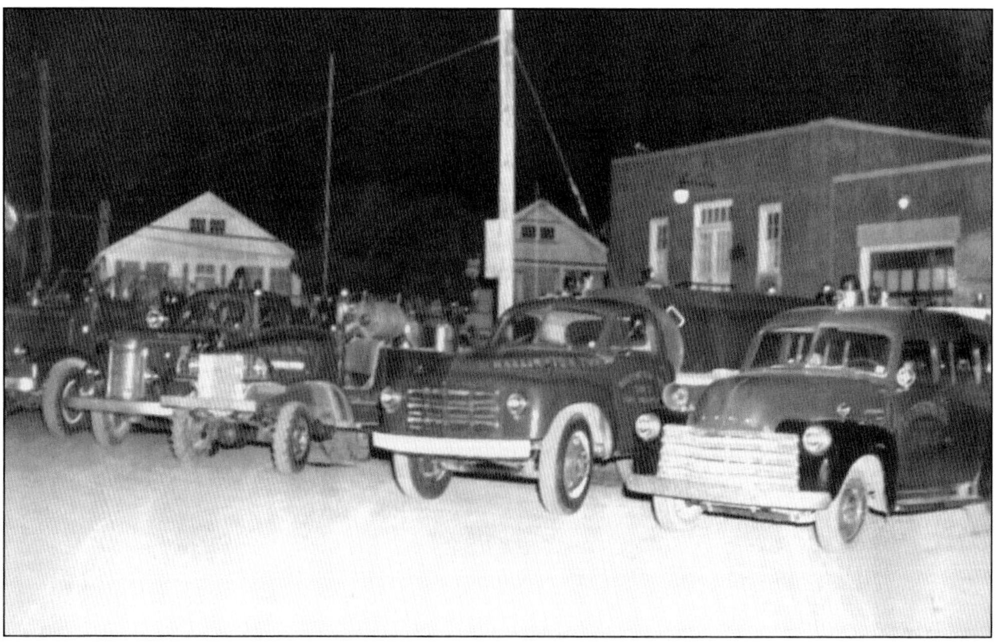

Shown above is a night picture, taken around 1955, on Maple Avenue that shows the Warrington Fire Department's firefighting fleet. In the background, several houses located on Kansas Road can be seen. (Courtesy of Warrington Fire Department.)

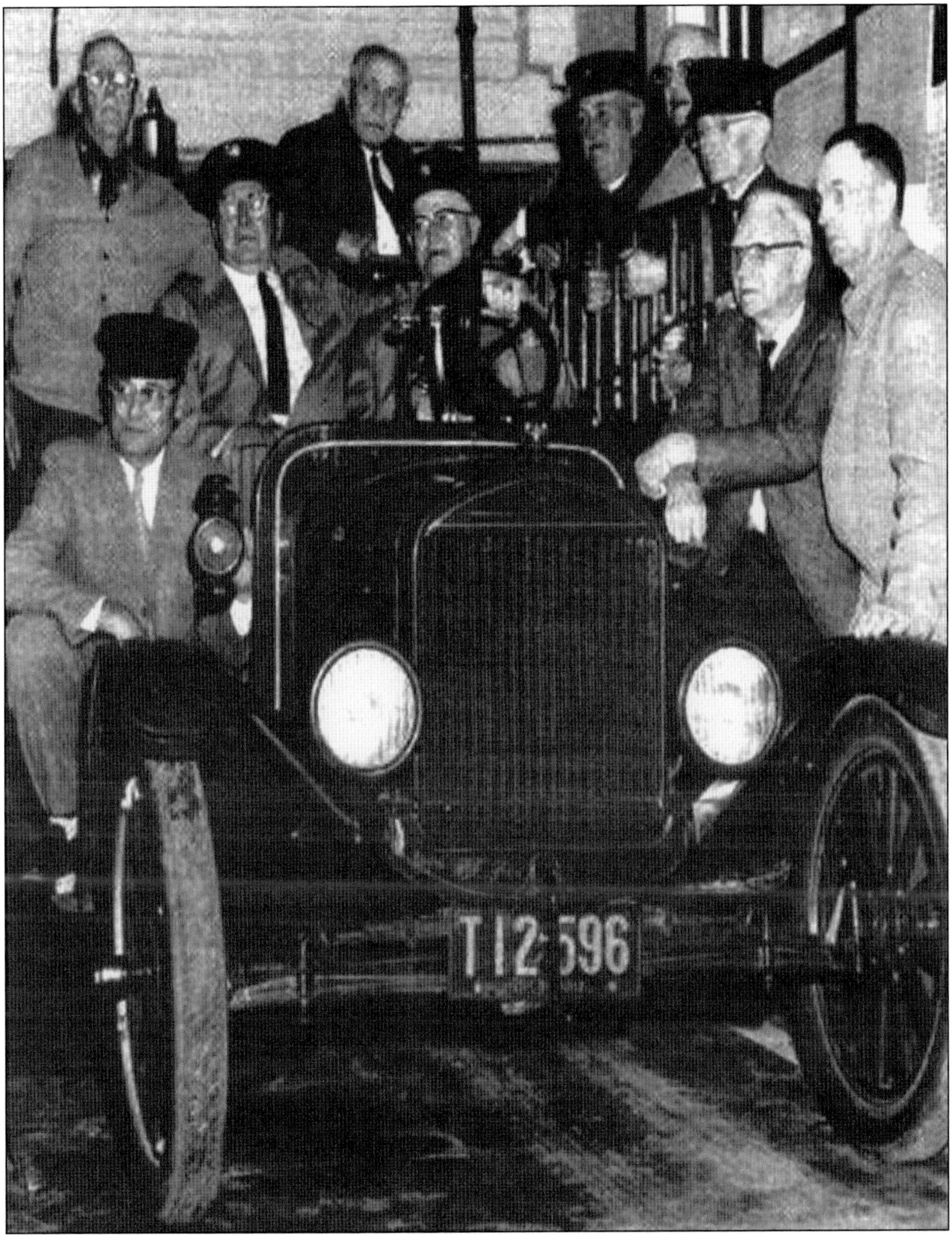

C. Leroy Murray sits at the wheel of Warrington's first fire truck. Other members of the company pictured are, from left to right, (first row) Ellis Lewis, Elmer Lewis, Irvin MacNair, and Joe Penrose; (second row) Charles Loux, Dave Worthington, Jim Kern, unidentified, and Sherman Perry.

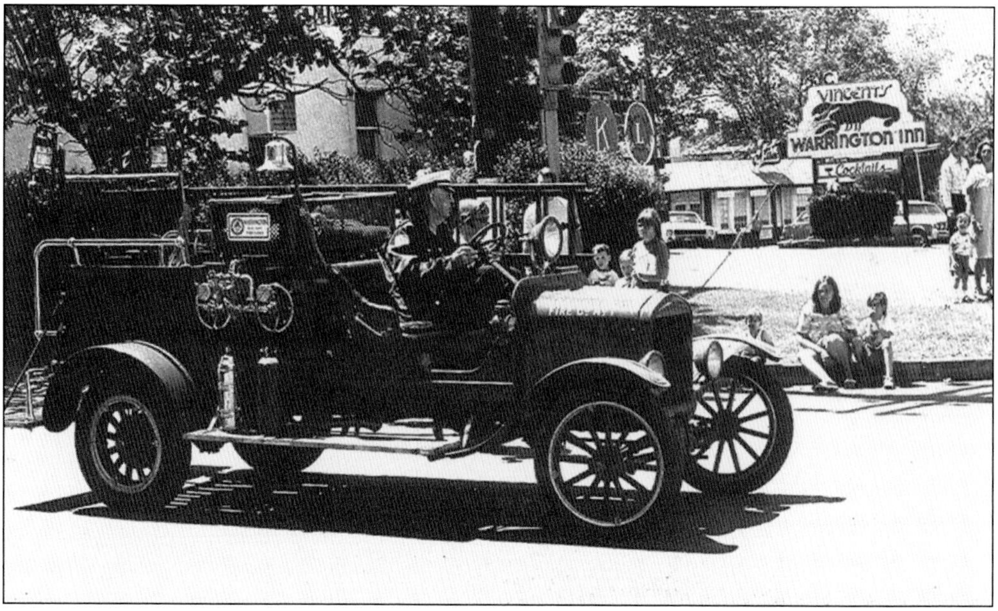

The first fire truck, a 1925 Ford Model TT American LaFrance chemical fire truck, was purchased for $2,083. It was in service until 1955. The 40-horsepower engine was not enough for the hills in Warrington, so the fire company voted to give the truck to Joseph Penrose Sr. It was owned by the Penrose family from 1955 until May 2008 when it was given back to the fire department.

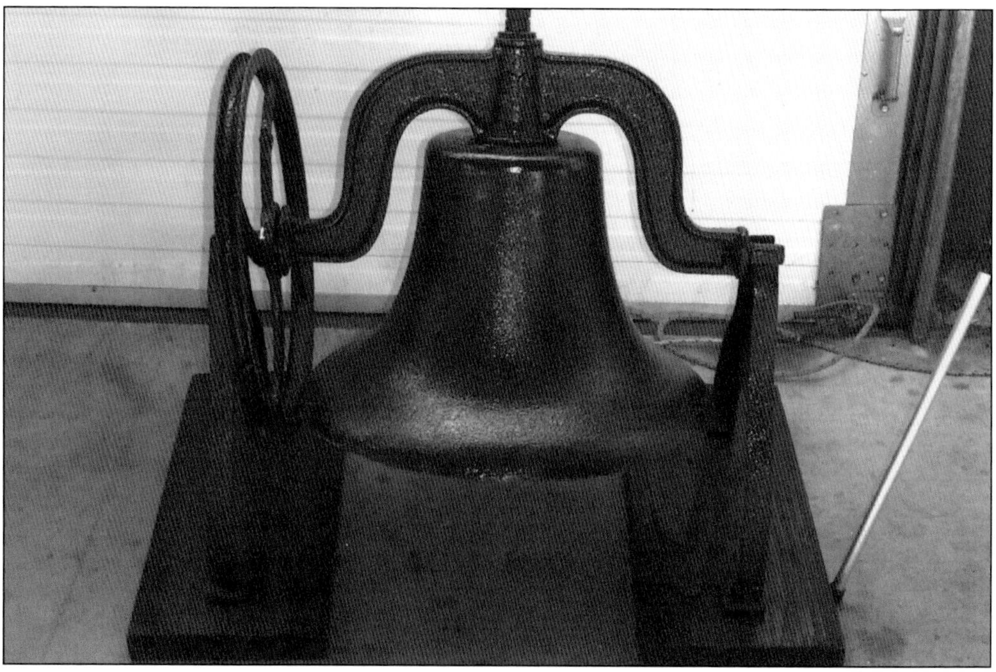

Atop the garage, behind the general store, sat a bell that was rung to summon the firefighters. When the firehouse was opened on Maple Avenue, the bell was no longer used, as a siren tower was installed. The Riley family purchased the bell at auction when the general store was torn down. In 2006, Donald Riley donated the bell to the fire department.

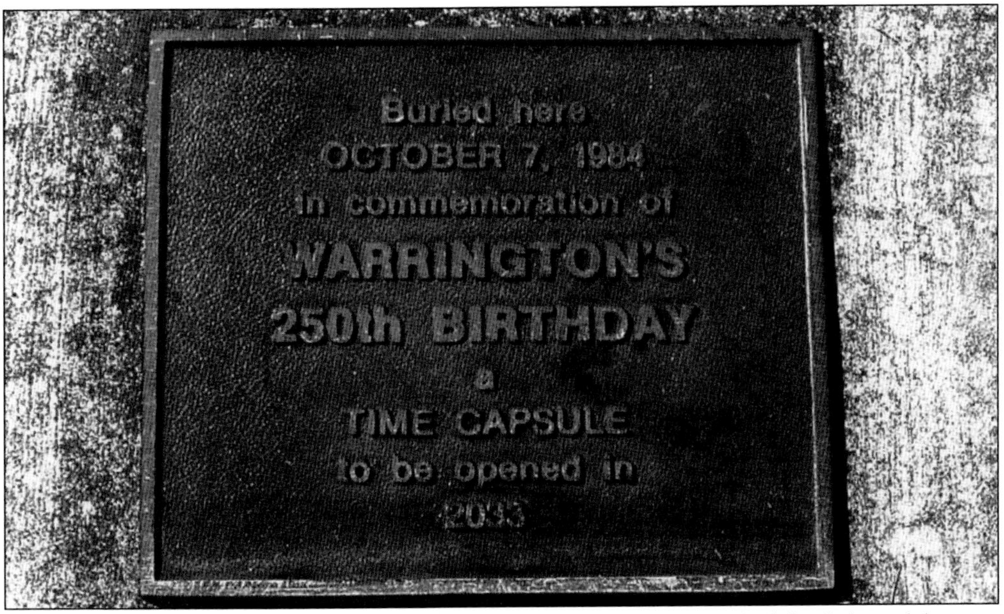

A time capsule was buried on October 7, 1984, as part of Warrington's 250th birthday celebration on the grounds of the firehouse located on Easton Road. The capsule is to be opened in 2033 when Warrington turns 300 years old. Some of the items buried included a Tamanend Junior High School yearbook, fire department membership list and patch, Lions club newsletter, and Warrington Woman's Club yearbook.

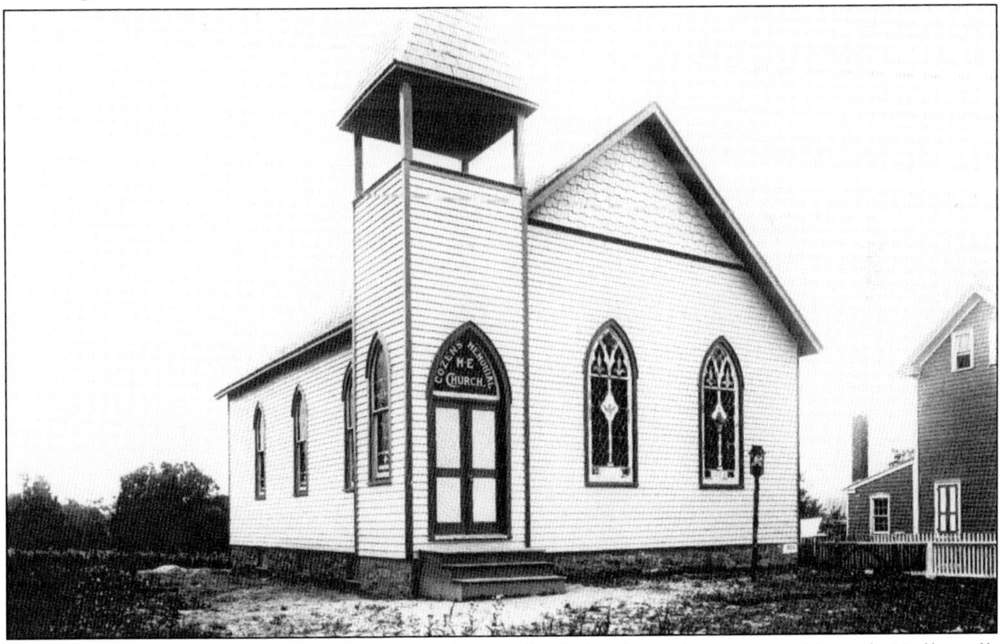

In 1894, the lot on Easton Road was purchased for $150 from the estate of Joseph Hallowell. Determined to build a chapel, the residents, under the direction of Rev. Wilmer Gray, former pastor from Willow Grove Methodist Church, organized. In 1905, the Neshaminy Methodist Episcopal Church, later renamed Cozens' Memorial Chapel, was opened. This served the needs of their congregation until 1963 when ground was broken on a new building.

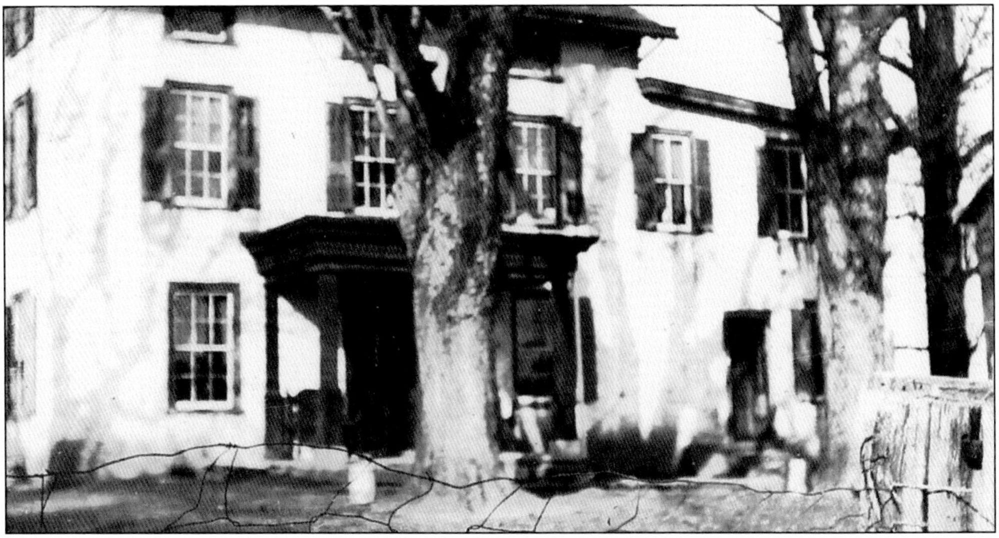

On November 2, 1727, Joseph and Elizabeth Paul purchased property in Warrington. The purchase consisted of 300-plus acres, for which they paid one shilling for every 100 acres. Son James Paul married Mary Worth and constructed the original homestead that is today located at 213 Easton Road in 1749. This picture shows the house as it stood in the late 1920s. (Courtesy of Joseph Penrose Jr.)

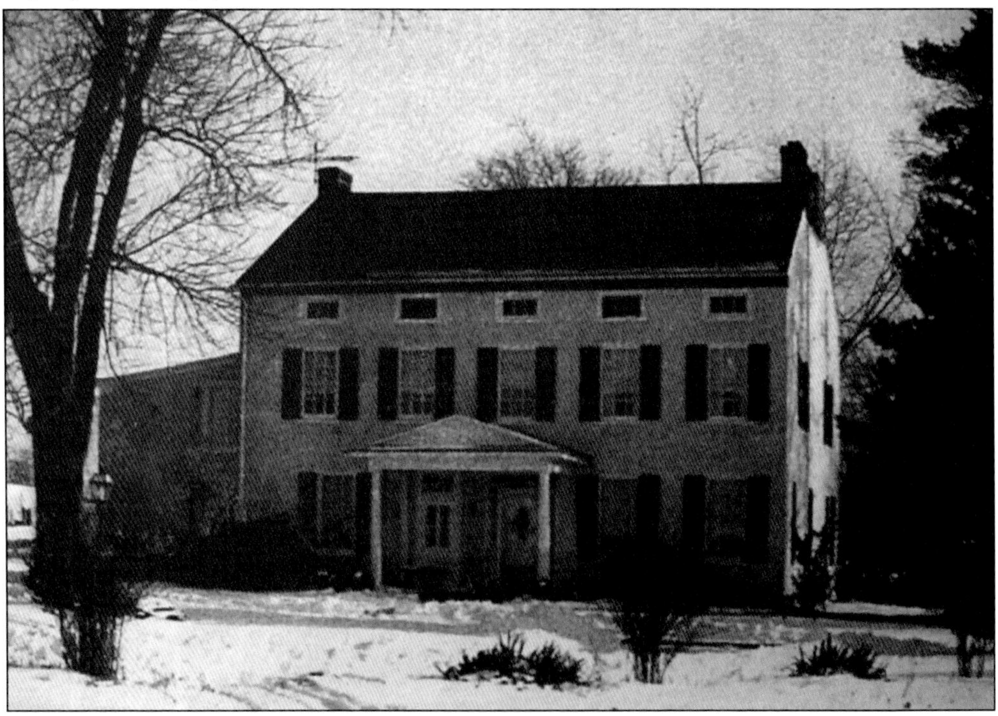

In 1846, James's sons, Joseph and Morris Paul, built the house today located on Costner Drive (pictured here). In 1847, Morris Paul inherited 120 acres of the original 300 acres, including this house. Later Morris's daughter, Hanna Paul, came to own the property and married William Penrose Sr. This home received a certificate and plaque from the Bucks County Heritage Conservancy in 1976. (Courtesy of Edward Knell.)

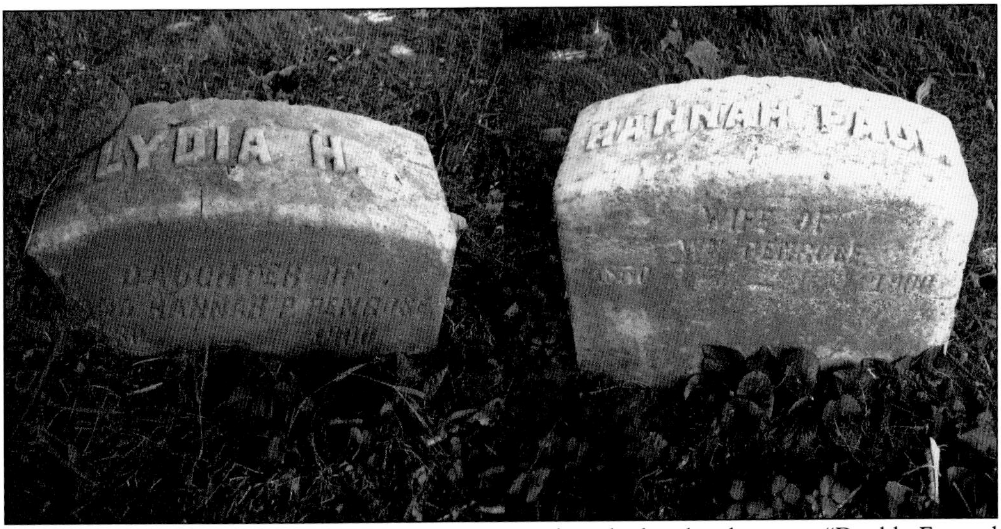

Penrose's family suffered terrible losses in 1900, as described in local papers, "Double Funeral in Warrington: One of the largest funerals that ever took place in Warrington occurred on Wednesday afternoon, the 2d, when Mrs. William Penrose and her daughter, Miss Lydia H. Penrose, both of whom died under peculiarly sad circumstances from typhoid fever, were buried in the Horsham Friends' burying ground."

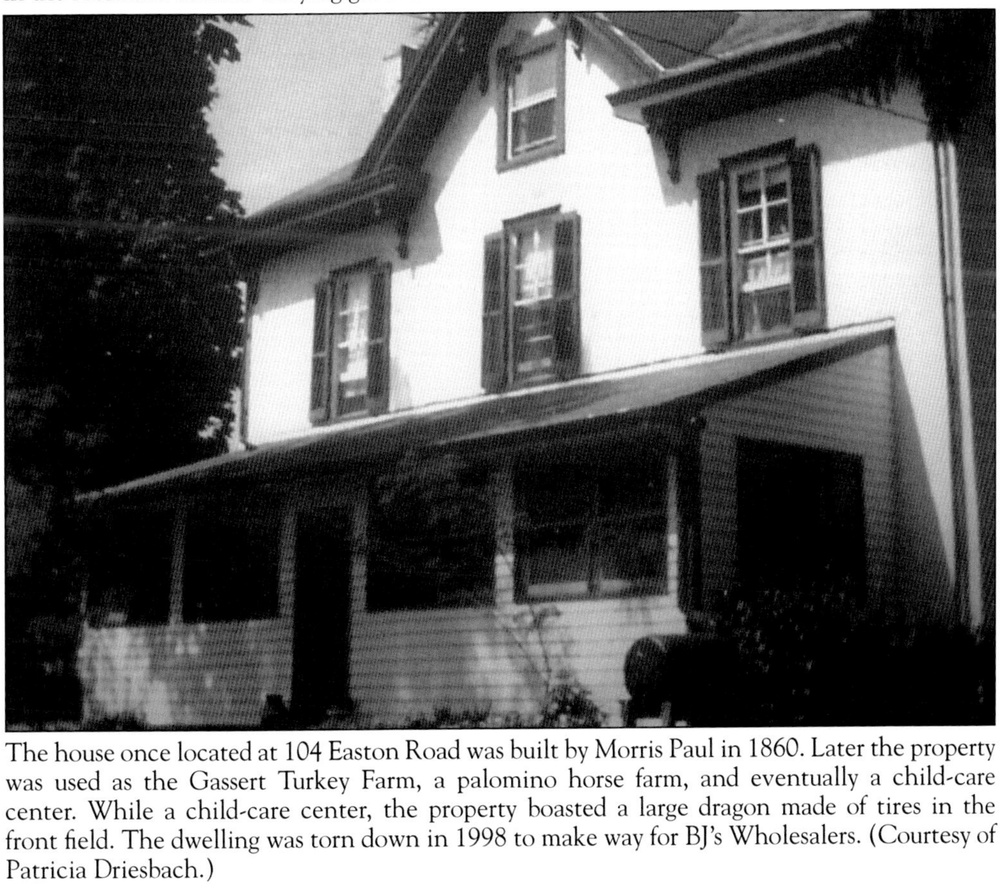

The house once located at 104 Easton Road was built by Morris Paul in 1860. Later the property was used as the Gassert Turkey Farm, a palomino horse farm, and eventually a child-care center. While a child-care center, the property boasted a large dragon made of tires in the front field. The dwelling was torn down in 1998 to make way for BJ's Wholesalers. (Courtesy of Patricia Driesbach.)

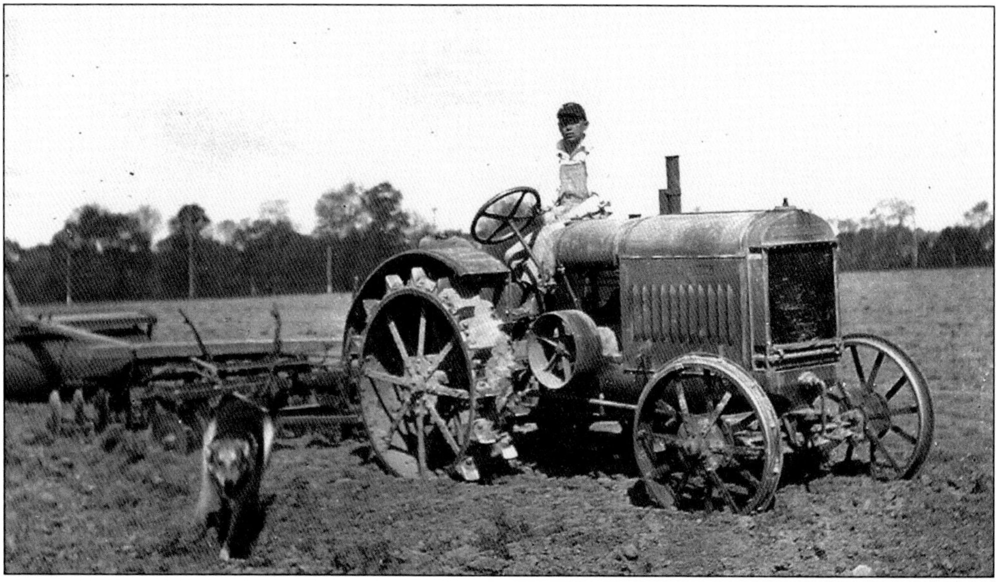

Seen above is a tractor owned by the Penrose family. On November 26, 1965, a suspicious fire destroyed a then 206-year-old barn (built 1759 with an addition in 1847). There was livestock killed, and a dozen antique automobiles were destroyed. The value placed on the loss was over $100,000 (1965 value). An empty gas can that did not belong to the Penroses was located near the scene. (Courtesy of Joseph Penrose Jr.)

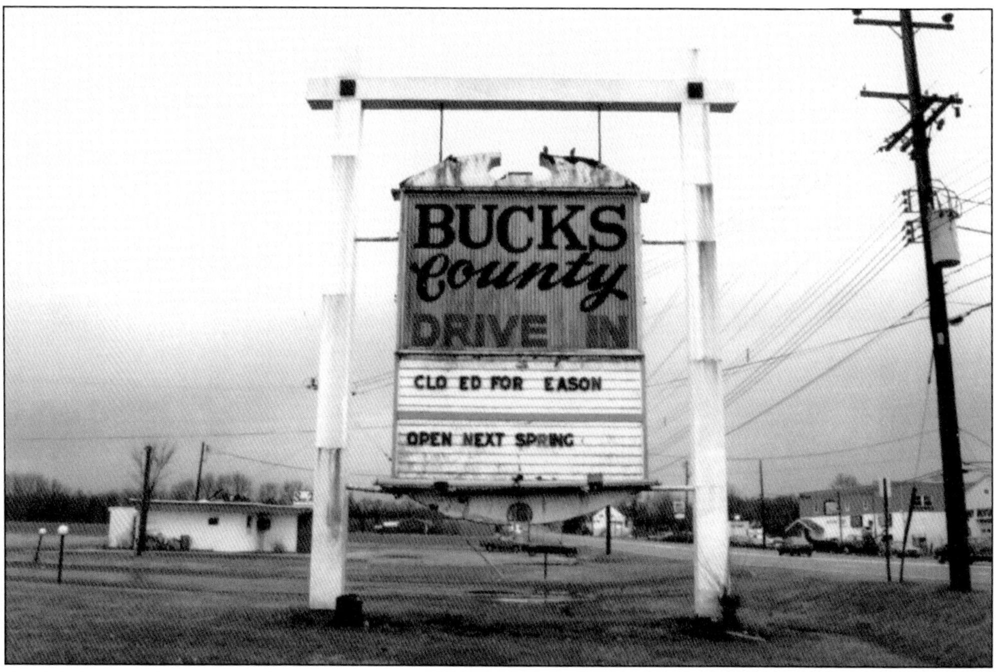

In 1951, Joseph Penrose Sr. opened a drive-in movie theater at 401 Easton Road. The Bucks County Drive-In originally had one screen and no snack bar (just a fish stand out front). This was the first drive-in in the area to install in-car air-conditioning. Later the drive-in housed two screens, a snack bar, bathrooms, and a playground. The drive-in closed in 1999. (Courtesy of the John Lewis Collection/Cinematour.com.)

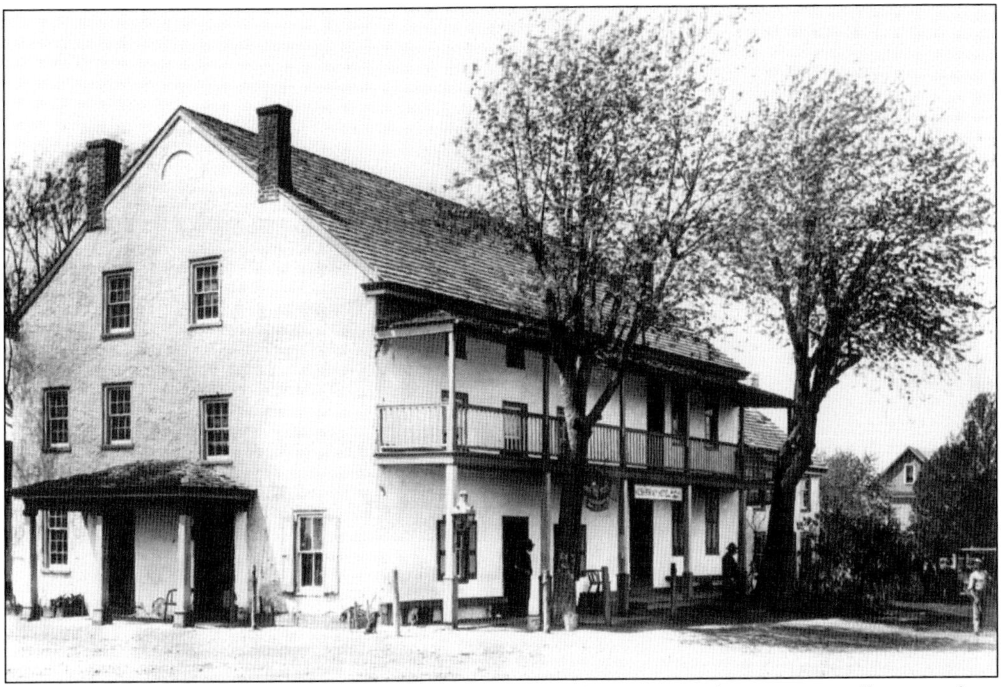

A tavern, located at 308 Easton Road near the Little Neshaminy Creek, was an excellent site for a hotel since the stagecoaches had to cross the stream located close by. For many years, the hotel was called Paul Valley Hotel, after Joseph Paul. In the late 1800s, the inn was called the Farmers Inn and later Frog Hollow Inn/Hotel. The inn would eventually be called the Neshaminy Inn/Hotel.

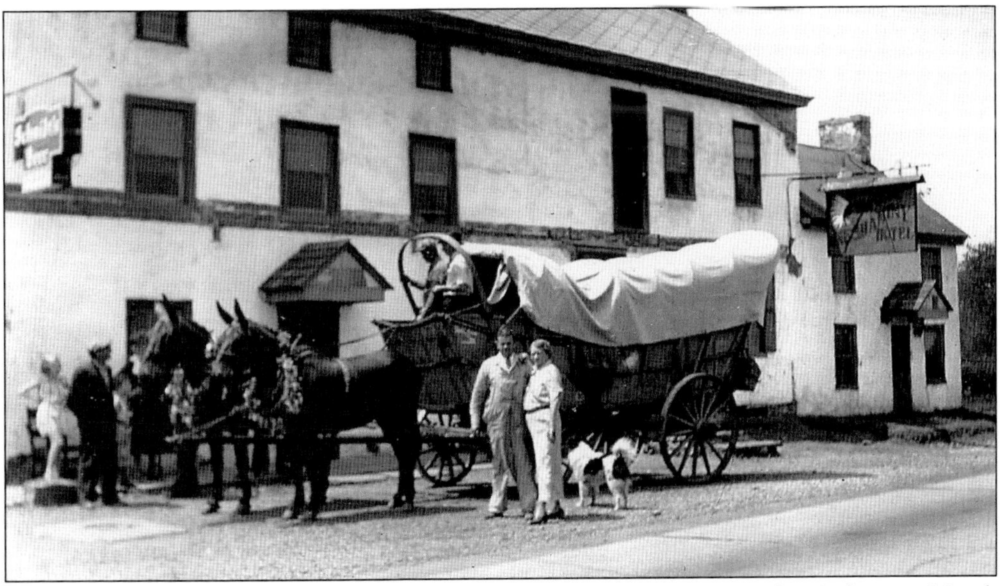

From 1914 through 1941, the township supervisors held their meetings at the Neshaminy Hotel. Joseph Hirsch bought the hotel in 1964. He opened a go-go bar in 1965 named the Old Time Hotel. In the early 1990s, Hirsch painted the building a series of brightly colored stripes in response to the township supervisors' attempt to amend an ordinance banning signs depicting nudity. (Courtesy of Joseph Penrose Jr.)

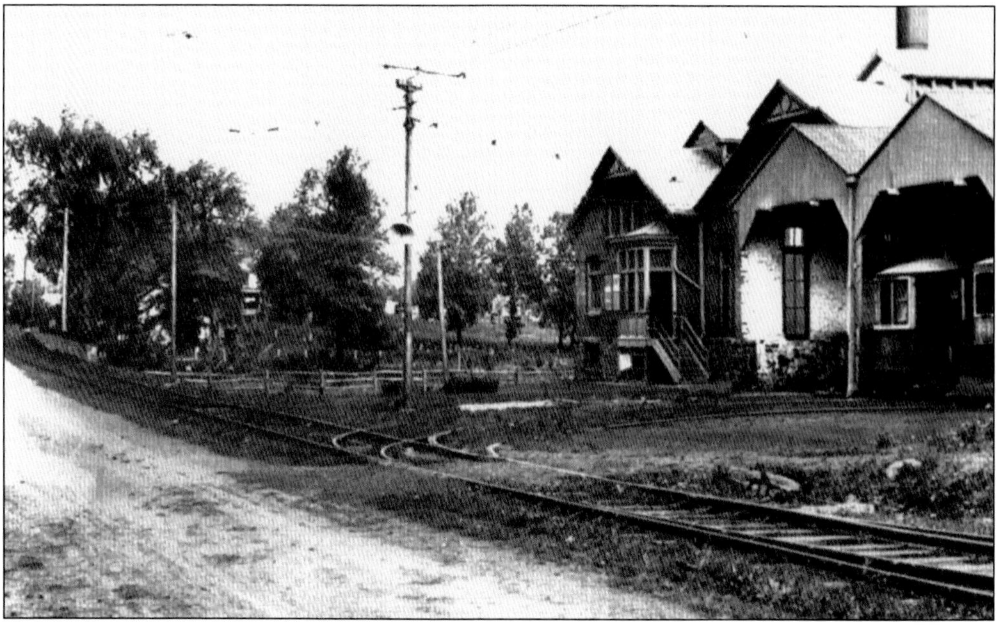

On May 26, 1898, the Bucks County Railway Company began to run a 12.18-mile trolley line on Easton Road. This line ran from Doylestown to Willow Grove on the northbound side of the road. Later the Doylestown and Willow Grove Railroad Company would run the line, followed by the Philadelphia Rapid Transit Company. The line was discontinued on February 14, 1931.

On July 1, 1903, Easton Road was leased to the Philadelphia Rapid Transit Company for 999 years. Warrington was a stop along the way and had trolley carbarns and a powerhouse at 401 Easton Road. The trolley barns were dismantled, but the powerhouse that used the water from the Neshaminy Creek still stands with "Bucks Co. Railway Powerhouse Paul Valley Erected 1897" engraved in a build stone on it.

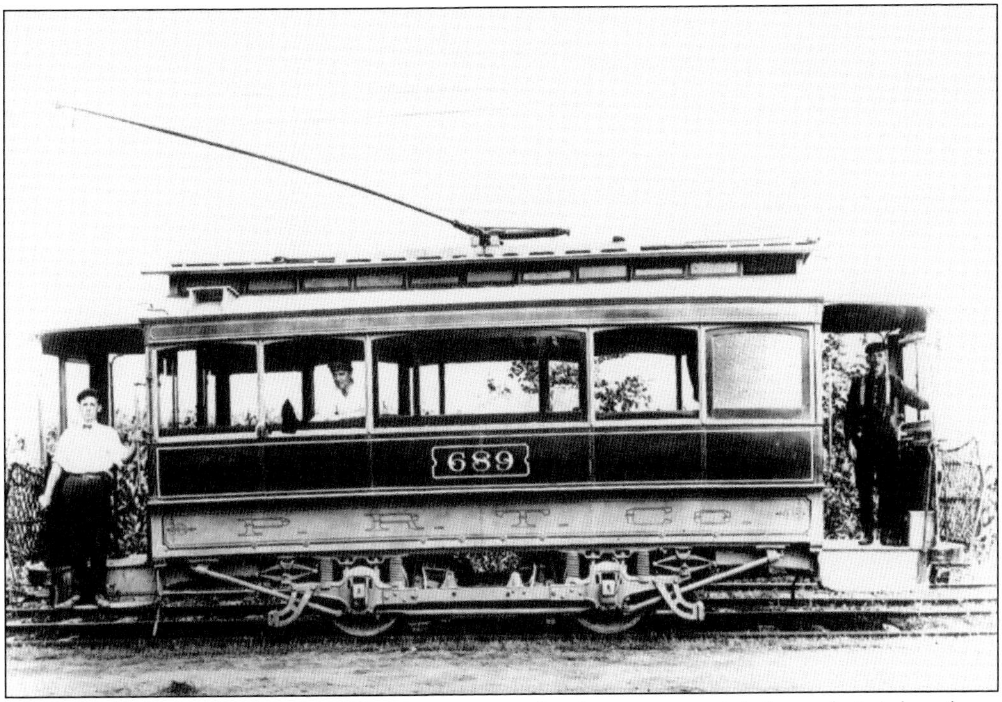

The trolley cars were of a great advantage to people who commuted daily to their jobs, places of business, or shops. The passenger cars ran on a schedule of every 36 minutes each way during the week and 18 minutes on weekends. There was a freight car that traveled each morning and afternoon during the week, delivering and picking up freight from the depots in the villages.

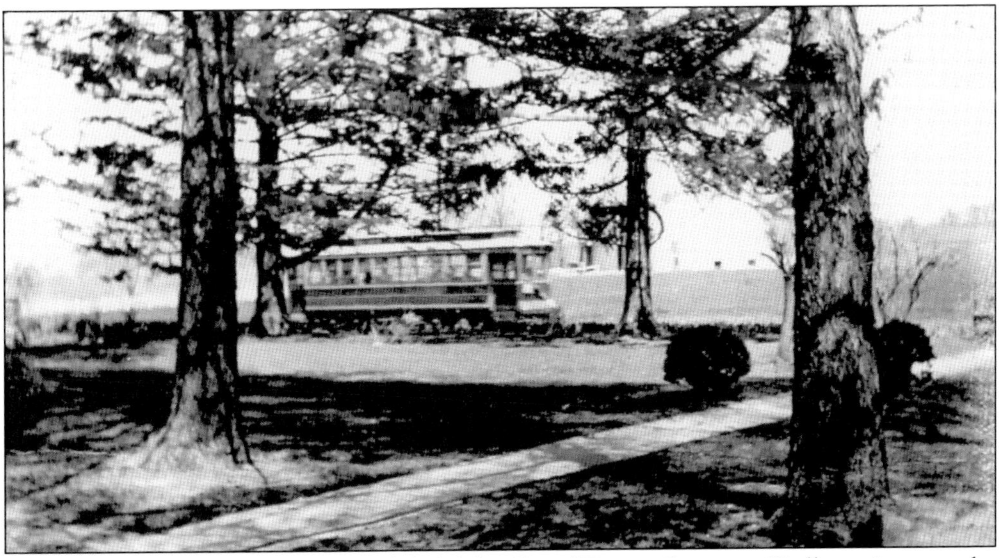

Pictured here in the mid-1920s is a Philadelphia Rapid Transit Company Trolley as it passes the Penrose Farms on Easton Road. As of 2008, for 281 years this property had been continuously owned by descendants of Joseph Paul, who purchased the property in 1727. Currently there are plans for the remaining property to be sold out of the family in 2009. (Courtesy of Joseph Penrose Jr.)

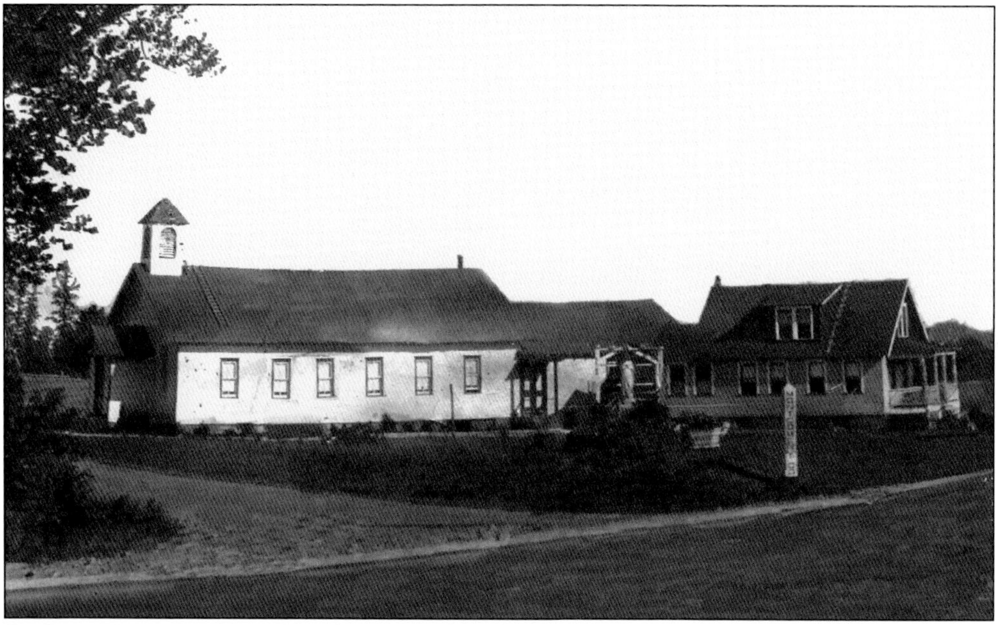

On June 16, 1922, St. Joseph's Church was founded with Fr. Joseph Gallen as pastor. The original parish church building was built on the western side of Easton Road, north of County Line Road. The church was a simple wood frame structure covered in white wood siding. In 1950, a new church was constructed on the east side of Easton Road. (Courtesy of St. Joseph's Church.)

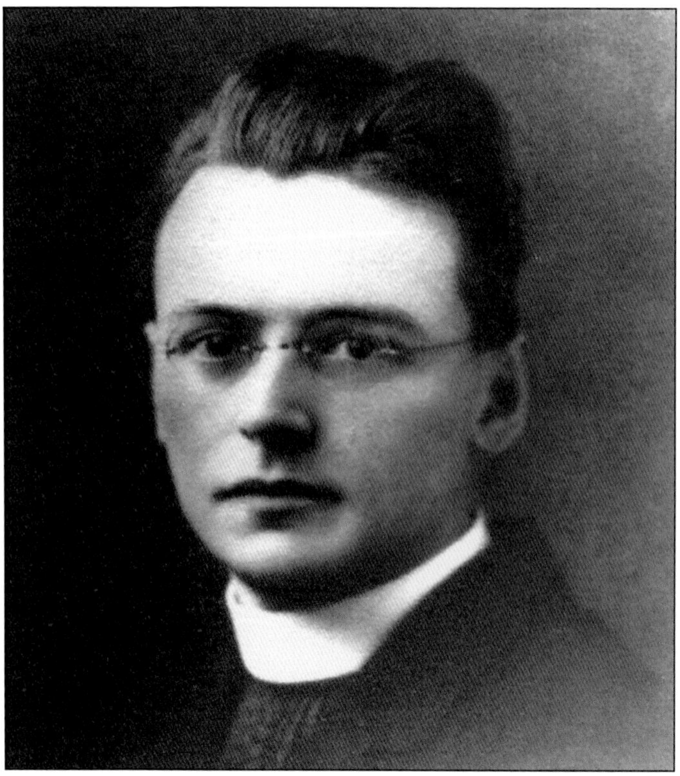

Gallen was known for taking in underprivileged boys. They became known around the area as "Father Joe's boys" or "Father Gallen's Gang." These boys tried their hands at everything on the farm and in fields; they learned to cook, sew, and bake bread. Some worked with plumbers and with electricians. (Courtesy of the Knights of Columbus, Father Joseph A. Gallen Council No. 5494, established 1964.)

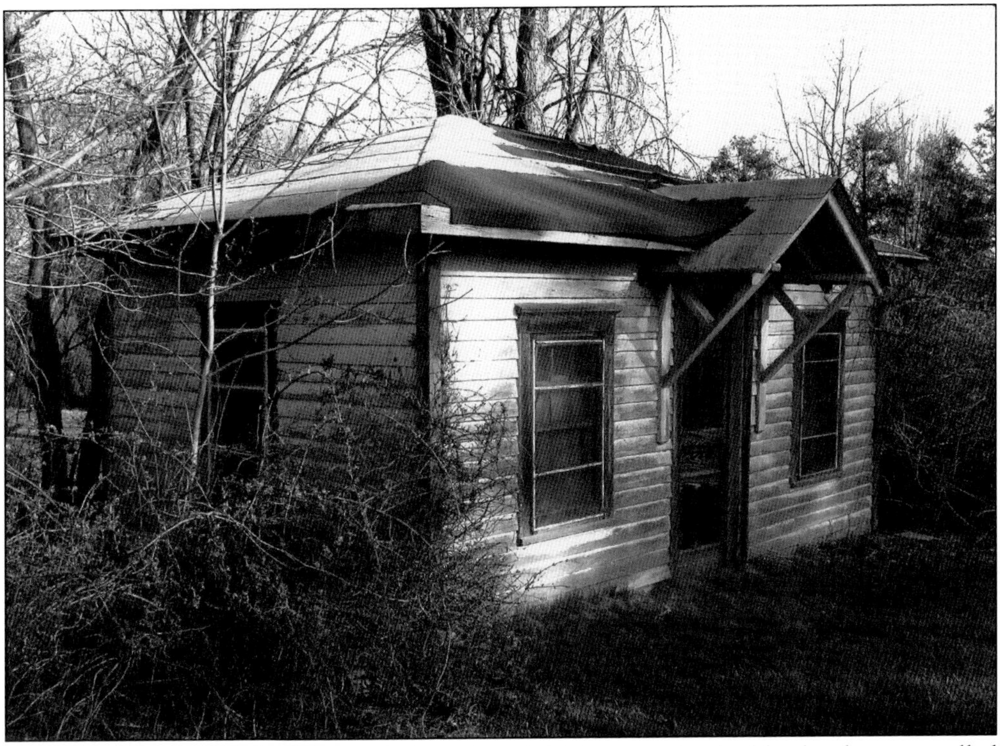

In 1926, George and Roland Schmidt, from Philadelphia, started to build a development called Crestwald off Easton Road, around Georges Lane and Crestwald Terrace. At this same corner sat a small building, which was the sales office. The sales brochures boasted all electric houses with built-in ironing boards.

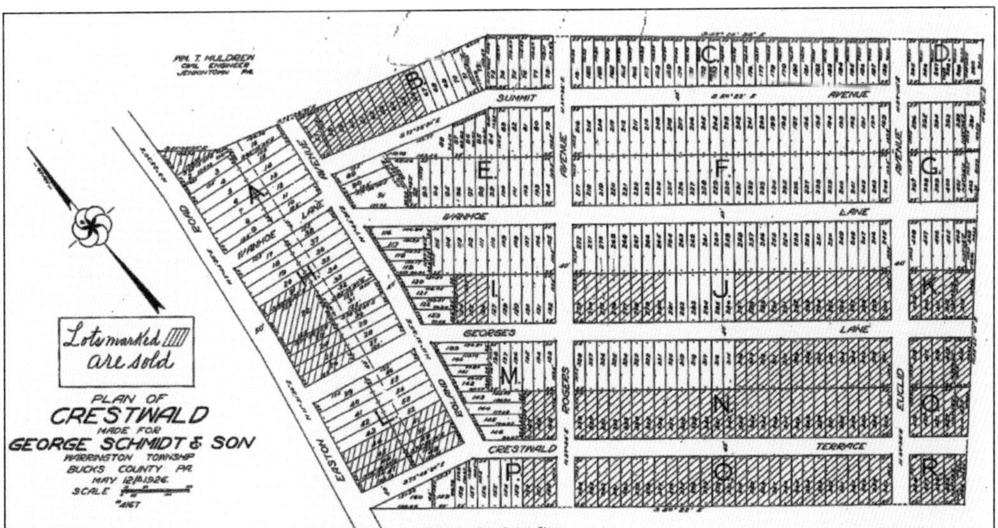

This plan for Crestwald Development shows the large amount of plots that were for sale. The development got as far as laying out the streets, placing curbs and sidewalks, and laying water access before the Great Depression got in the way of the plans. Only the four plots between 273 and 276 on Georges Lanes were actually built on. (Courtesy of Ronald and Viola Lewis.)

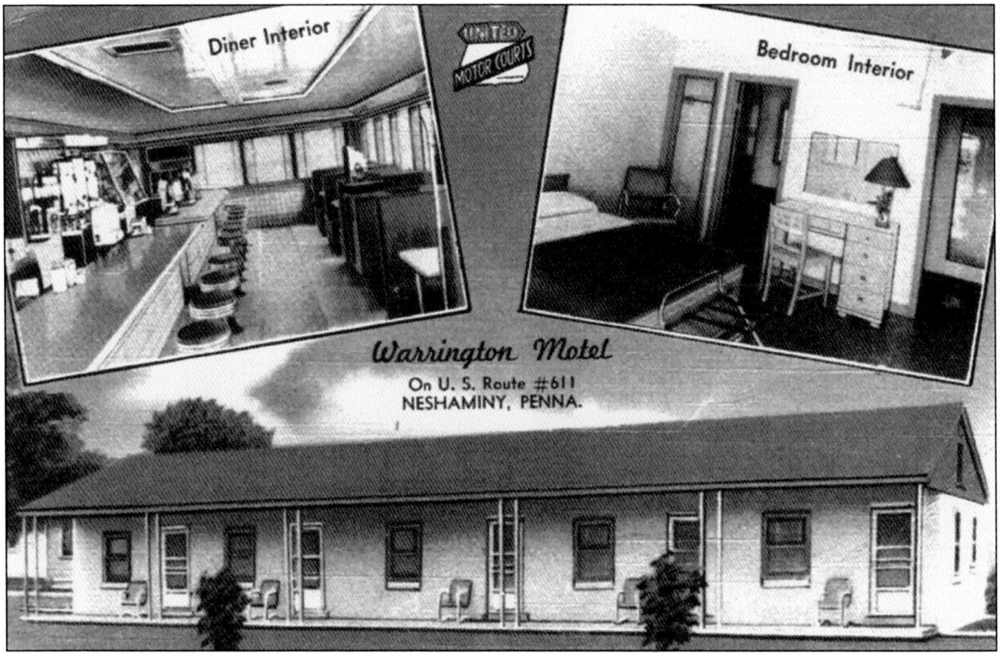

Joe Elnitski, a police officer from Philadelphia, started the Warrington Motor Lodge with a diner and a few motel cabins. Some of these cabins started their lives as chicken coops. Ann Leventhal bought the property in 1954. At one time, there was a multireligion chapel located on the property. Three generations of the Leventhal family managed the business for 50 years, until it finally closed in 2004.

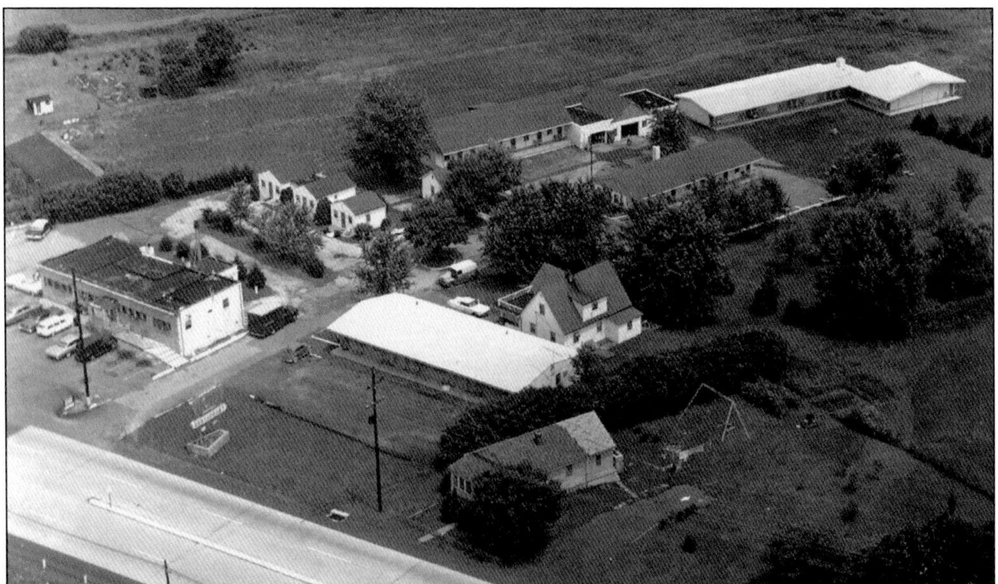

This aerial view, taken about 1961, shows the motel when there were 33 rooms and the diner before it was expanded to become a banquet hall and the Generations restaurant. It was a very popular diner and the only motel in the area. All the structures were torn down to develop the Valley Square Center. (Courtesy of Michael Leventhal.)

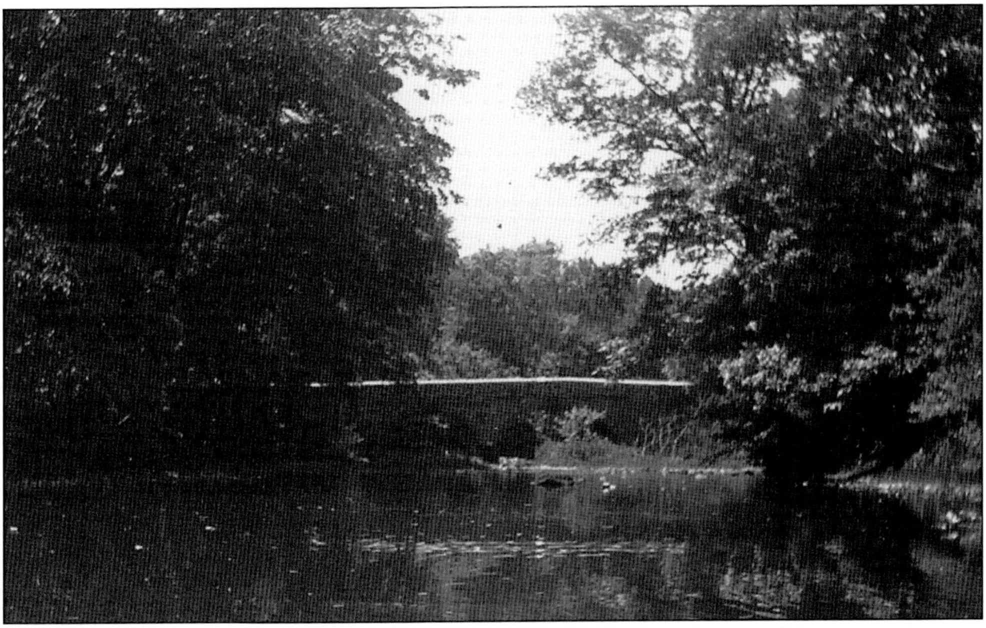

This picture, taken looking west on the Neshaminy Creek, gives a glimpse of the two-arch stone bridge that was once located on Street Road. This bridge was removed in 1960 when the state widened Street Road. (Courtesy of Harrison Delano Jr.)

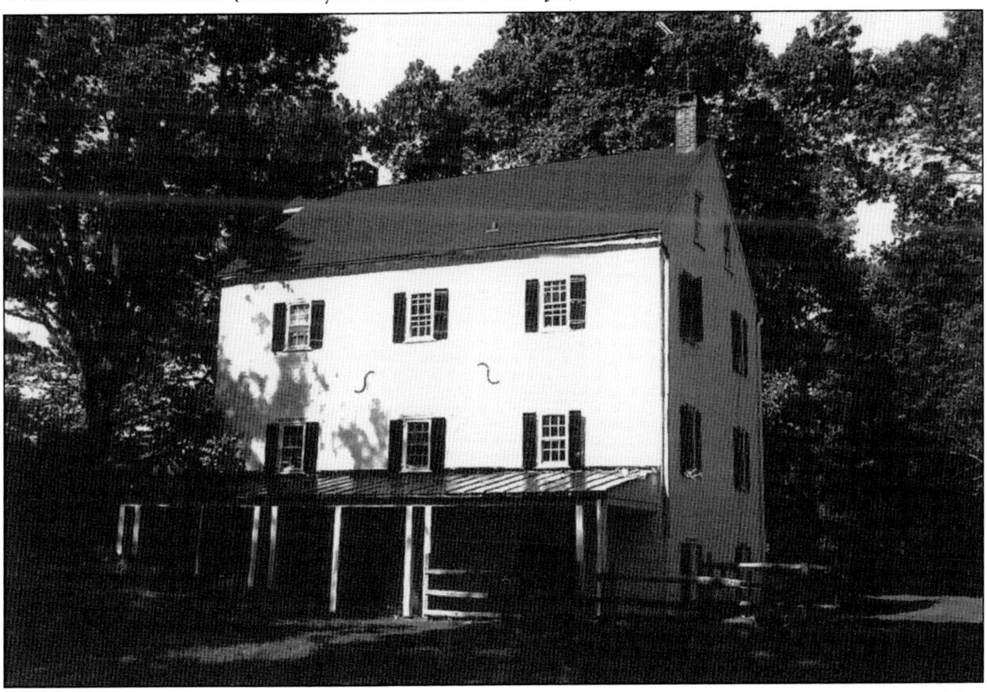

The gristmill pictured was built by Robert Tomkins, who owned the land from 1749 to 1759. The mill, located on Valley Road, operated under the name of the Long Merchant Mill when the Longs owned the property. In 1936, Adeline McCord converted the mill to a residence with plans drawn by A. Oscar Martin. The current owners operate the Old Mill Farm Nursery at this site.

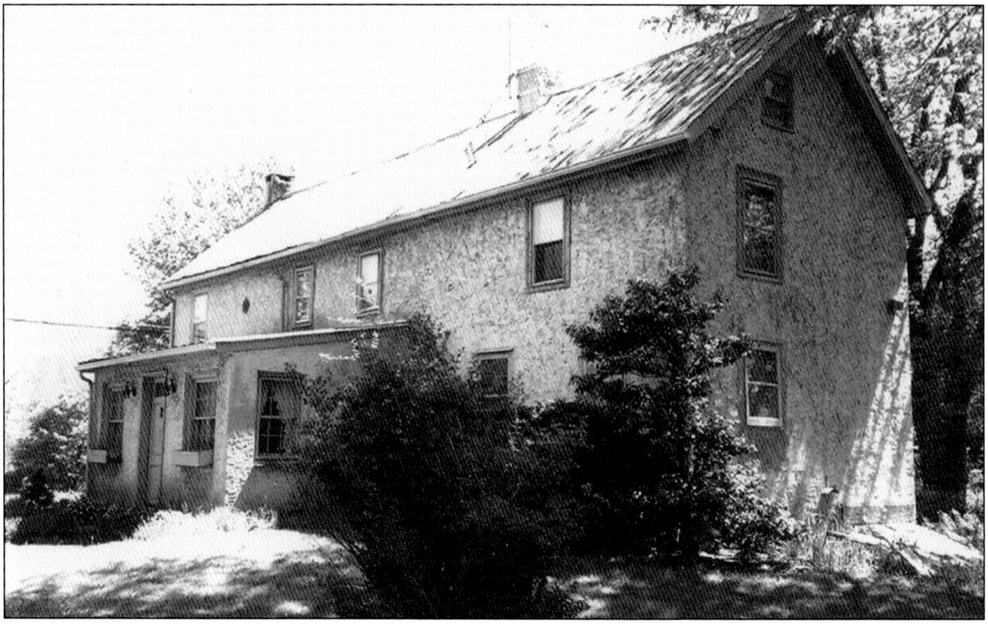

On March 13, 1911, Harry Cohen and his son Wolf Cohen purchased 63 acres of land on Street Road. Tomatoes made up much of the crop grown by the Cohen family and were bought by the Campbell Soup Company of Camden. Other crops, such as sugar corn and potatoes, were hauled to the markets in Philadelphia. Harry first held services in his farmhouse, located currently on Street Road, on Saturday mornings.

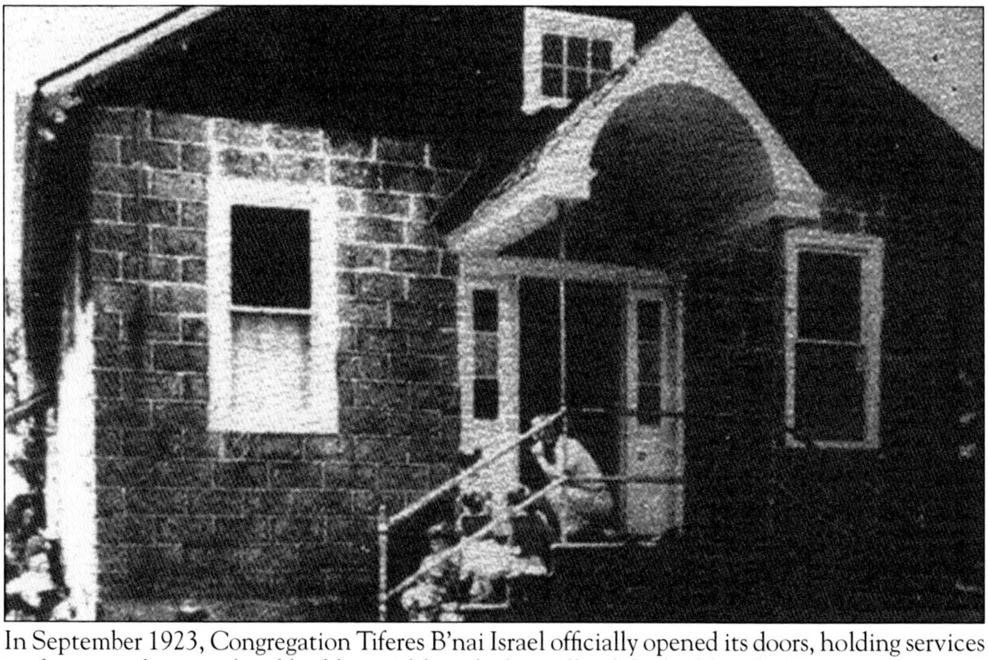

In September 1923, Congregation Tiferes B'nai Israel officially opened its doors, holding services in the yet-to-be-completed building. Although the walls of the building had been constructed, the roof was unfinished. A tent, borrowed from Delaware Valley College, was draped over the building to protect the worshipers in case of rain. People came from near and far for the building's dedication. (Courtesy of Congregation Tiferes B'nai Israel.)

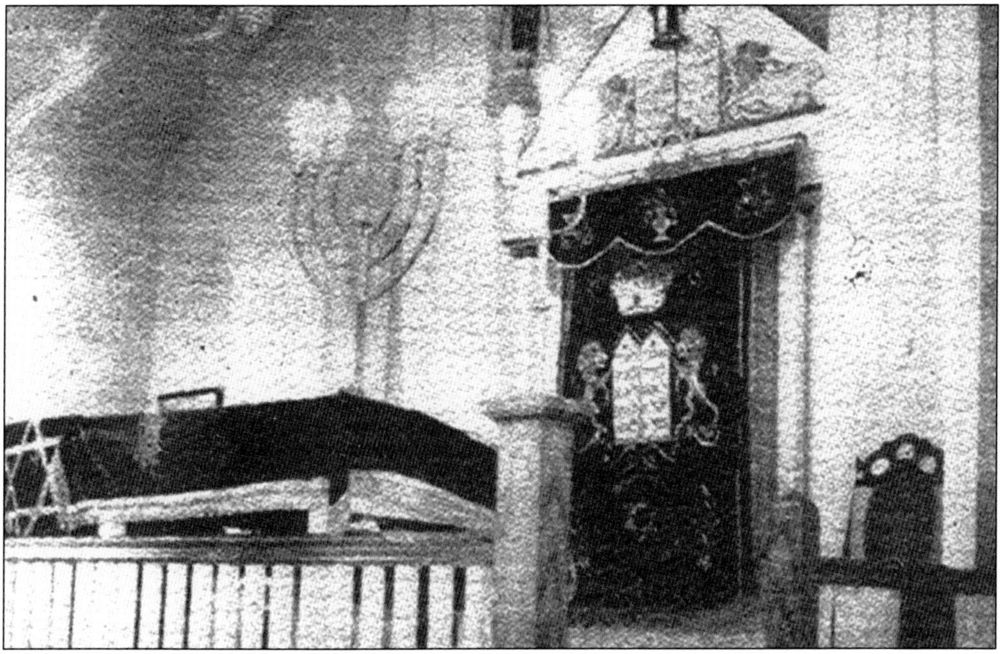

On March 26, 1924, Congregation Tiferes B'nai Israel was chartered at a court session of common pleas in Doylestown, making it the oldest synagogue building in Bucks County. Today the fifth generation of the Cohen family attends the same synagogue that their elder Harry had dreamed of over 85 years ago. (Courtesy of Congregation Tiferes B'nai Israel.)

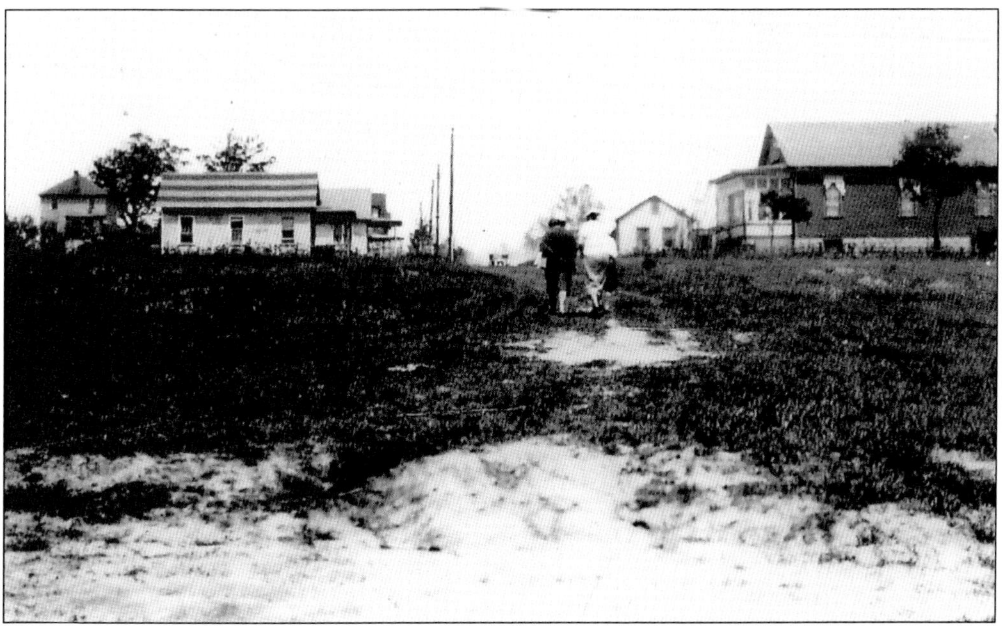

This view is looking north on Oak Avenue from Evergreen Avenue, probably in the 1930 era. All these houses are still standing. The large house on the left is on Street Road and was owned by the Cohen family. The people on Oak Avenue are Sarah Simons and her daughter Mary walking to take the trolley on Route 611 to Willow Grove. (Courtesy of Joseph and Marjorie Simons.)

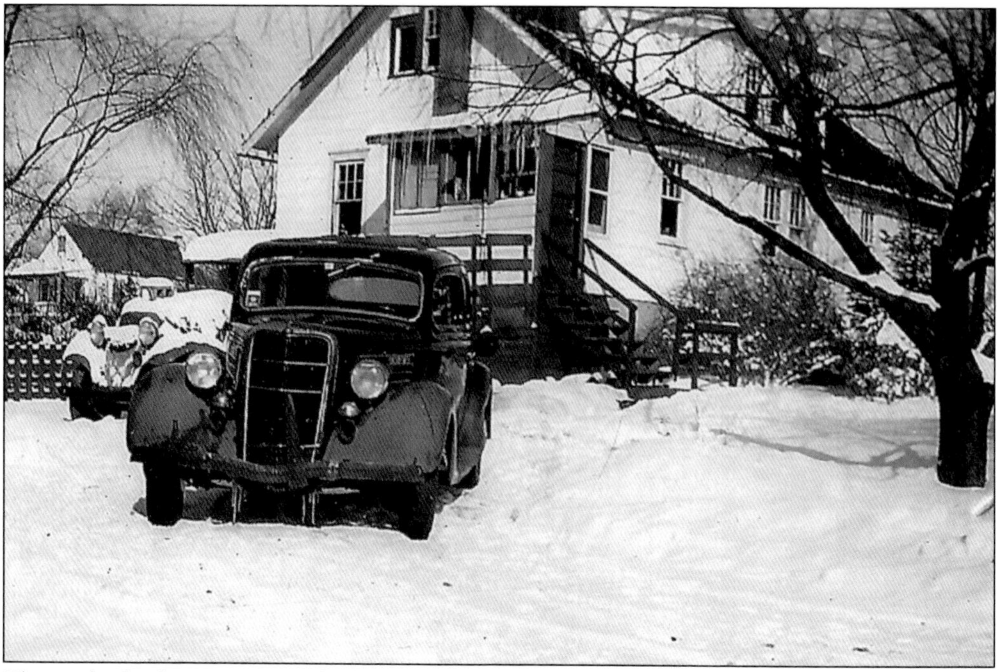

This is the back entrance to the home built in 1922 by Joseph L. Simons for his wife, Sarah, and their four children. The house still stands at the corner of Oak and Evergreen Avenues and is occupied by his oldest son, Joseph P., and his wife, Marjorie. The other home shown is still standing on Evergreen Avenue. (Courtesy of Joseph and Marjorie Simons.)

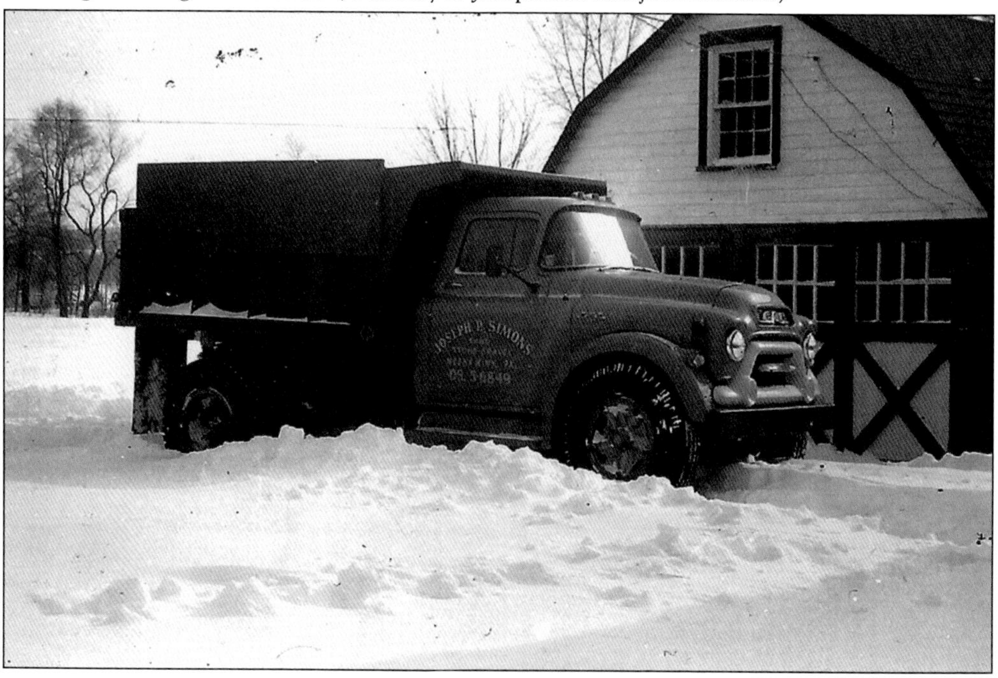

Pictured here is the dump truck of Joseph P. taken in 1958. He provided the stone for many homes and driveways in Warrington and the surrounding towns. The barn pictured still stands on Oak Avenue. (Courtesy of Joseph and Marjorie Simons.)

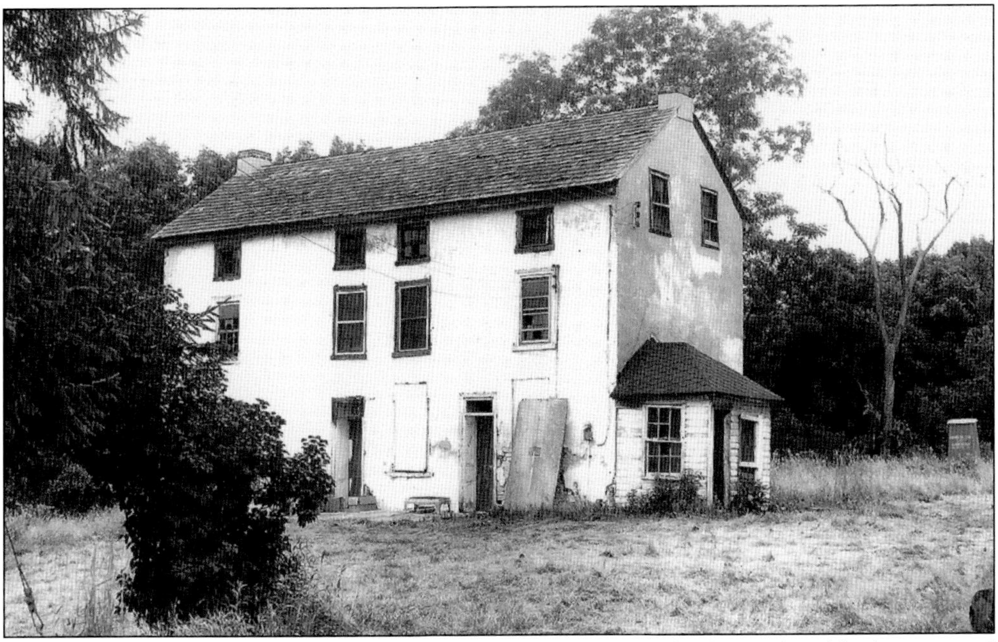

The Karpovitch homestead was located off Bradford Avenue. The house dated back to around 1870. The property was purchased by Jacob and Heonila Karpovitch in 1922. It was demolished in 1979, when this farm was taken by the county to build the Bradford Dam to control the flooding that occurred along the Neshaminy Creek during the storms of the 1950s and 1960s. (Courtesy of Alex Karpovitch.)

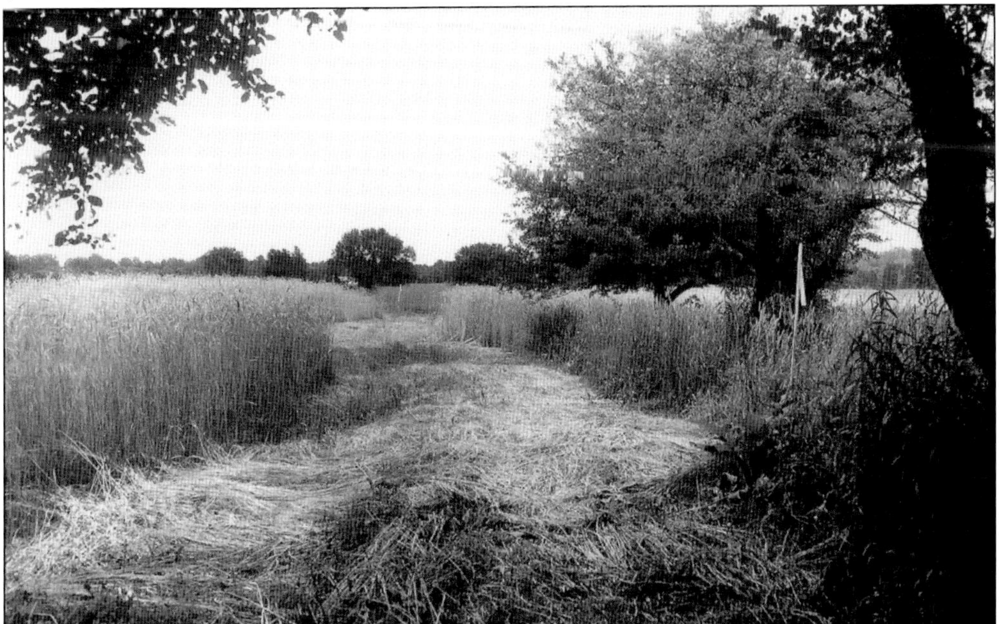

This is the lane behind the Karpovitch farm showing the county surveyor's stakes where the dam would be placed. All this ground is now flooded and is part of the Bradford Dam (also known as Bradford Lake or Warrington Lake or Floodwater Retarding Dam PA-611), a 22-acre impoundment located off County Line Road. (Courtesy of Alex Karpovitch.)

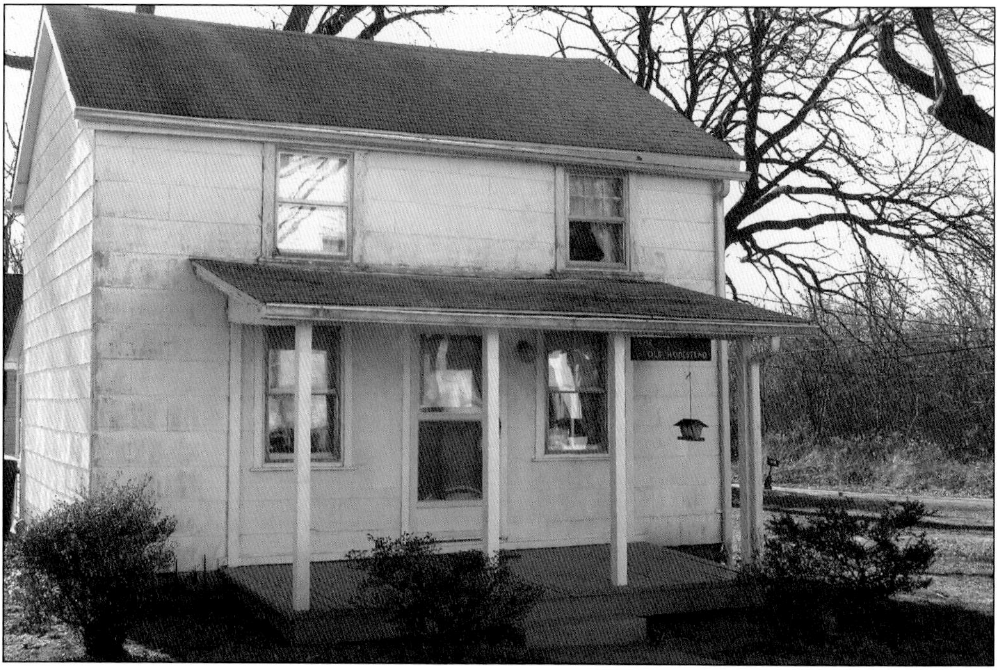

This house, located on Bradford Avenue, was built by Michael Riley around 1841. It was constructed of log with stone mortar. In 1929, owners Albert (son of Michael) and Anna Riley subdivided the five-acre lot into 30 lots. The plan on file with the township was called Riley's Terrace. Most of the houses that were built on this land were built by Riley descendants.

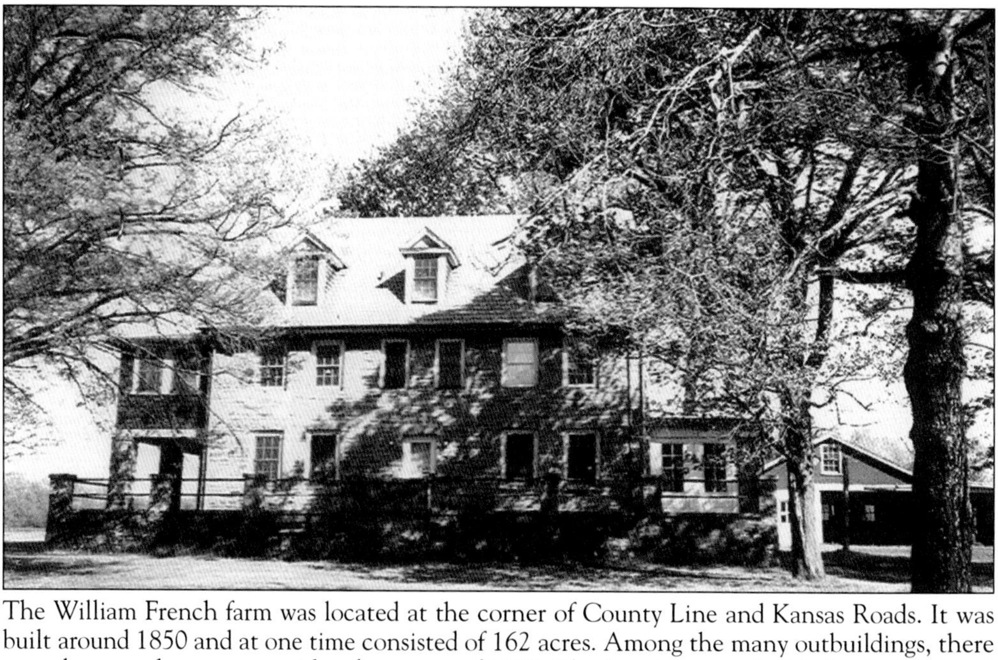

The William French farm was located at the corner of County Line and Kansas Roads. It was built around 1850 and at one time consisted of 162 acres. Among the many outbuildings, there was a barn on the property with a date stone of 1868. The farm became eligible for the National Register of Historic Places in 1998. It was razed in early 2000 to make room for the Bluestone Creek development.

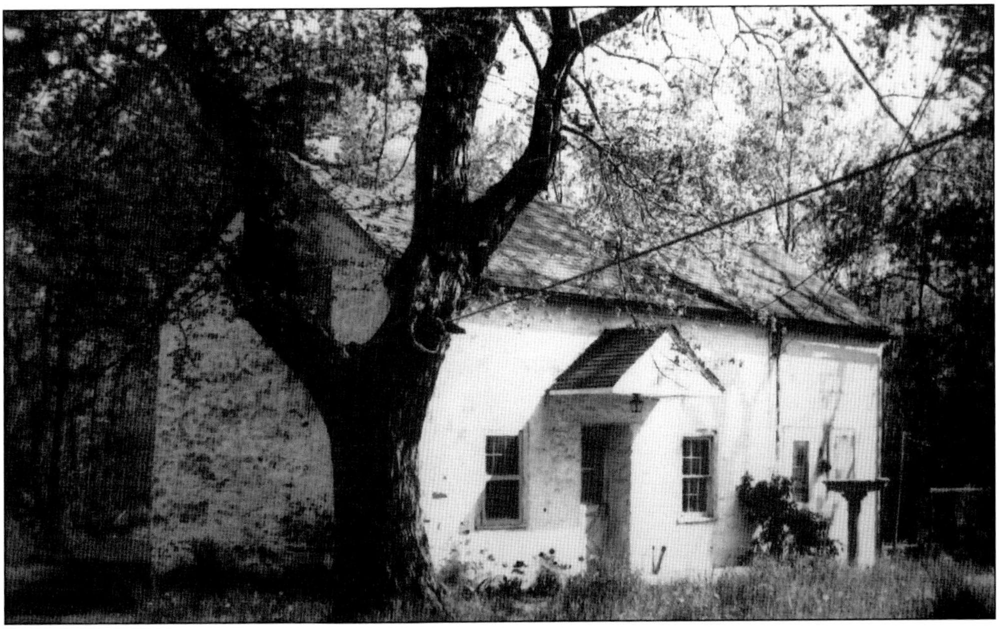

Part of the French farm, this is possibly the oldest photographed structure in Warrington Township. This one-and-a-half-story stone house was once located on County Line Road and had a date stone that stated "Built 1738 RM 1954" (*RM* means remodeled). The dwelling is mentioned in a deed dated December 1, 1766. It was razed in early 2000 to make room for the Bluestone Creek development.

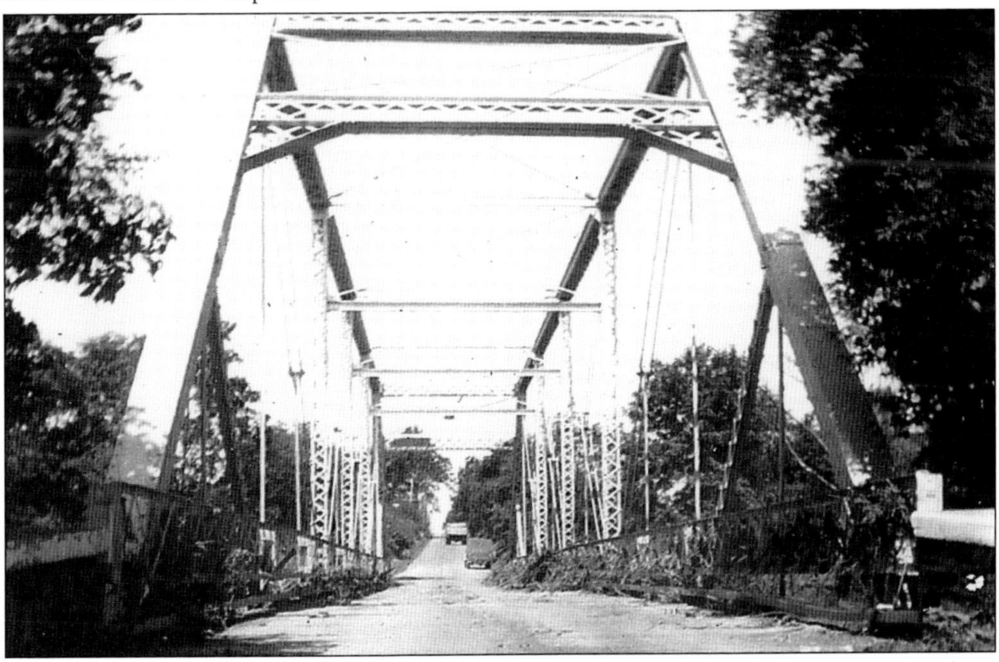

This bridge (known as County Bridge 142) once spanned over the Little Neshaminy Creek on Kansas Road. It was a stone-and-iron structure with timber-plank decking. It is pictured here in 1954 shortly after Hurricane Diane. It was replaced by a modern structure in 1981. (Courtesy of Jeanne DeLong and Frank Ace.)

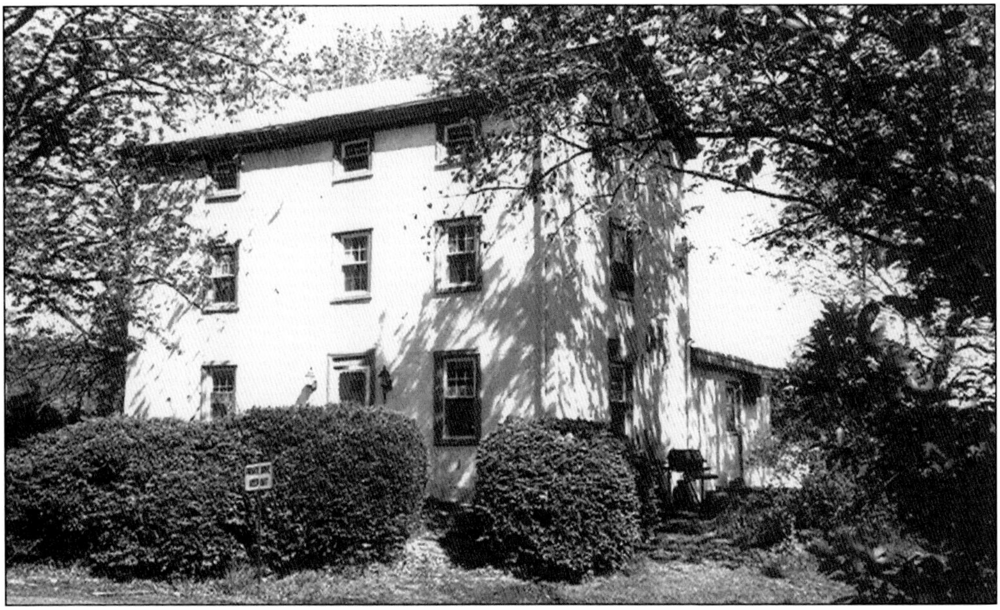

At the corner of County Line Road and Bradford Avenue is one of the oldest known homesteads in the township; it was built around 1750. The stucco had been removed to expose the stone exterior seen today. The foundation of the main section sits on logs visible in the dirt basement. About 1875, the house was owned by Henry and Elizabeth Arnold (brother and sister). Henry was a well-known local farmer, butcher, and merchant.

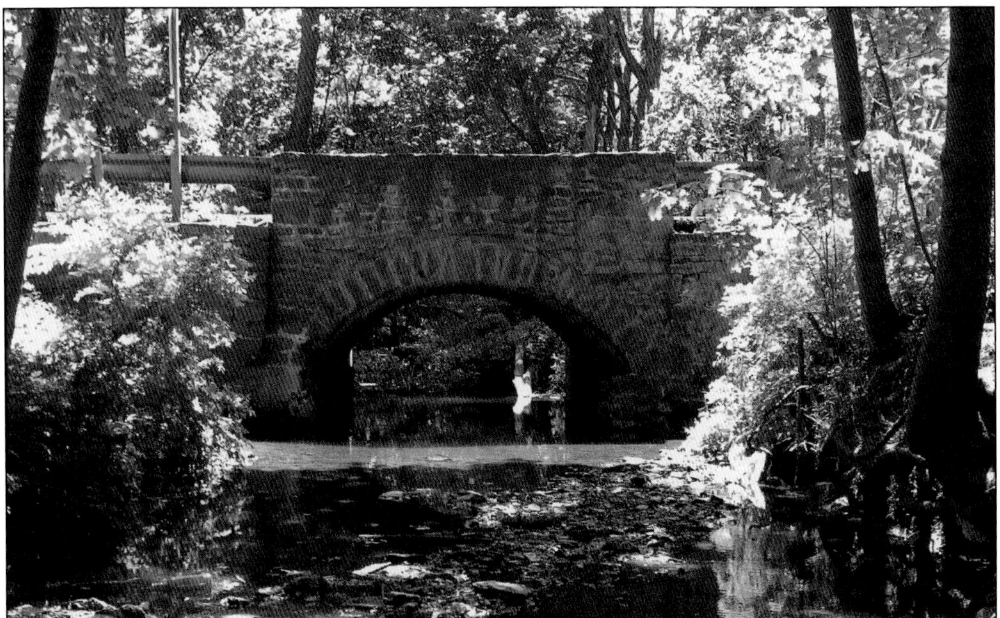

Pictured here is a stone bridge that was built in 1853 spanning over the Little Neshaminy Creek. Still used today, the bridge is located on County Line Road just south of Fairmount Road. This single-arch bridge probably will not survive the forthcoming plans to widen County Line Road to four lanes.

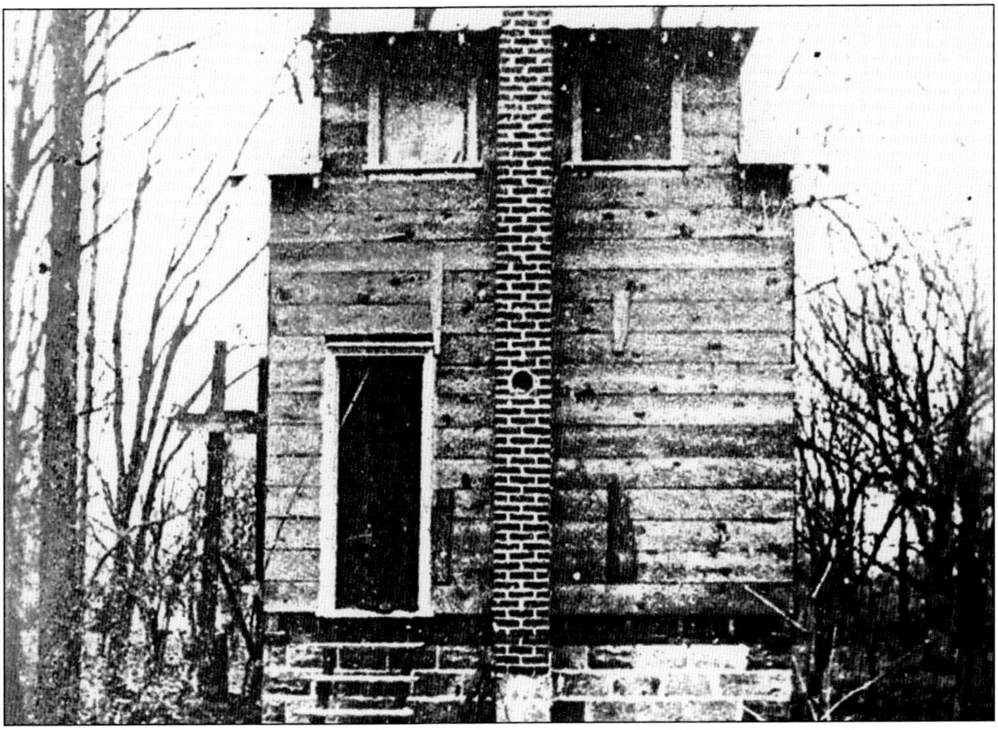

Seen here is one of the early summer homes located along the Neshaminy Creek. This house, pictured in the mid-1920s, has since been updated and still stands on Brinkworth Avenue off Street Road (Courtesy of Harrison Delano Jr.)

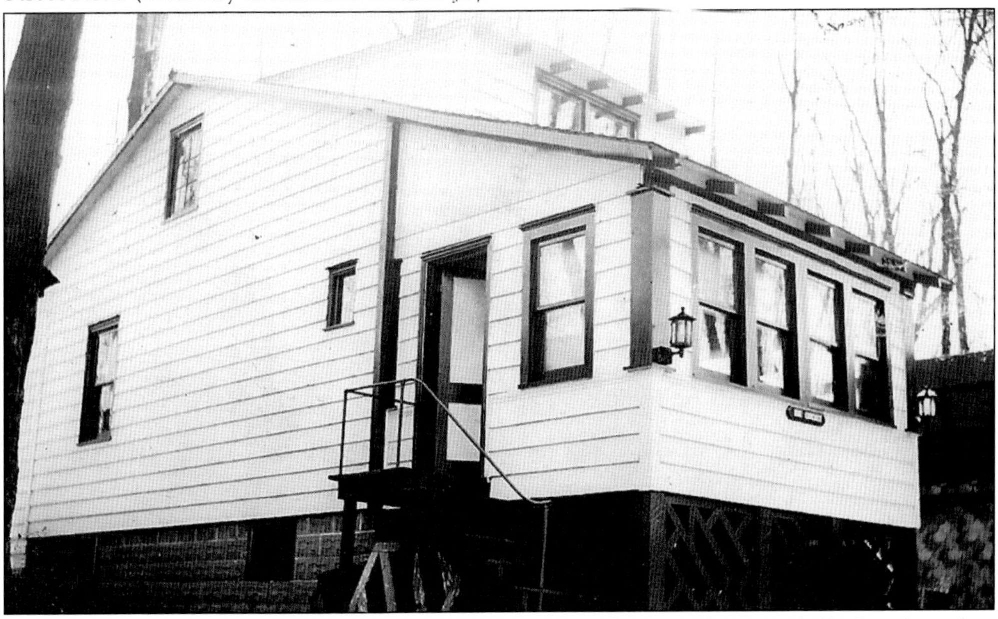

The house on Brinkworth Avenue is pictured here again, this time from 1942. Enclosed porches and the side of the house are pictured as improvements. Past owners had given the home names such as Buena Vista and Cricket. These summer homes over time have become year-round residences. (Courtesy of Harrison Delano Jr.)

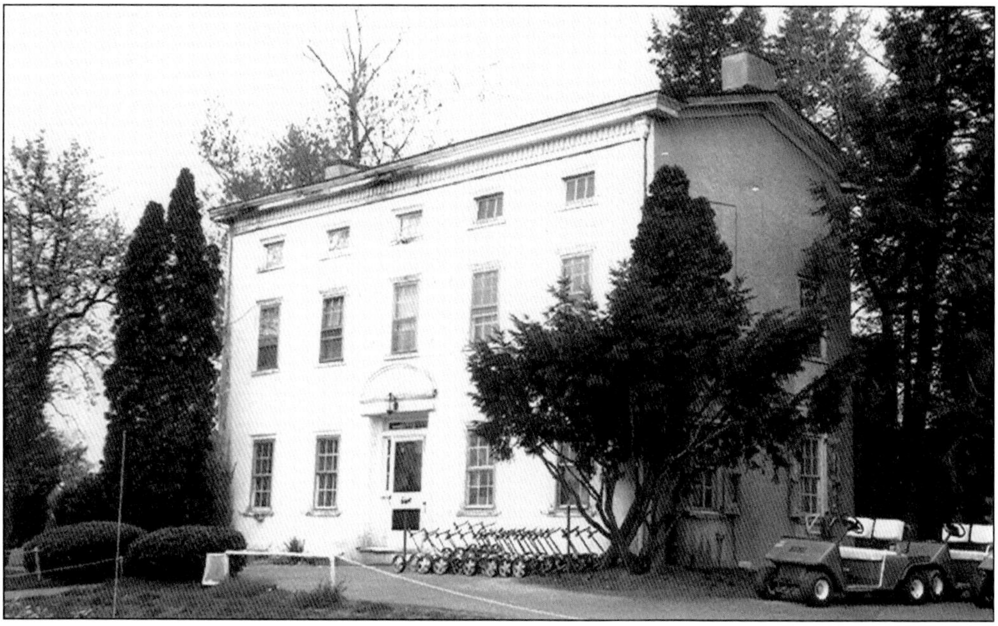

In 1965, the land formerly known as the Dolly Farms was developed. It included the property that today is located on Country Club Lane, the Fairways Golf and Country Club. Dolly Farms once had a grand entrance on Street Road that included columns on either side of the lane with "Dolly" on the left column and "Farms" on the right side.

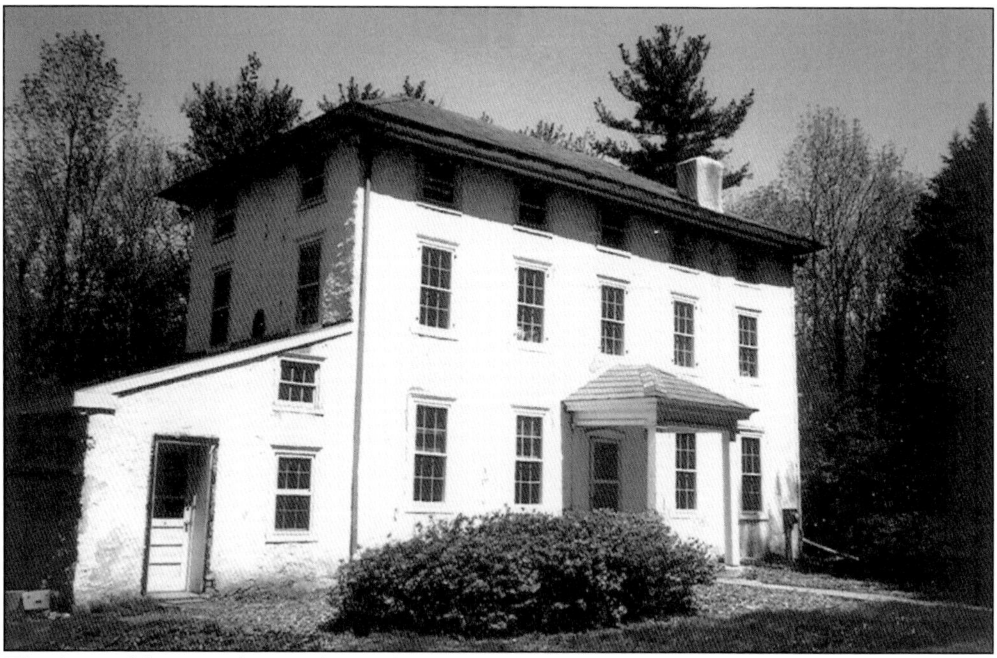

This beautiful manor house, dating from around 1840, still stands on Harvard Drive in the middle of the Woodlands development off Street Road near Elbow Lane. One of the outstanding features on this house is the windows. There are a total of 48 of them. Before the development of the property, the address of this dwelling was 2708 Street Road. At one time, a nursery operated at this location.

Three

Village of Eureka

Eureka Village, originally called Pleasantville, is located at the intersection where Limekiln Pike, Lower State Road, and County Line Road meet (half the village was in Montgomery Township, Montgomery County). A story is told how one traveler, weary from hours of searching for Pleasantville, was finally assured by a local shopkeeper he had arrived. "Eureka" he shouted. "What was that word, son?" asked the shopkeeper. "Eureka, that is Greek for 'I have found it'" was the reply. So the village is known as Eureka to this day. Prior to 1850, the center of Eureka was actually part of New Britain Township, as Warrington's border ended at County Line Road and just above Lower State Road. The post office located on the Montgomery side opened about 1871 and closed on July 30, 1955, as its functions were taken over by the Chalfont Post Office. This building, which once housed the post office and general store, was removed after a car hit the structure around 2001.

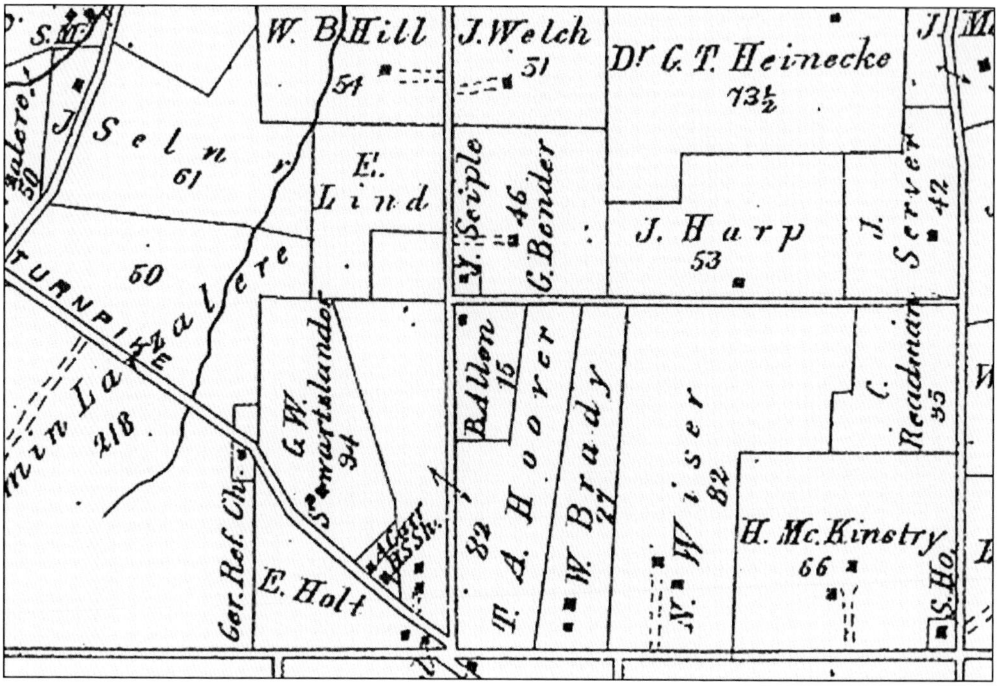

Pictured here is a village of Eureka map from the 1876 atlas of Bucks County by J. D. Scott.

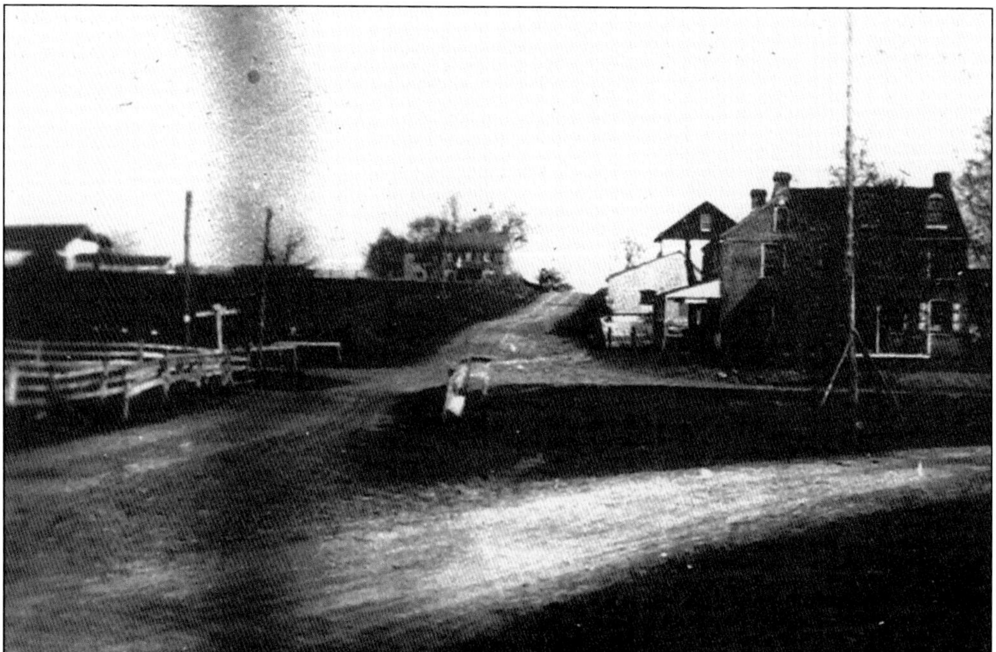

A 1910 view shows Eureka Village (County Line Road, Lower State Road, and Limekiln Pike) looking southeast toward Neshaminy. Seen here is the "Eureka Triangle." Up on the hill is the McKinstry/Kohler house. To the right, located in Horsham Township, is the general store and post office. (Courtesy of Jane Henderson.)

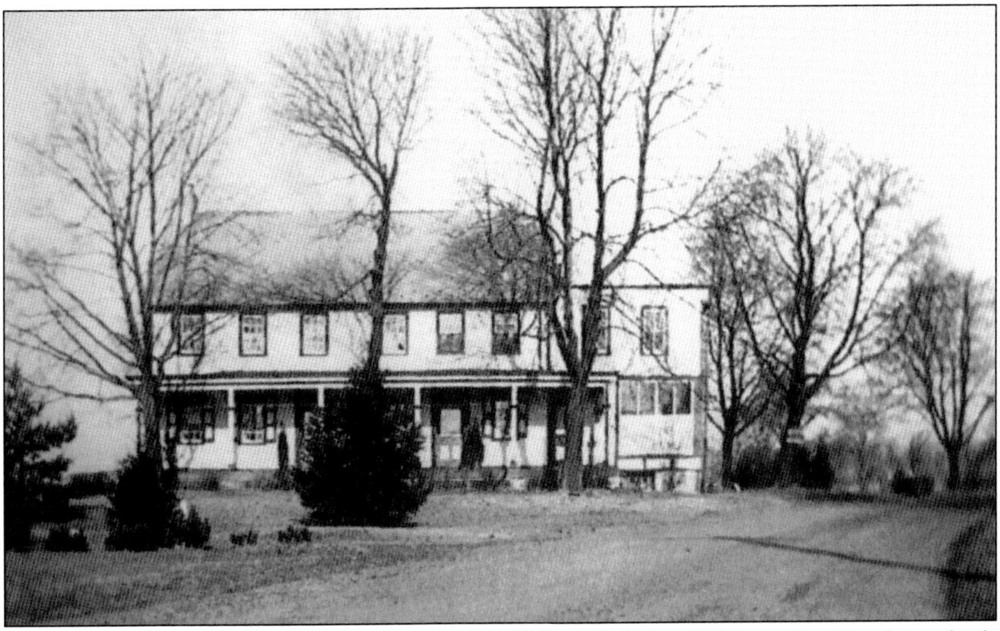

The Green Tree Tavern/Inn, earlier known as Eells Foot and the Old Turnpike Hotel, was built about 1834. The inn at one time was run by John and William Snare. Later the inn was the home of the Nash family. The inn was torn down in 1984. While the demolition was being done, documentation was found that stated, "T.C Waters Shenandoah Penns July 29th 1892, Bought Green Tree March 1892." (Courtesy of Barbara Case.)

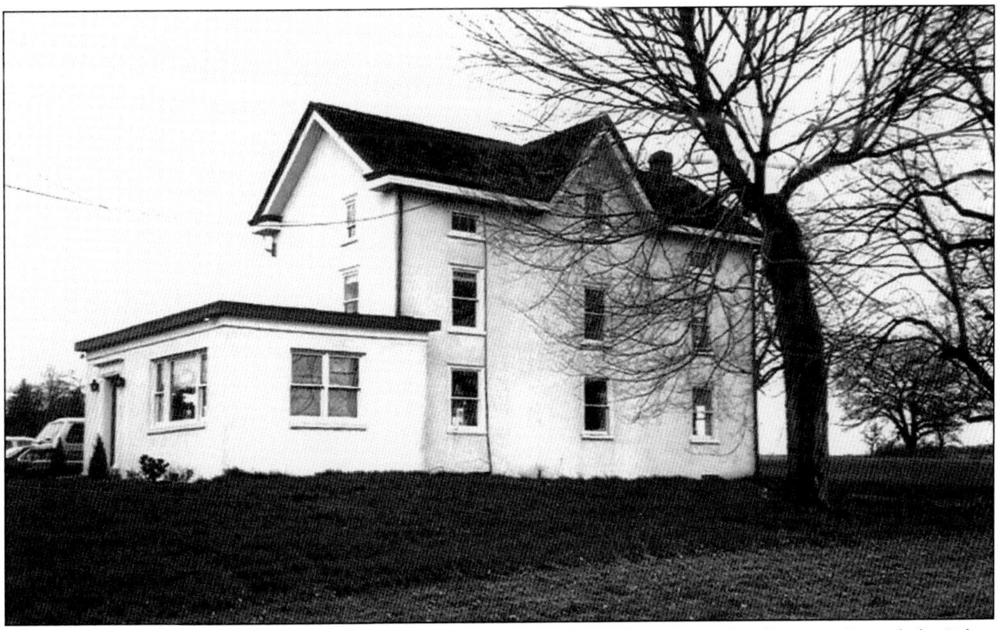

Frederick W. Hoover purchased a tract of land and made his home on the farm on Limekiln Pike. He was one of the founders and organizers of the German Reformed Church as well as one of its pillars, taking a most active part in its work and serving as an elder. Possessing marked musical talent, he was a lead singer in the church and also played different musical instruments.

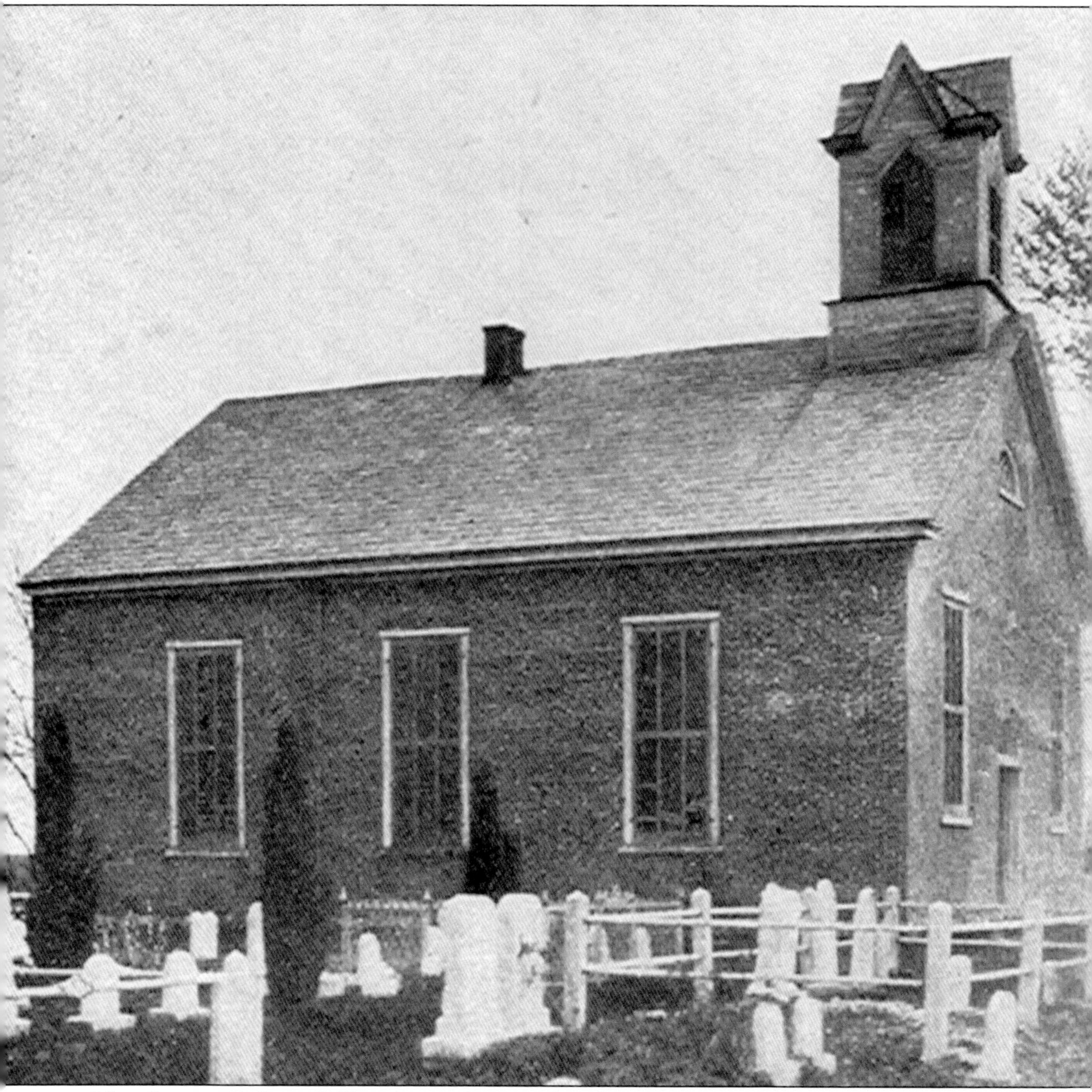

The German Reformed Church was the first church to be established in Warrington. It started as a series of evangelistic meetings held in the grove of Jacob Cassel and in the barn on the property later owned by Tilghman A. Hoover. As a result of these meetings, an organization was effected in the County Line Schoolhouse in the latter part of September 1840. John Dunlap donated two acres on Limekiln Pike; on October 19, 1840, the cornerstone was laid. It was a plain substantial brick structure, 60 feet by 51 feet. The dedication took place on May 19, 1841. The cost of the church was about $3,000. Around 1850, a bell was added to the belfry. The church was known as the Brick Reform Church. (Courtesy of Pleasantville United Church of Christ.)

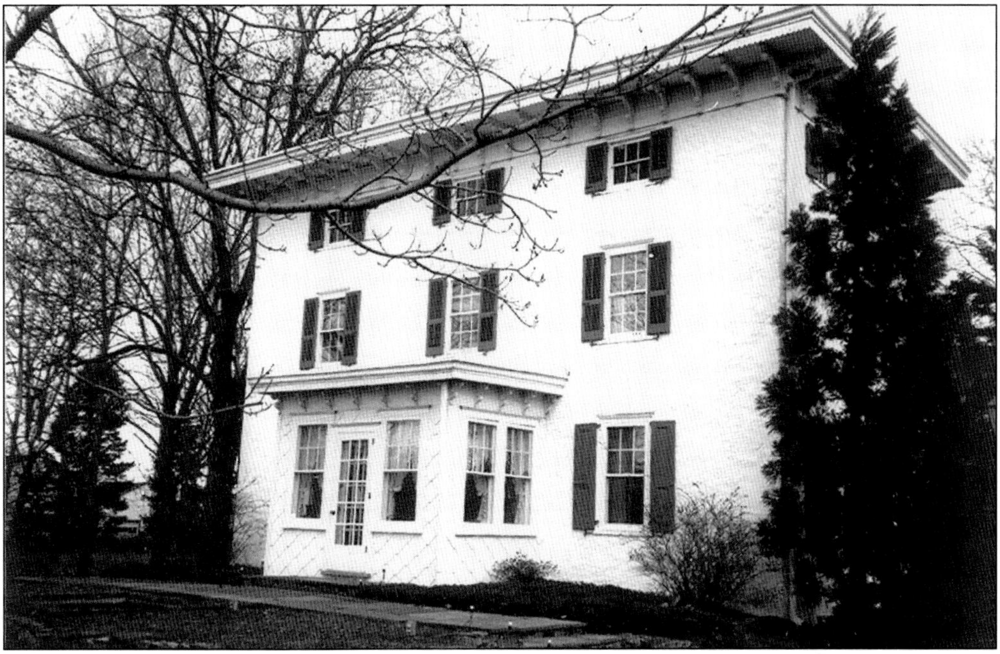

The first parsonage house of the German Reformed Church was located on Lower State Road. During the years 1872 and 1873, great improvements were made to the church property. Benjamin Larzalere gave one acre of land for shedding purposes and a parsonage when needed. More ground was also added to the cemetery. It still stands and is part of a landscape business.

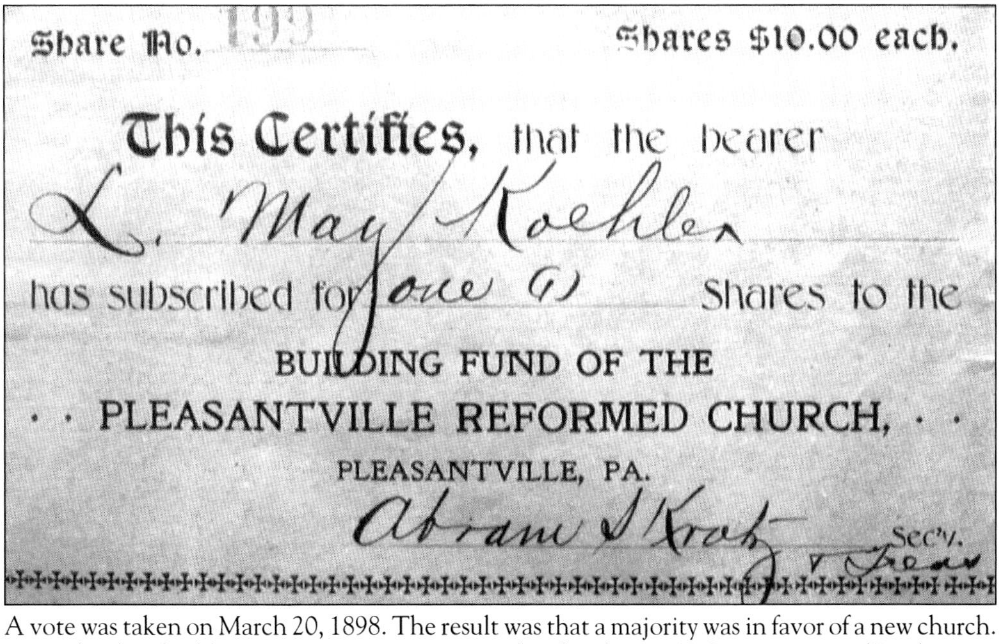

Share No. 199 Shares $10.00 each.

This Certifies, that the bearer

L. May Koehler

has subscribed for one (1) Shares to the

BUILDING FUND OF THE

· · PLEASANTVILLE REFORMED CHURCH, · ·

PLEASANTVILLE, PA.

Abram S Kratz Sec'y. & Treas

A vote was taken on March 20, 1898. The result was that a majority was in favor of a new church. Accordingly, a building committee was appointed and architect A. Oscar Martin of Doylestown was employed to present plans for the new edifice. His plans were accepted, and on June 5, 1898, subscriptions were sold to raise money for the construction. (Courtesy of Jane Henderson.)

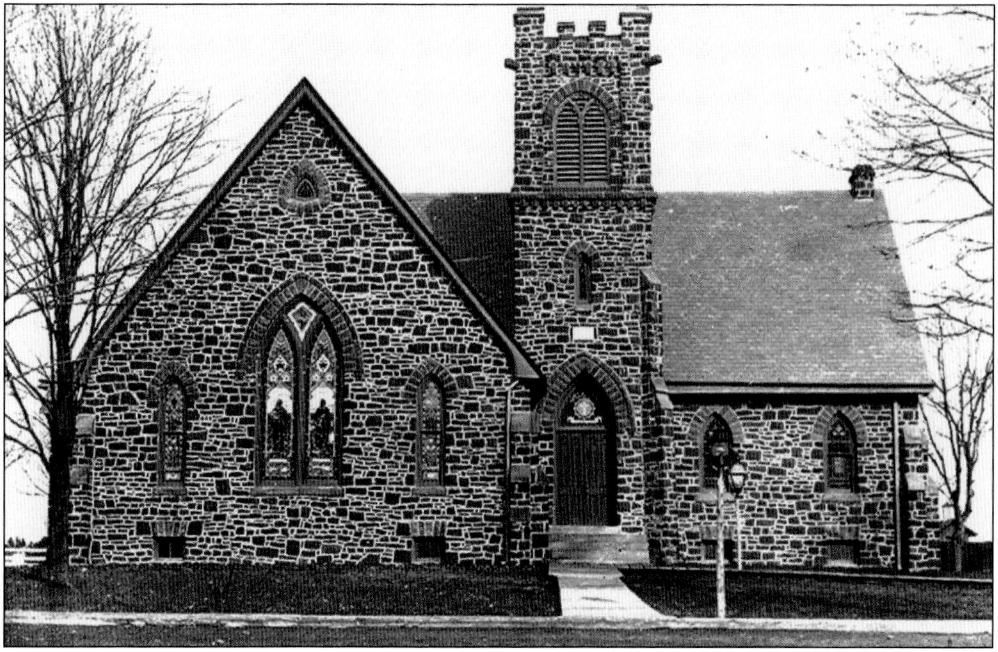

The first service in the new church was held on Christmas Day 1898. The cost of the new building was $7,000. In 1934, the church merged with the Pleasantville Evangelical and Reformed Church. In 1957, it merged again, becoming the Pleasantville United Church of Christ. The bell in the belfry, dated 1850, is from the original church on the site. (Courtesy of Jane Henderson.)

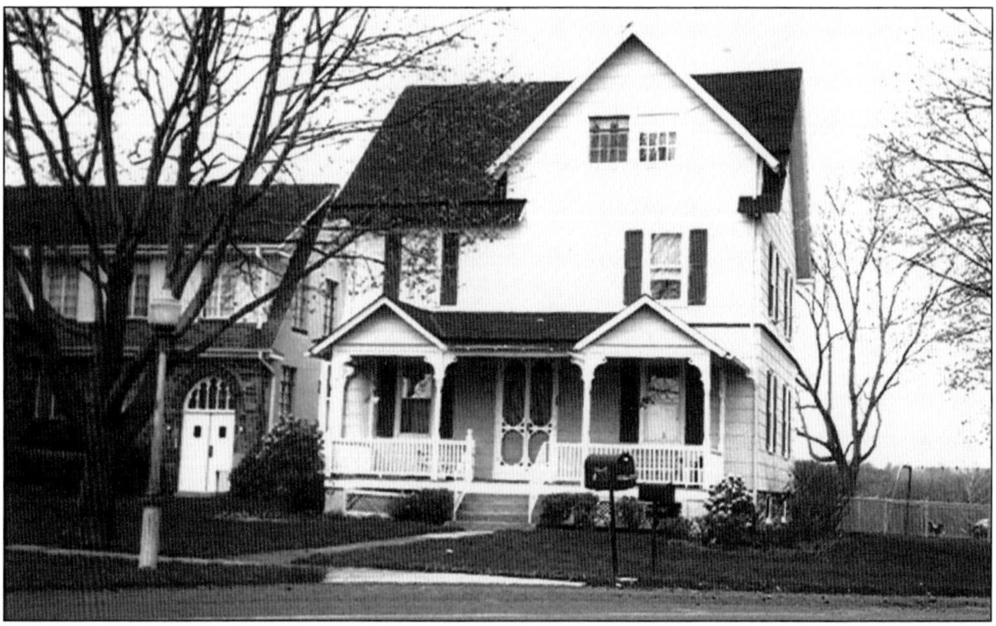

In 1890, a parsonage house (seen here) was built next to the church. Around 1901, a portico was added to the front entrance of the church and a pipe organ was installed in the sanctuary, in memory of Tilghman A. Hoover. Three additions have been made to the 1898 church building, one in 1915 to add the Sunday school annex, the second in 1956, and the last in 1987.

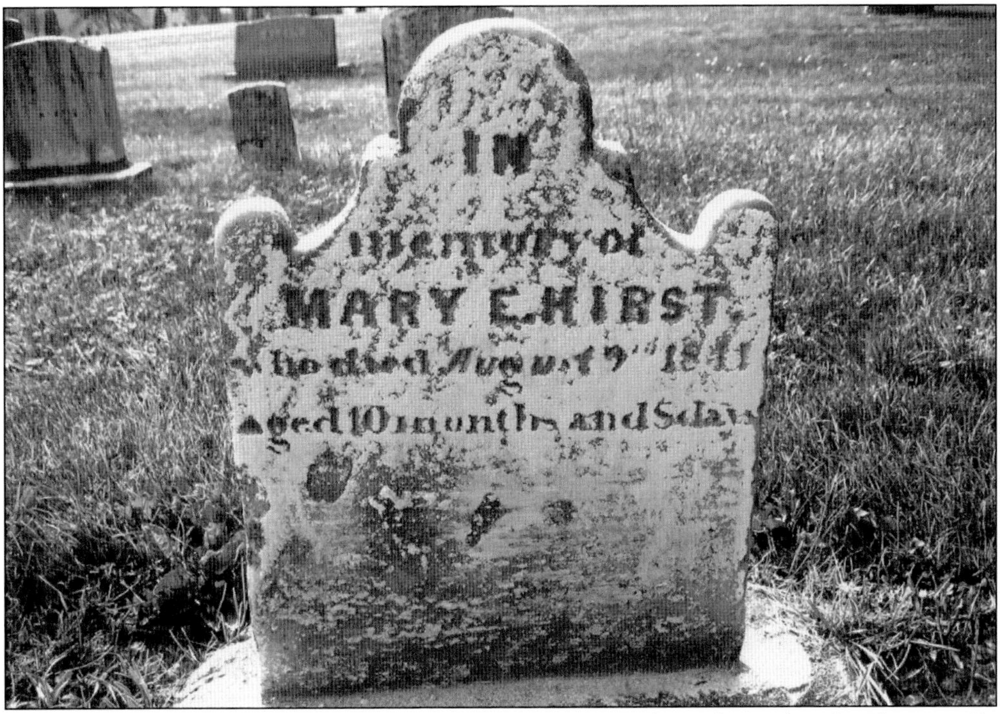

The only 19th-century cemetery known in Warrington Township is located at the Pleasantville Church. The cemetery began its operation shortly after the church was formed in 1840. This cemetery, which still conducts services, consists of over 300 marked graves. The oldest known marked grave reads, "In memory of Mary E. Hirst, who died on August 9th 1841, aged of 10 months and 8 days."

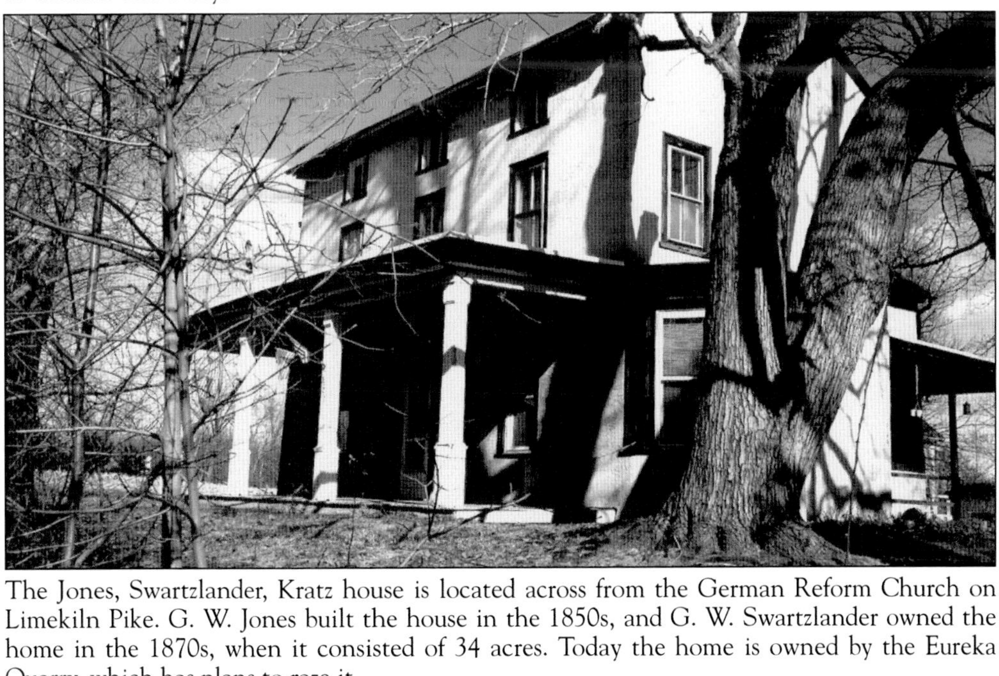

The Jones, Swartzlander, Kratz house is located across from the German Reform Church on Limekiln Pike. G. W. Jones built the house in the 1850s, and G. W. Swartzlander owned the home in the 1870s, when it consisted of 34 acres. Today the home is owned by the Eureka Quarry, which has plans to raze it.

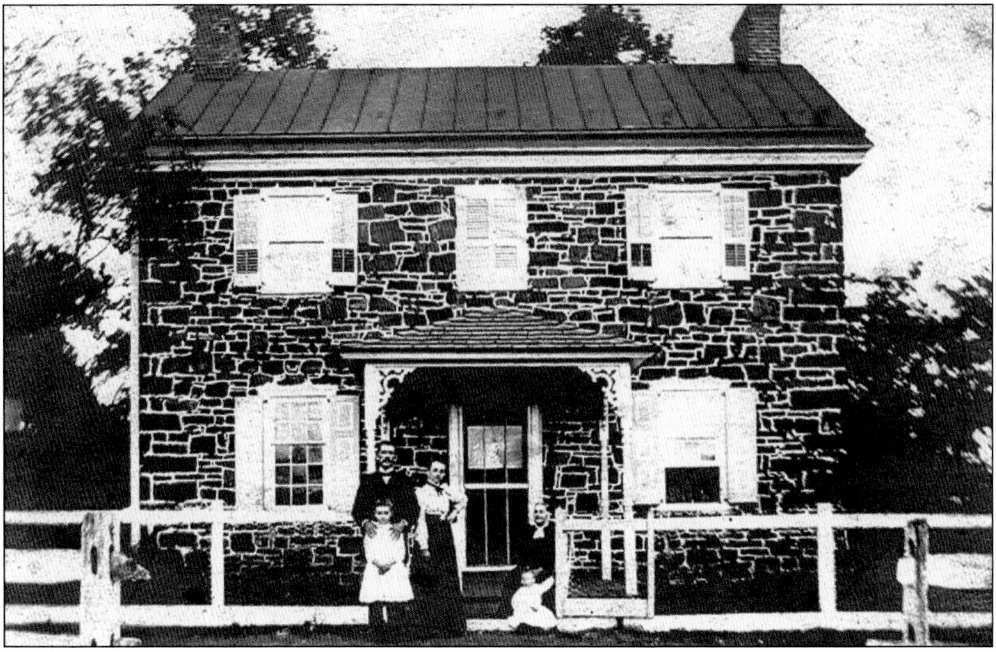

Up the hill, on County Line Road, is a home that has been continuously occupied by six successive generations since its construction. In 1823, John McKinstry purchased the property (27 acres) so that he and his brother Nathan McKinstry could live in a log cabin while doing carpet weaving and farming. Around 1825, they constructed the original portion of the house. (Courtesy of Jane Henderson.)

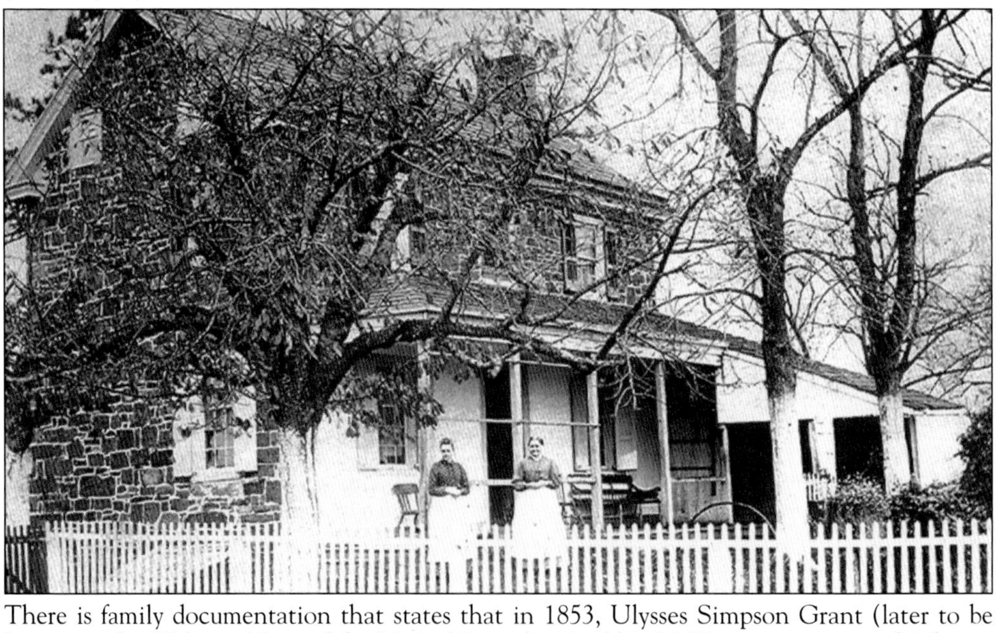

There is family documentation that states that in 1853, Ulysses Simpson Grant (later to be known as the 18th president of the United States) visited his McKinstry cousins at this house while in the area visiting his grandparents on Limekiln Pike in Horsham Township. During William and Jennie Kohler's ownership (around World War I), the wood frame additions were wire-lathed and the entire house was stuccoed. (Courtesy of Jane Henderson.)

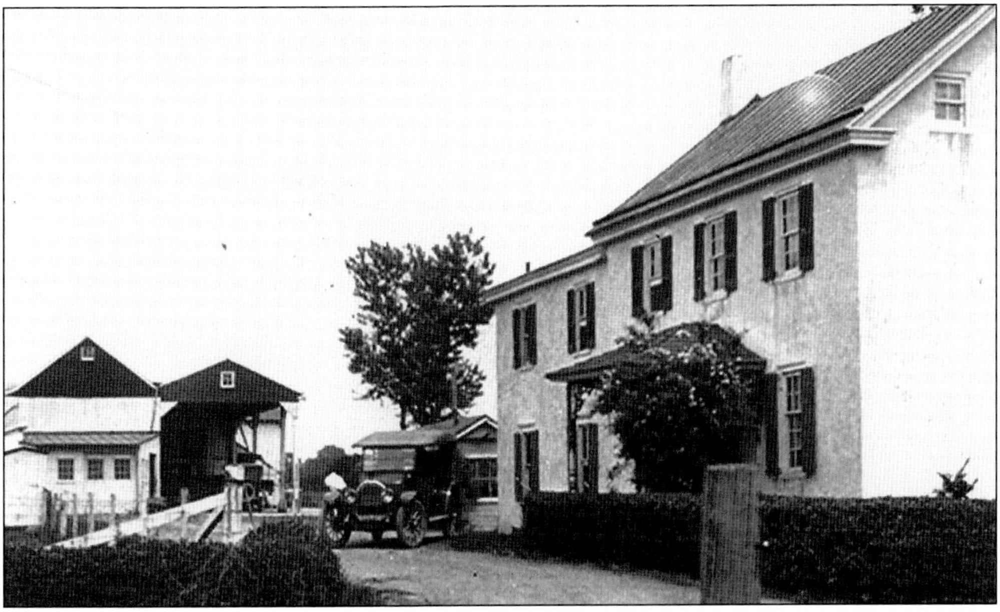

Several times throughout the home's history, the state/county government for road improvements has claimed the property facing County Line Road. The house today, minus a wraparound porch, is much closer to the road than it had been in past years. This home received a certificate and plaque from the Bucks County Heritage Conservancy in 1982. (Courtesy of Jane Henderson.)

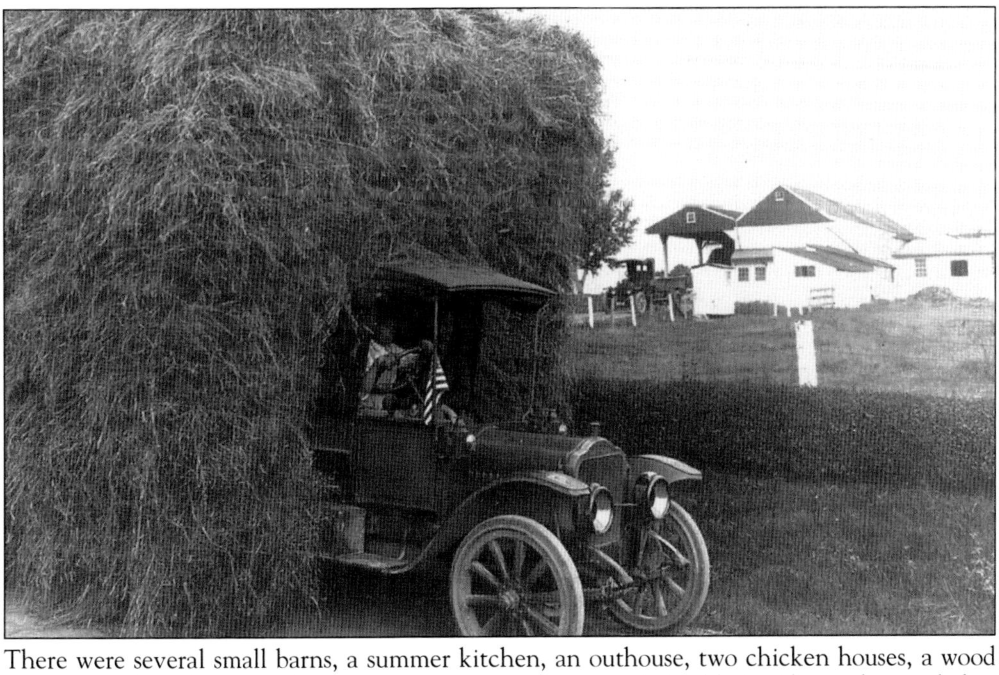

There were several small barns, a summer kitchen, an outhouse, two chicken houses, a wood shed, and a large hay barn. The large hay barn (built around World War I) was dismantled in 2000 to make way for a housing development (Warrington Hunt). William Kohler conducted a large hay and farm products business from the home. Seen here is a hay truck loaded for the market. (Courtesy of Jane Henderson.)

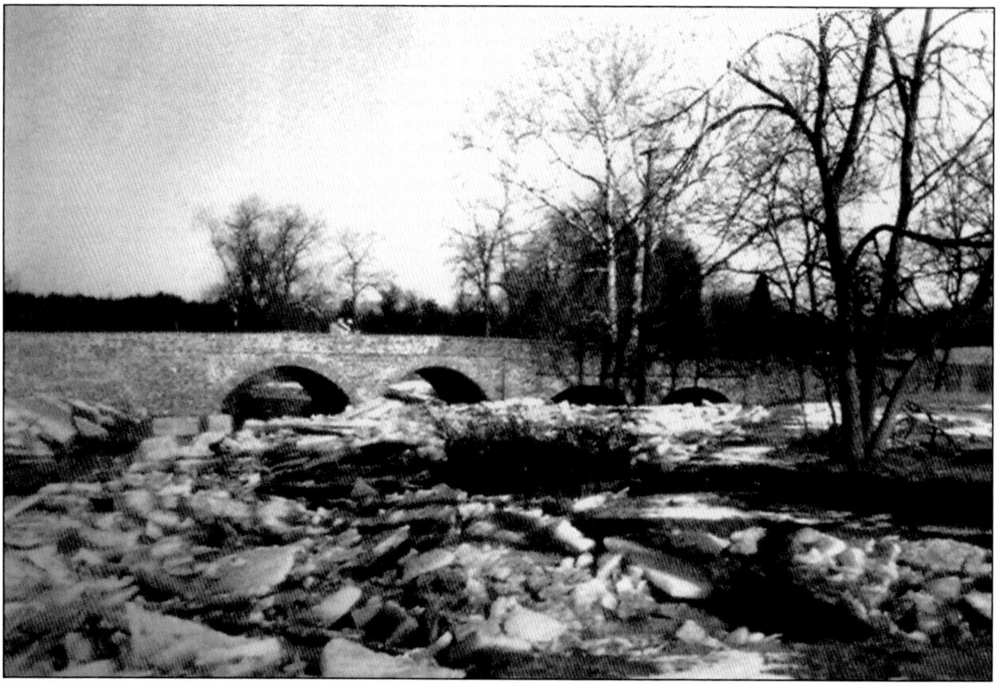

The County Line Bridge that once spanned over the Little Neshaminy Creek was built in 1865. It was a four-arch stone structure and was 236 feet long. In 1984, the deteriorating bridge was replaced with a modern structure. (Courtesy of Jane Henderson.)

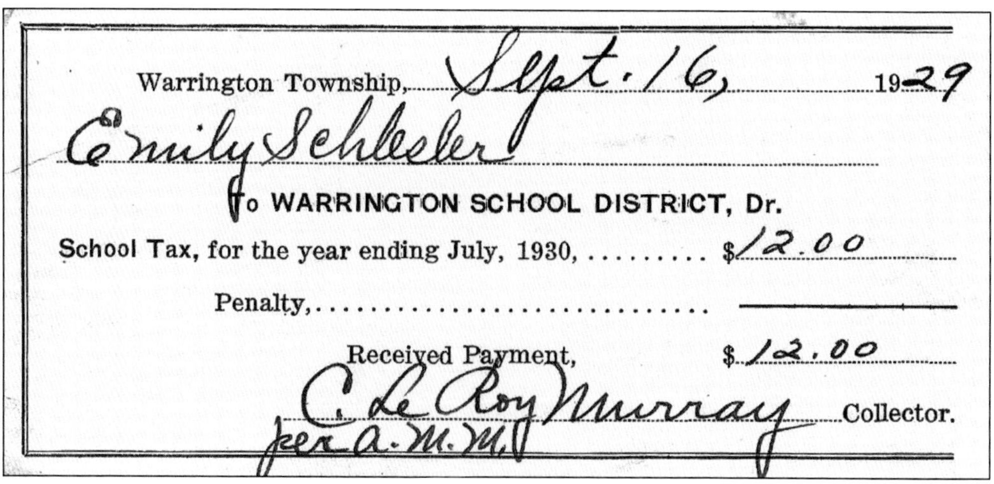

Warrington Township, Sept. 16, 1929
Emily Schlecter
To WARRINGTON SCHOOL DISTRICT, Dr.
School Tax, for the year ending July, 1930, ... $12.00
Penalty, ...
Received Payment, $12.00
C. LeRoy Murray Collector.
per A. M. M.

Shown here is a township school tax bill from 1929. This tax was due for the property located at 10 Folly Road after the township sold the County Line Schoolhouse and one acre to the Schlecter family in 1928. (Courtesy of the Schlecter family.)

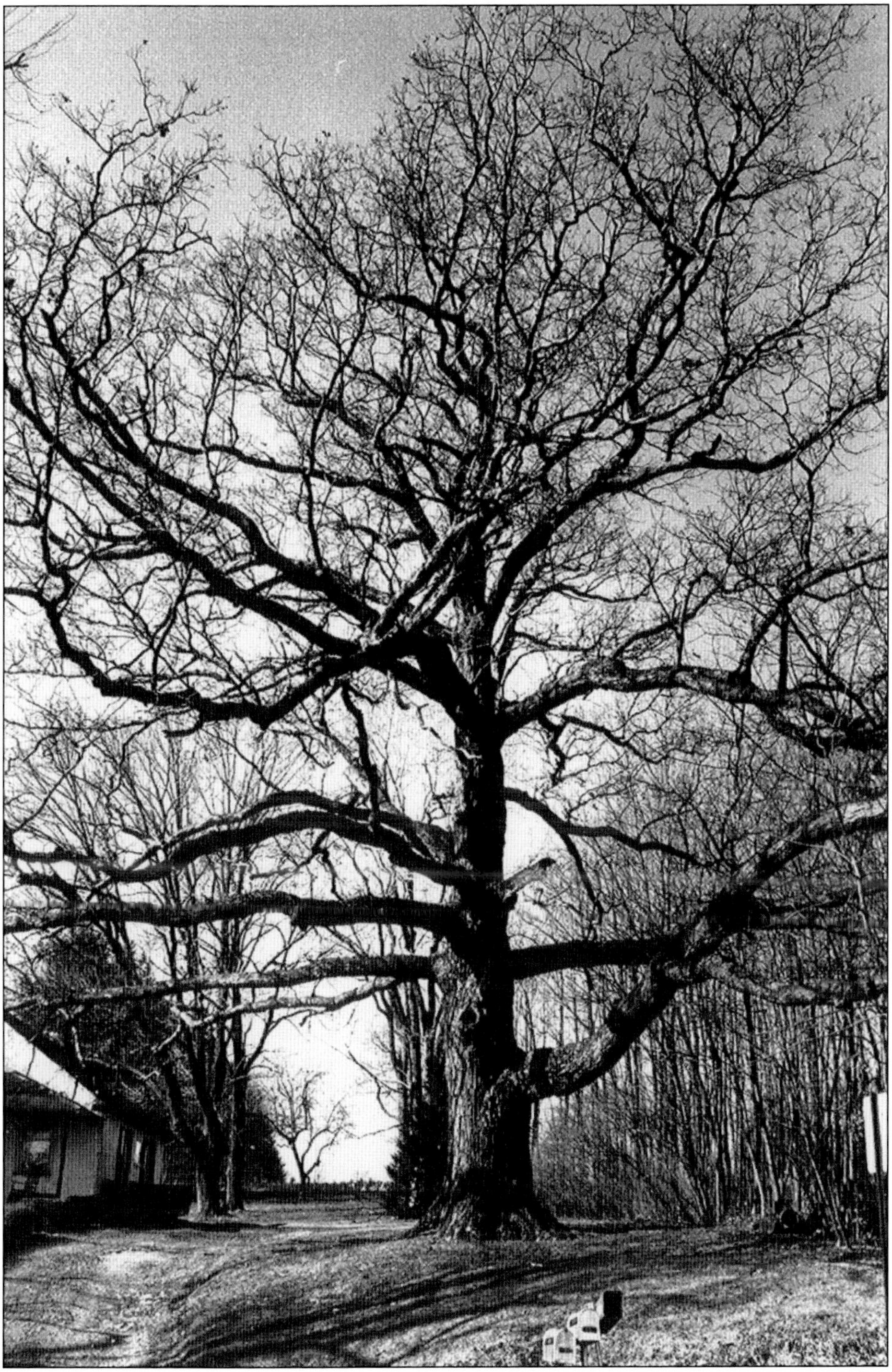

On October 27, 1932, the tree located at the County Line Schoolhouse was recognized as an authentic William Penn Pin Oak. The tree is estimated to be over 300 years old. During the 19th and early 20th centuries, children who attended the school played under its spreading limbs, which span over 120 feet. Its trunk has a diameter of over 17 feet.

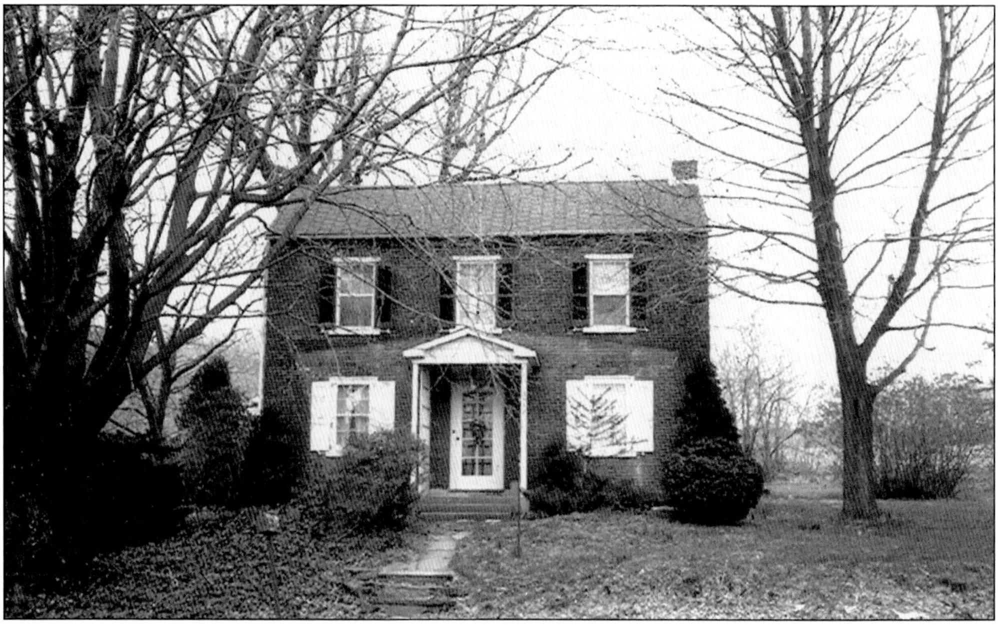

The Charles Haldeman and Irvin MacNair farmstead is one of the first constructed of brick in the township. One of the owners, Irvin MacNair, a justice of the peace, lived in and farmed the property from 1917 until his death in 1977. His father, Howell E. MacNair, was justice of the peace from 1879 to 1912, while Irvin was justice of the peace from 1915 to 1967, when the position was eliminated.

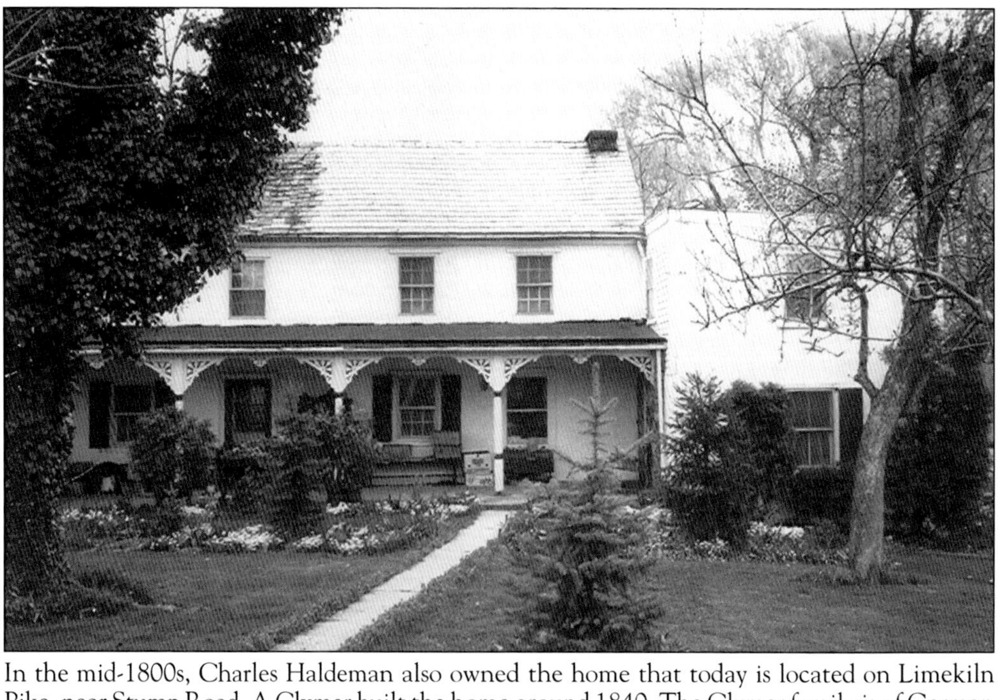

In the mid-1800s, Charles Haldeman also owned the home that today is located on Limekiln Pike, near Stump Road. A Clymer built the home around 1840. The Clymer family is of German origin, the name having been formerly spelled Klemmer. The dwelling became eligible for the National Register of Historic Places in 1994.

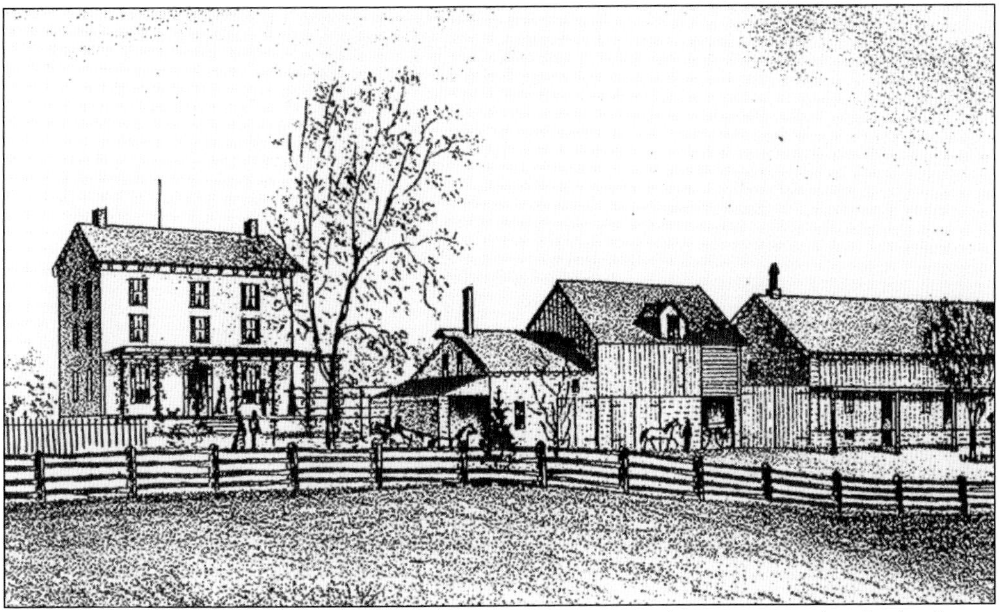

Benjamin Larzelere bought John Dunlap's property in 1855 for $11,000. Larzelere built a house (shown above) in 1865 on the site of Dunlap's old house, which was built in 1750. Eventually Larzelere would accumulate a total of 400-plus acres. He at one time owned all the property between County Line Road, Stump Road, and Limekiln Pike. This drawing is from the 1876 atlas of Bucks County.

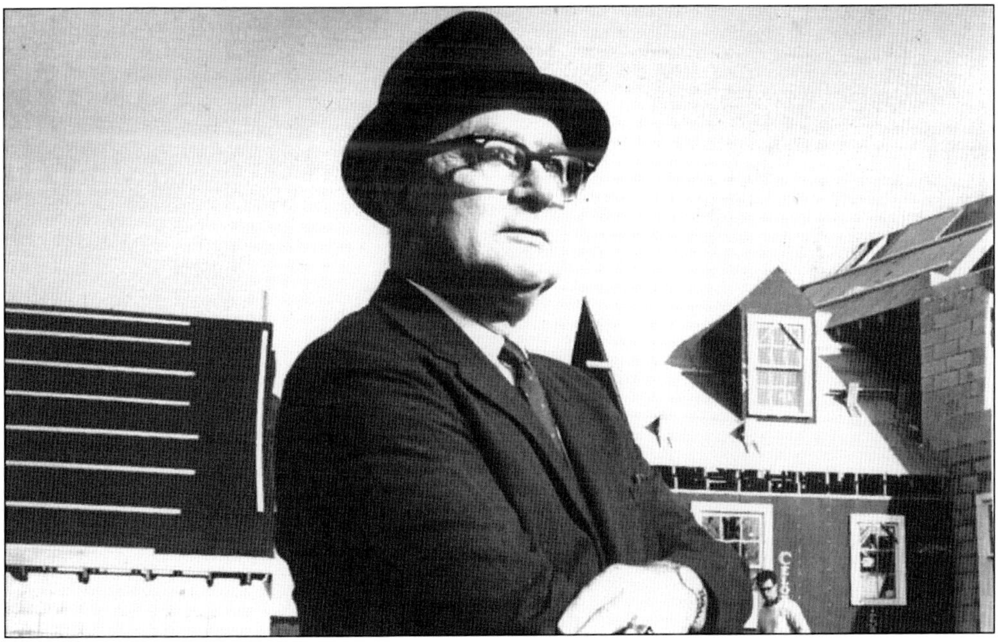

Called Woodlawn Homes, this development, submitted to the township by Abram and Bertha Elizabeth Nash, was the first "housing development" in Eureka Village. Built in 1933, it was located on Woodlawn Avenue. Luther Nash (pictured above), a Doylestown contractor, built and shortly lived in the first house built. Many of the other houses on the street were built by the Nash family. (Courtesy of Barbara Case.)

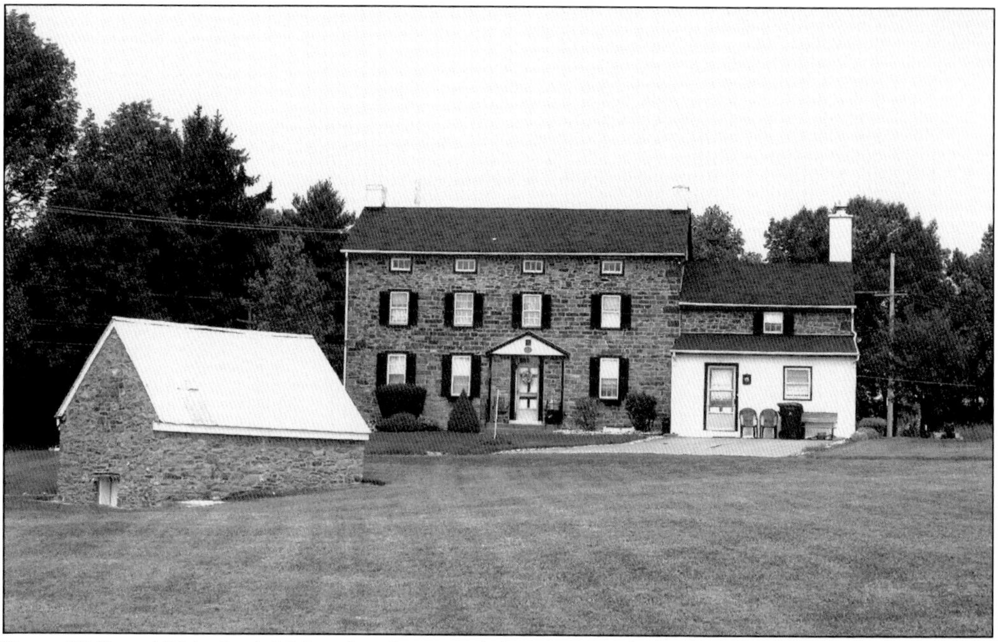

From 1843 to 1921, the McNair family owned the property located at the corner of Street and Folly Roads. The house seen today was built around 1845. In 1947, the McNaney family bought the 37 acres. Produce is still sold at the Truck Patch stand, which opened in 1968. This home received a certificate and plaque from the Bucks County Heritage Conservancy in 1981.

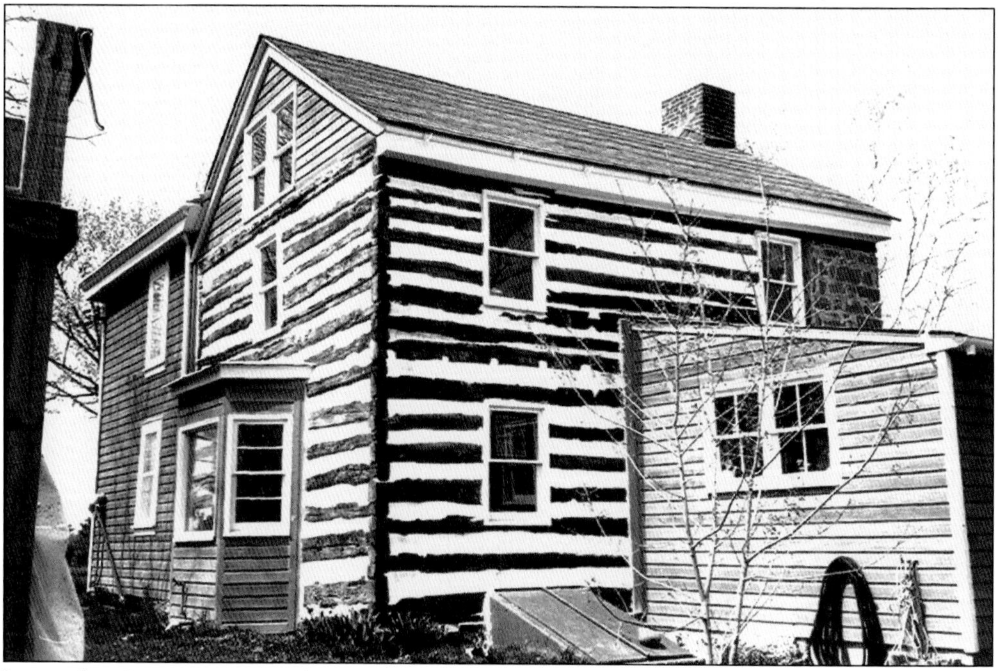

Located on Lower State Road is a home built about 1810. The original house is constructed on stone and logs. This is the only known exposed-log home in the township. It was probably built by Michael Hartman, who owned the property from 1808 to 1825. The Carver family held the property for 36 years. During this time, Warren Carver operated a blacksmith business.

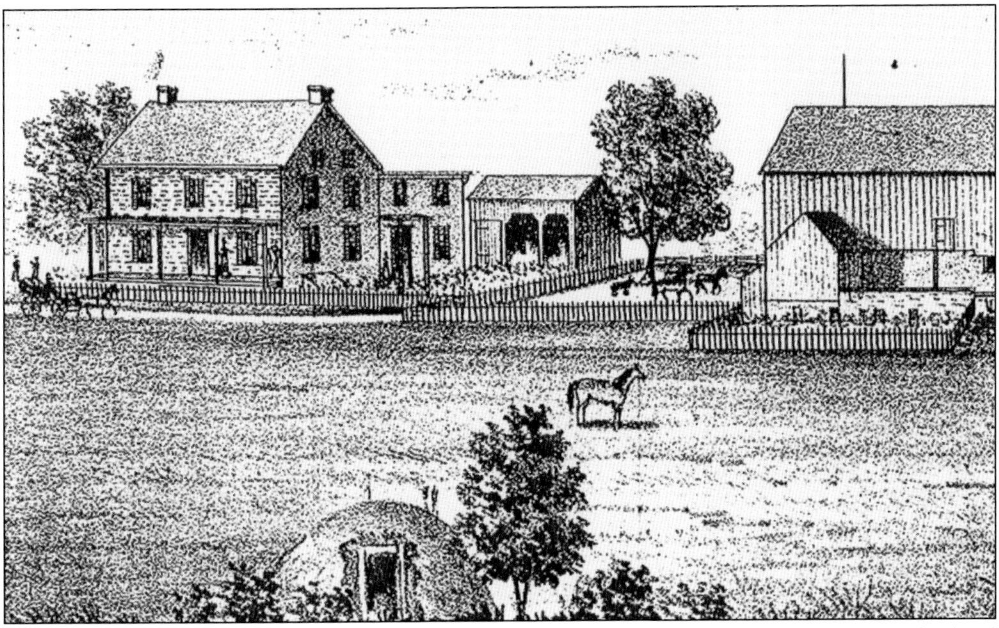

Late in life, John George Weisel settled in Warrington Township. In 1828, he bought the land from Michael Moyer where he built a sawmill in 1842 (that gave Mill Creek Road and the creek their names). A chopping mill was constructed in 1844. Up until the 1950s, Mill Creek Road was known as Weisel Road. This drawing is from the 1876 atlas of Bucks County.

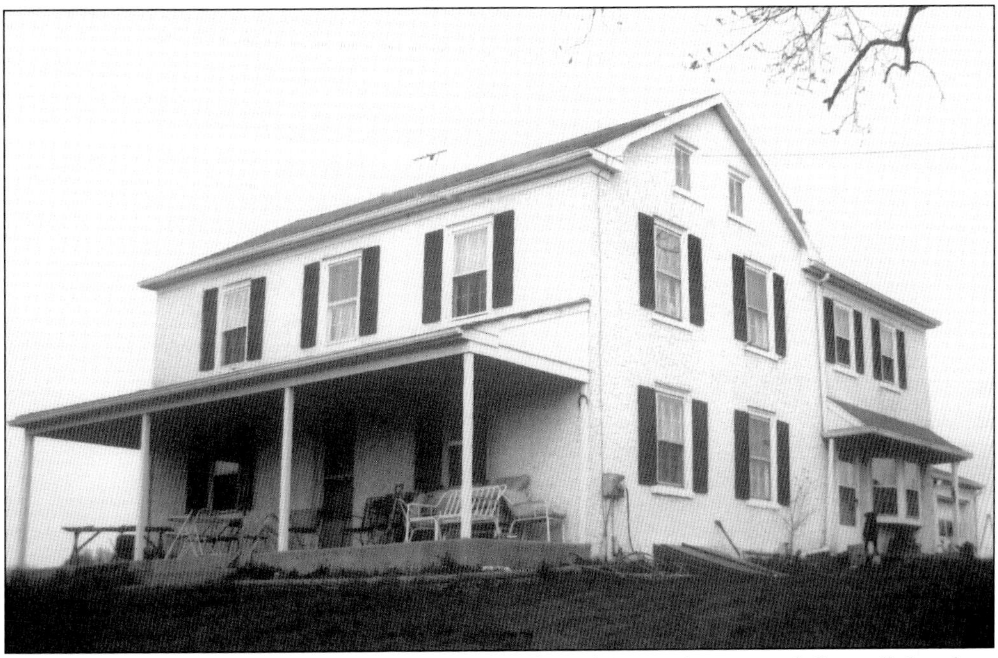

In the mid- to late 1800s, the three Weisel brothers (Henry, Aaron, and Samuel) lived on adjoining farms between Mill Creek, Stump, and Pickertown Roads. Henry owned 69 acres along Pickertown and Mill Creek Roads. The attic wall was engraved "H. Weisel 1850." The house and farm buildings were razed in 2000. Today it is designated open space and is the site of a waste management plant.

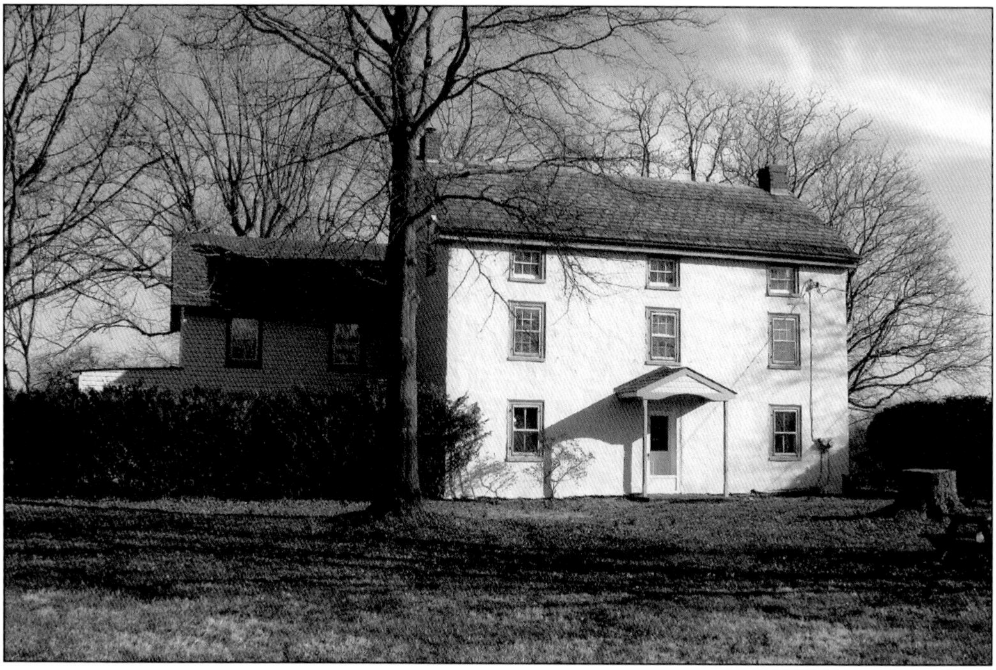

This house, located on Stump Road, was once owned by Aaron Weisel. There is a build stone in the basement that states that the house was built in 1854. At one time, the farm consisted of 55 acres of land. A large bank barn with a slate roof is still located on the property.

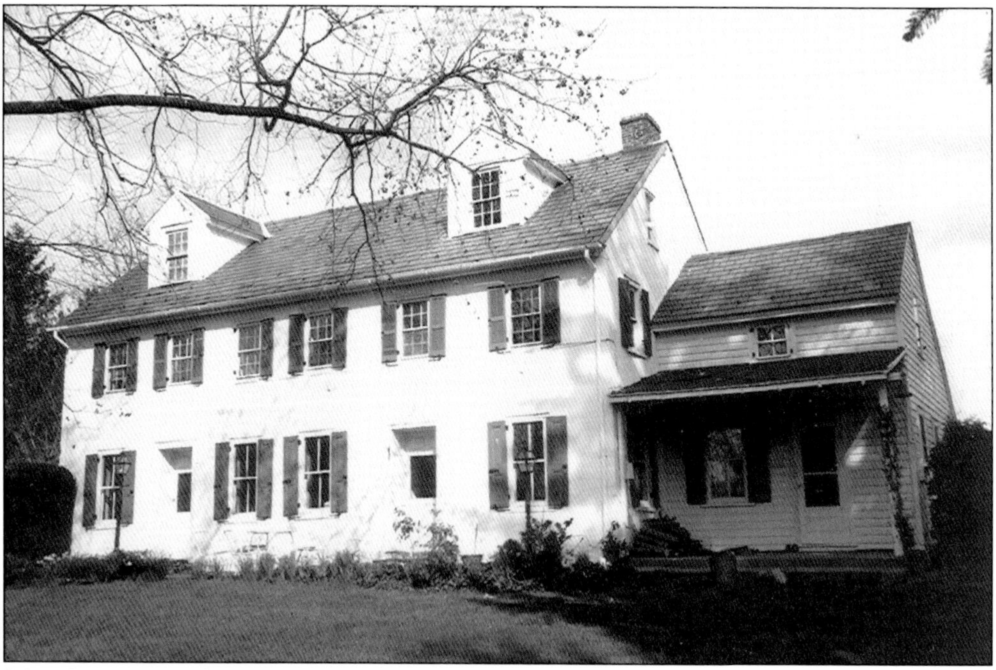

John George Weisel's son, Samuel, lived in this house. It was built in the mid-1750s. The house is mentioned as being new in the 1798 federal direct tax assessment, with Michael Moyers owner of the farm and consisting of 170 acres. Later in the 1870s, the property when owned by the Weisels consisted of 86 acres.

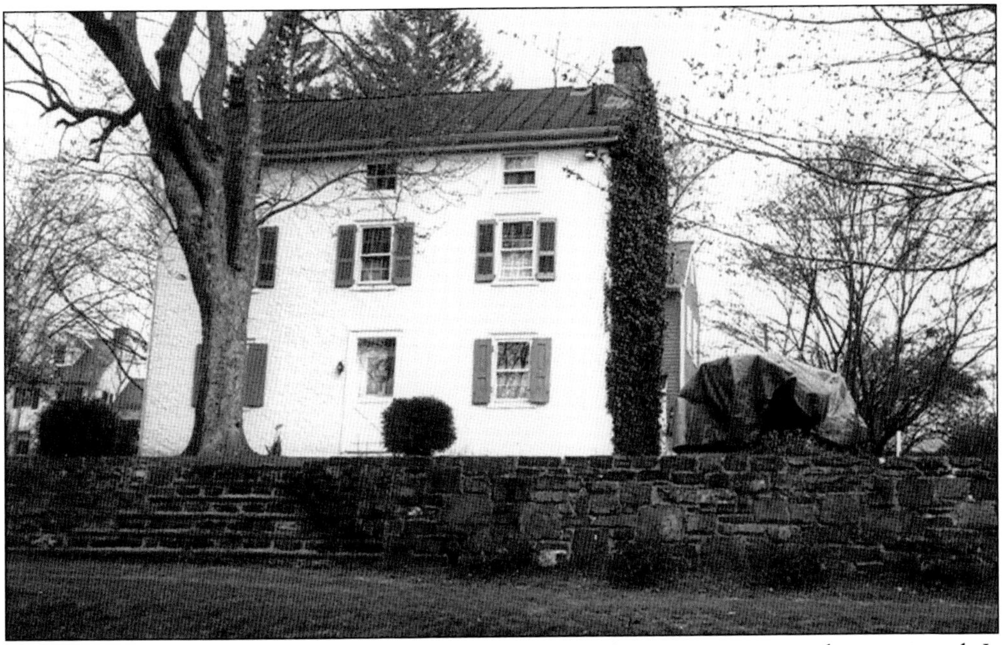

This is the second house that was located on the Weisels' 86 acres previously mentioned. It was built in the 1790s and sat closer to the property's lane and the Mill Creek. The property included a sawmill and chopping mill that drew their power from the Mill Creek. The mills were torn down by 1906.

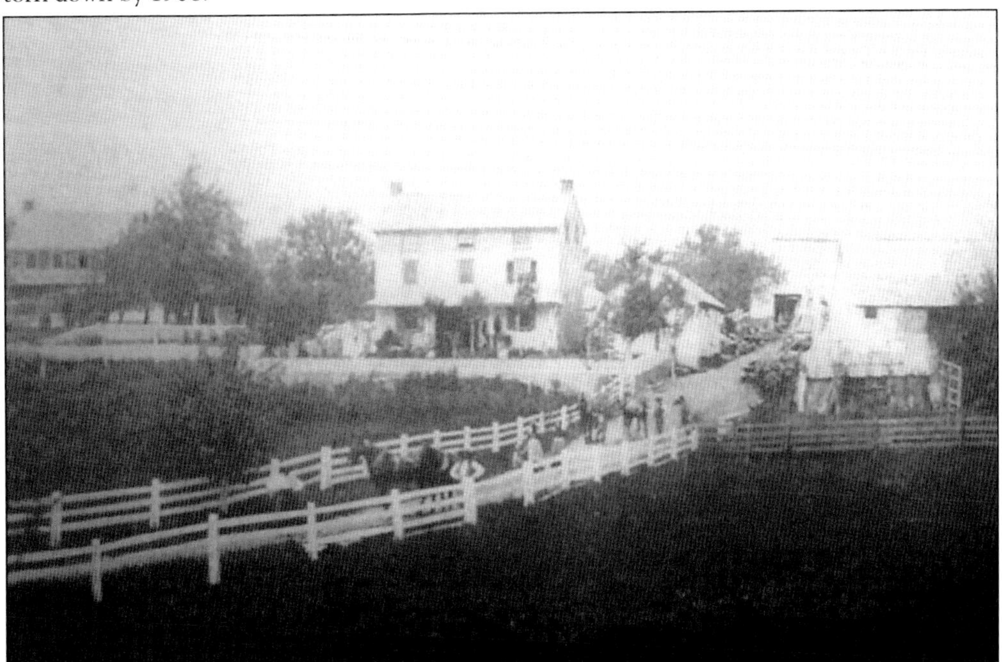

An early-1900s picture shows the Samuel Weisel farm located on Mill Creek Road. (Up until the mid-1950s, Mill Creek Road was known as Weisel Road.) Today these houses are barely visible from the road during the summer months due to the large amount of trees in the once farmed fields. (Courtesy of Thomas Knotts.)

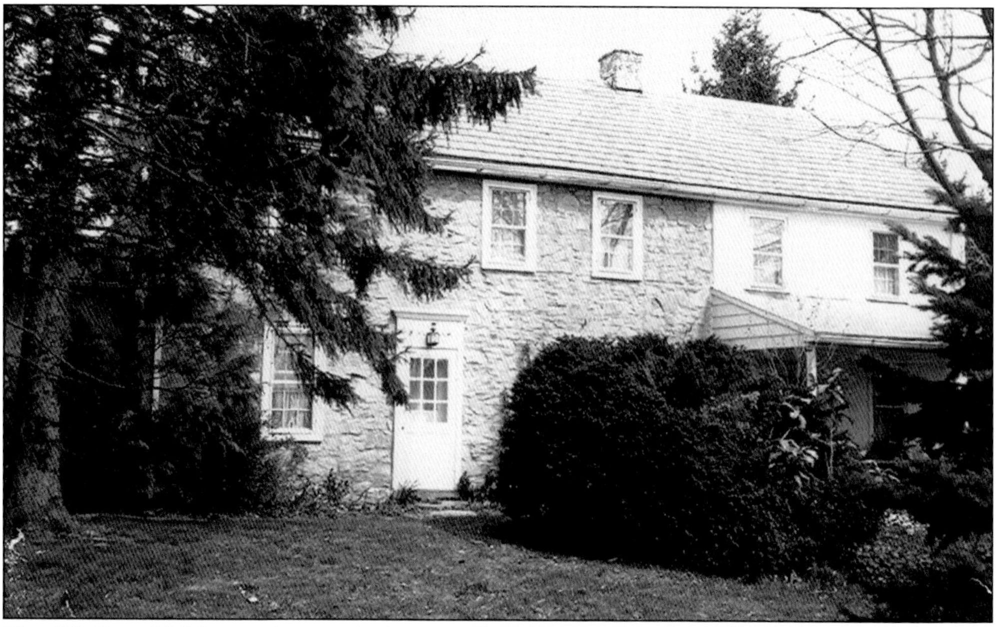

The William Haldeman house, built around 1840, is located at the corner of Stump and Pickertown Roads. A barn, corncrib, milk house, wagon shed, and hog house are also located on the property. It became eligible for the National Register of Historic Places in 1994.

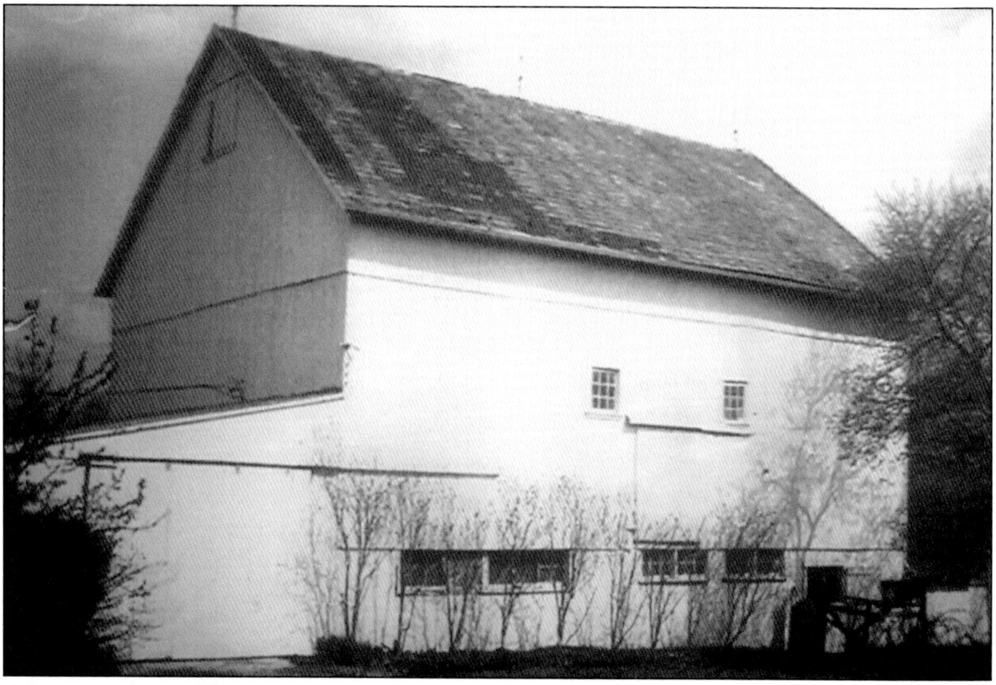

A barn on the Haldeman property is considered a typical Pennsylvania barn. They appeared late in the 18th century and flourished from about 1820 to about 1900. It is most common in the southeast and central parts of the state. The Pennsylvania barn exemplifies a highly mechanized, diversified grain-and-livestock agriculture. The Pennsylvania barn type is most closely associated with the Pennsylvania Germans.

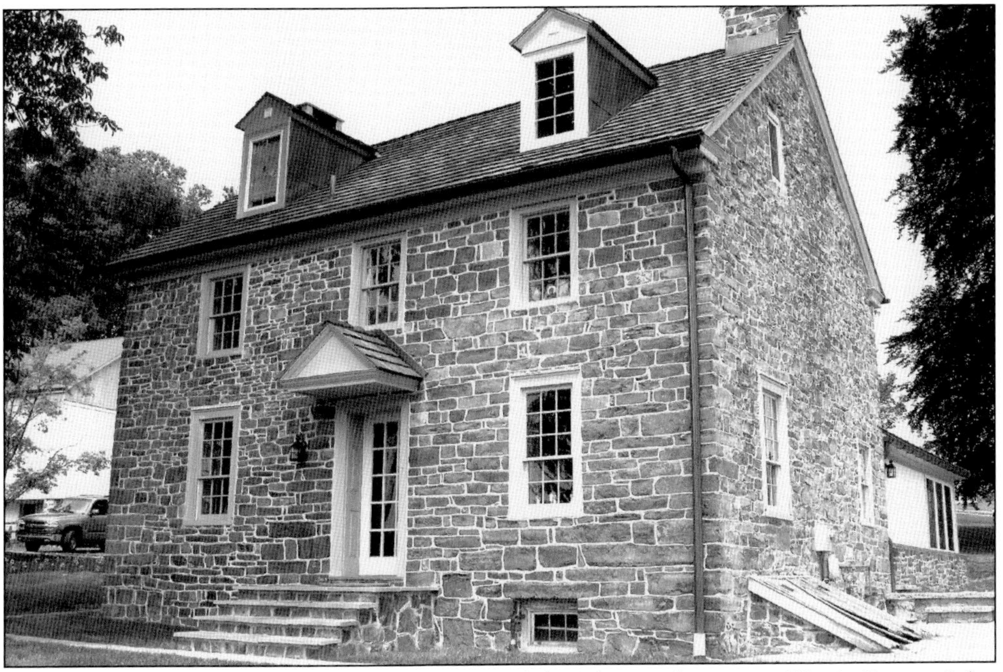

The intersection of Upper State Road and Limekiln Pike was known as Weir's Corner. John Weir's home, named Field of Praise, was built on the southerly slope of Spruce Hill around 1795. Weir's younger sister Rebecca married John Roberts Simpson Jr. Their daughter Hannah Weir Simpson married Jesse Root Grant and had a son, Pres. Ulysses S. Grant.

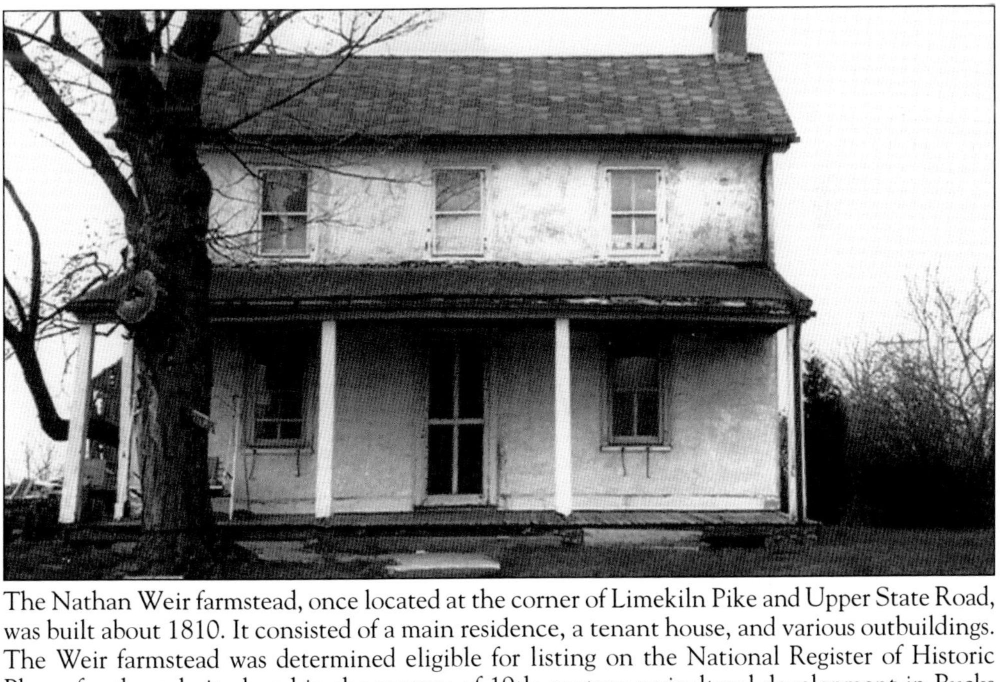

The Nathan Weir farmstead, once located at the corner of Limekiln Pike and Upper State Road, was built about 1810. It consisted of a main residence, a tenant house, and various outbuildings. The Weir farmstead was determined eligible for listing on the National Register of Historic Places for the role it played in the pattern of 19th-century agricultural development in Bucks County. The Weir Farmstead was razed in July 2007.

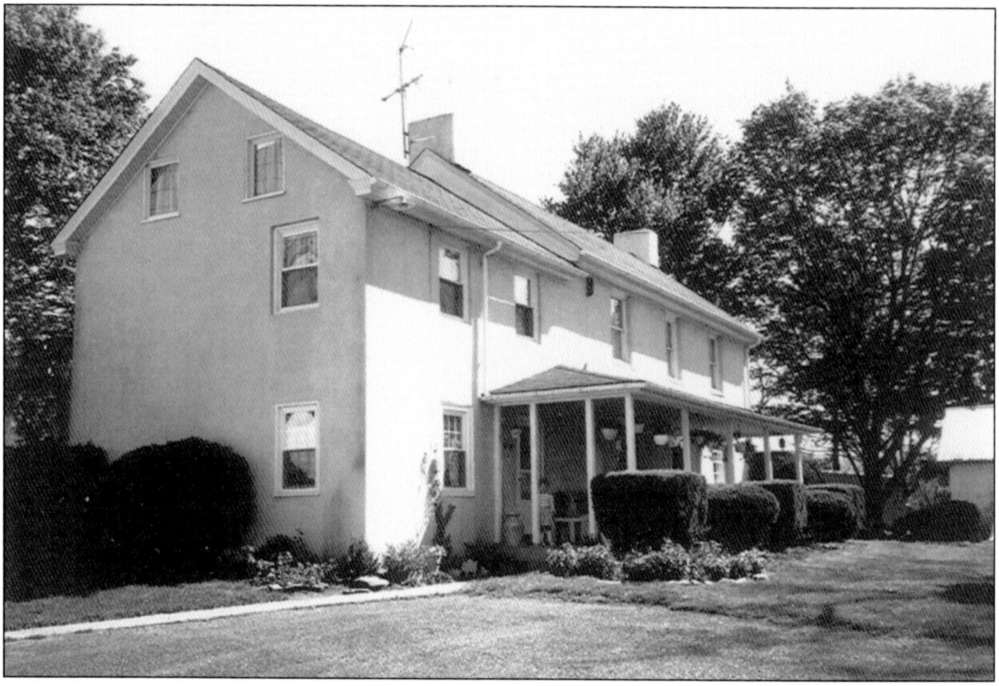

In the 1820s, James and Lewis Thompson built the house that today is located on the corner of County Line and Folly Roads. The home has a very uncommon feature of curved window sashes on the main floor. A housing development is planned for much of the property, but the house and many of the farm buildings will remain.

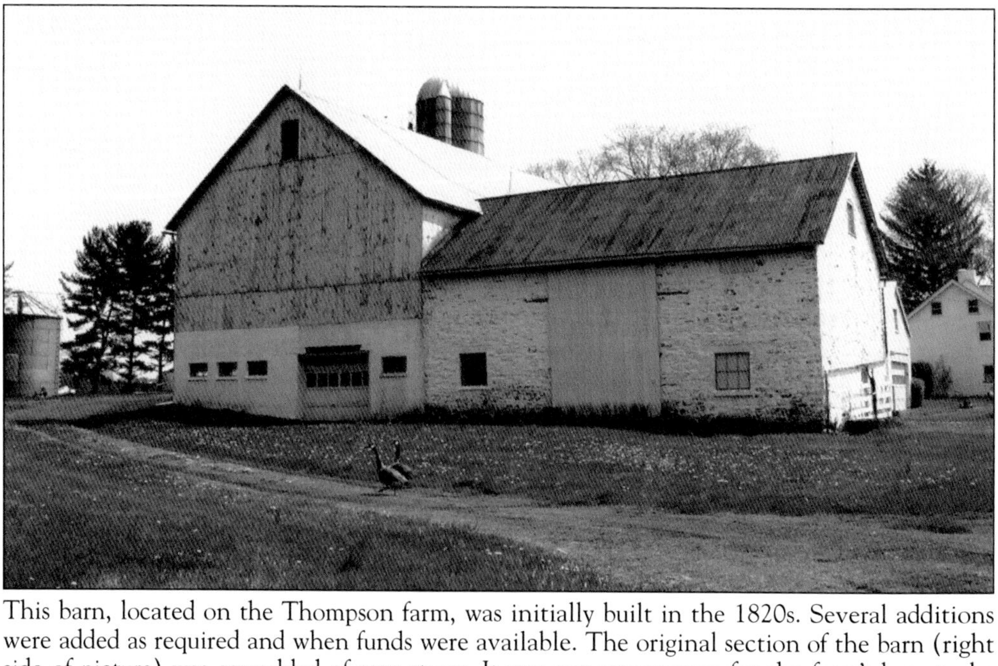

This barn, located on the Thompson farm, was initially built in the 1820s. Several additions were added as required and when funds were available. The original section of the barn (right side of picture) was assembled of area stone. It was not uncommon for the farm's barn to be larger and more ornate than the home that the family lived in. Many farmers built their barns before they built their houses.

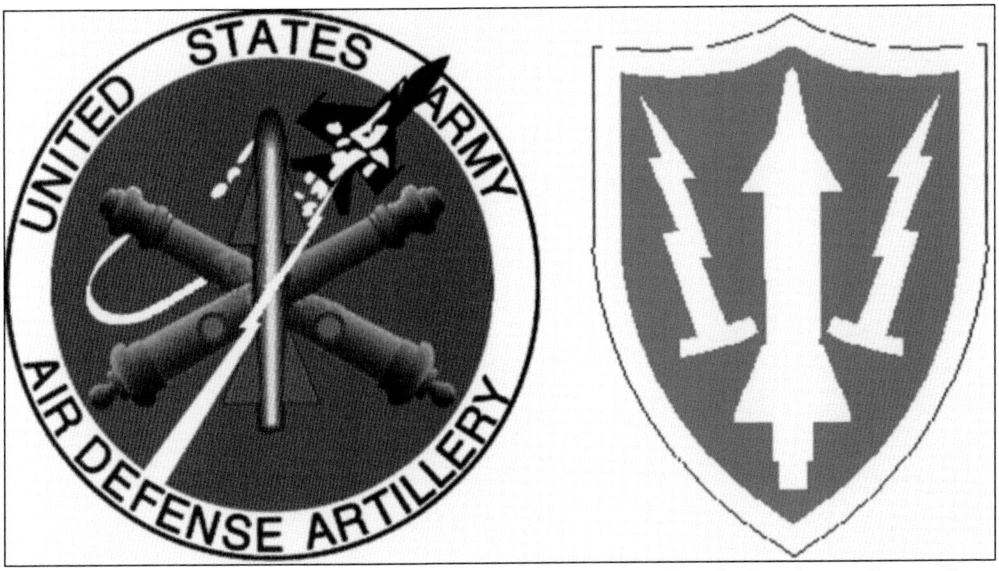

In 1954, two properties in the western part of the township, off Folly Road near County Line Road, were conveyed to the federal government. The soldiers of PH-99 watched the skies over the Philadelphia area from 1954 to 1969, a time when tensions were high between the United States and the Soviet Union. It was one of 12 sites around Philadelphia. (Courtesy of www.aradcomsite99.com.)

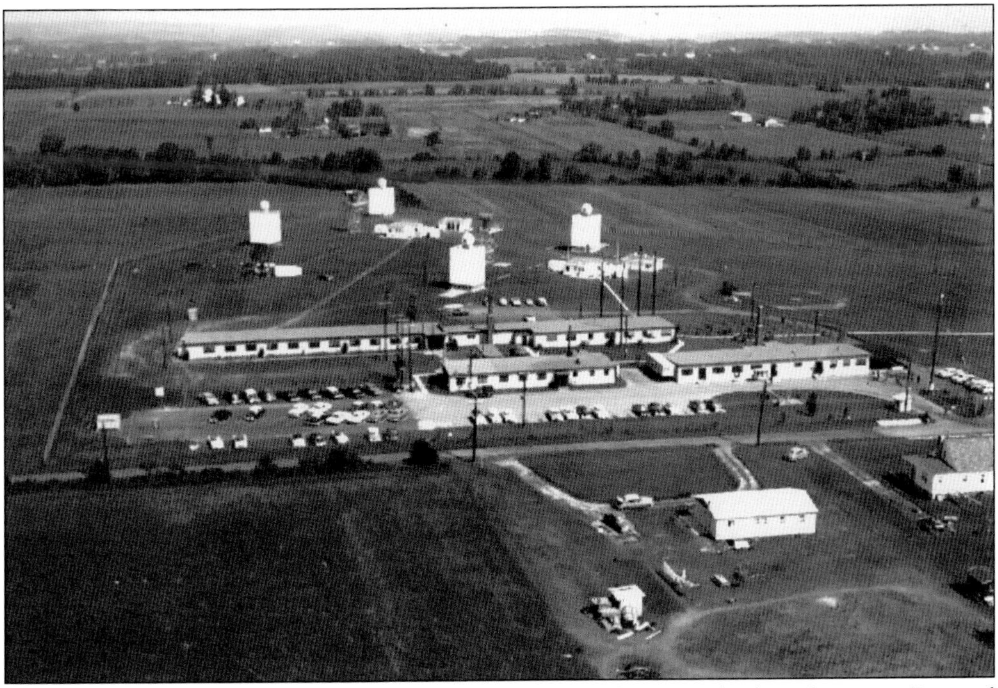

The site had two main sections, an integrated fire control area, and a launcher area. Pictured here is the former fire control area at the Warrington site, now known as Igoe-Porter-Wellings Memorial Park (named in the 1970s in honor of William John Igoe, Frank James Porter, and Edward Alfred Wellings, three Warrington Township residents killed while fighting in Vietnam), also known as Upper Nike Park. (Courtesy of www.aradcomsite99.com.)

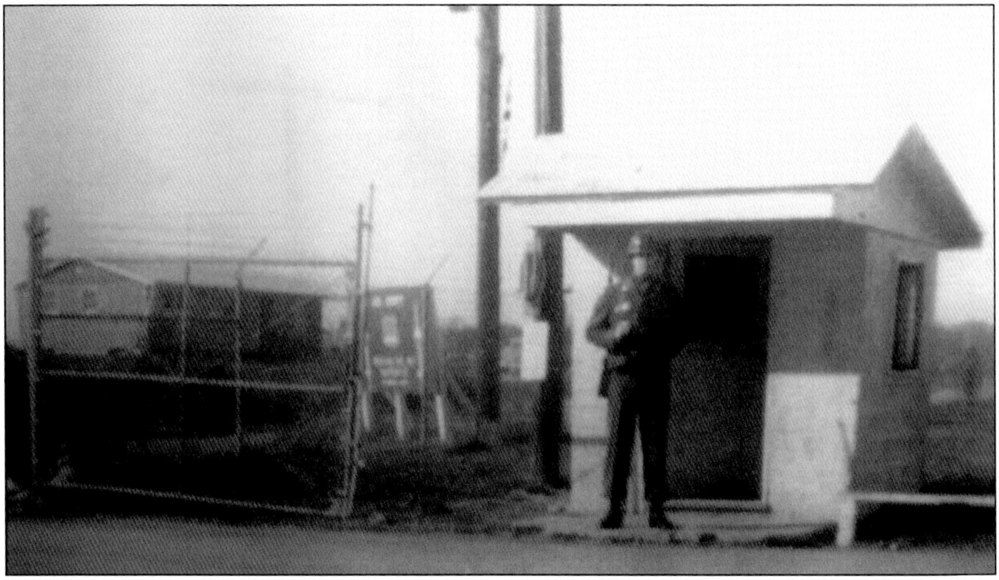

The 27.5-acre parcel was designated as the fire control area and included radar, barracks, a mess hall, two headquarter buildings, and fire control facilities. One of the headquarter buildings was occupied by the battery, which actually operated the site. It housed an orderly room, commanding officer's office, day room, supply room, barbershop, and post exchange. (Courtesy of www.aradcomsite99.com.)

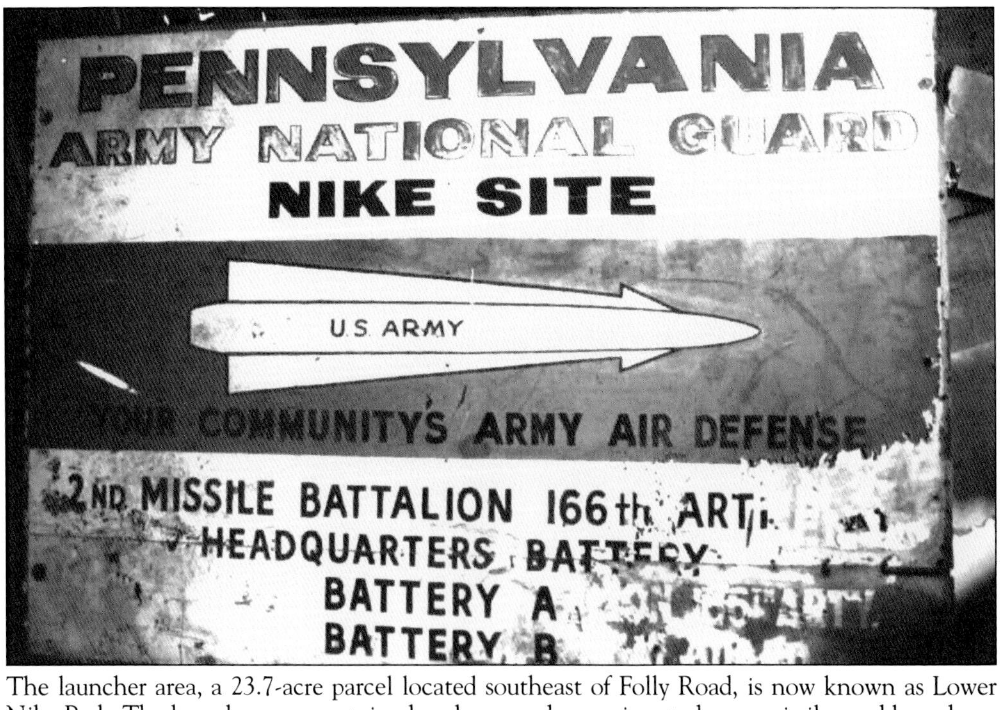

The launcher area, a 23.7-acre parcel located southeast of Folly Road, is now known as Lower Nike Park. The launcher area contained underground magazines to house missiles and launchers. The Warrington site was designated PH-99 and was a "dual site," meaning that it had launching facilities for both Nike Ajax and Nike Hercules missiles. (Courtesy of www.aradcomsite99.com.)

Four

Village of Tradesville

Tradesville Village is located at the intersection of Lower State and Bristol Roads. It was noted in 1887 that the village consisted "of four houses on opposite corners of the principal square at the crossing of Bristol Road and the State Road leading from Doylestown to Norristown." The village was also known as Brunnerville after a local family and later as Stuckert's Corner after a local storekeeper. This store was located in Doylestown Township and currently is the site of a gas station. Tradesville had its own post office, which operated from December 7, 1881. L. W. Walton as the postmaster until 1914. The name changed to Tradesville in 1884 for unknown reasons. But the name Tradesville was probably chosen because in 1682 William Penn offered the Free Society of Traders a nearly 20,000-acre tract of land made up from the then communities of Warwick, New Britain, and Hilltown. It was not considered a prosperous area at the time, and the prospect of growth was "not encouraging." An early history stated, "The only fraternity represented here is the loafer, who seems to be created for no other purpose than to perpetuate the ancient and honorable order of idleness." Prior to 1850, the west corner of Tradesville was actually part of New Britain Township, as Warrington's border ended at Bristol and Lower State Roads. The area at Upper State Road and Bristol Road was known as Prospect Hill, bestowed because of the vast extent of country to be seen from its heights. The Native American name for the hill was Machk-achsen-ing—*machkin* meaning "red," *achsen* meaning "stone," and *ing* meaning "at." Hence the name means "at the red stone," as the shale there is a noticeably rich dark red. Its earliest English name was Kelsa Hill, so named for the Kelsa family, early landowners. The hill would also be called Spruce Hill, from the abundant hemlock spruce on the steep slopes. Locally the northwestern division of the hill was known as Little Spruce Hill and the southeastern part as Big Spruce Hill. Chief Tamanend is presumed to be buried in a ravine at the northeast end of the hill (in New Britain).

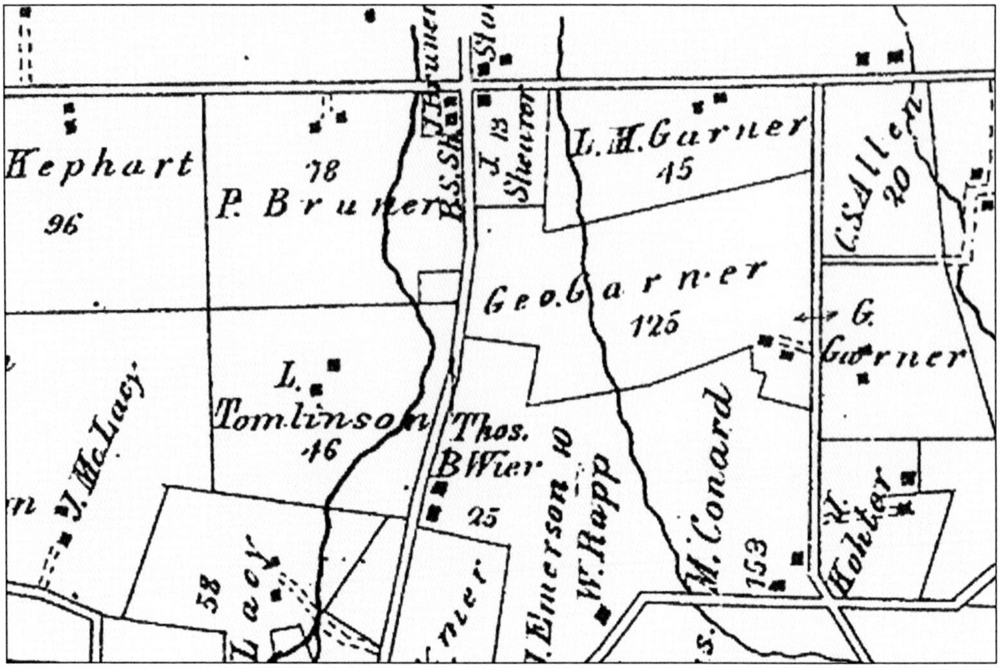

Pictured here is a village of Tradesville map from the 1876 atlas of Bucks County by J. D. Scott.

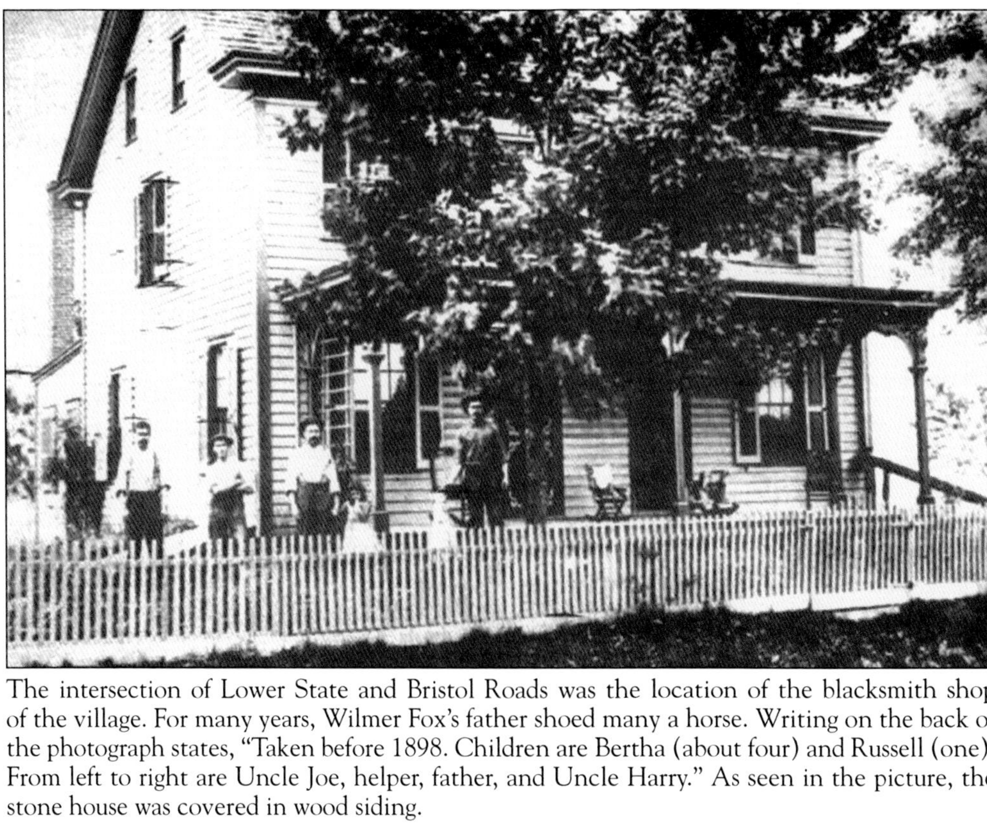

The intersection of Lower State and Bristol Roads was the location of the blacksmith shop of the village. For many years, Wilmer Fox's father shoed many a horse. Writing on the back of the photograph states, "Taken before 1898. Children are Bertha (about four) and Russell (one). From left to right are Uncle Joe, helper, father, and Uncle Harry." As seen in the picture, the stone house was covered in wood siding.

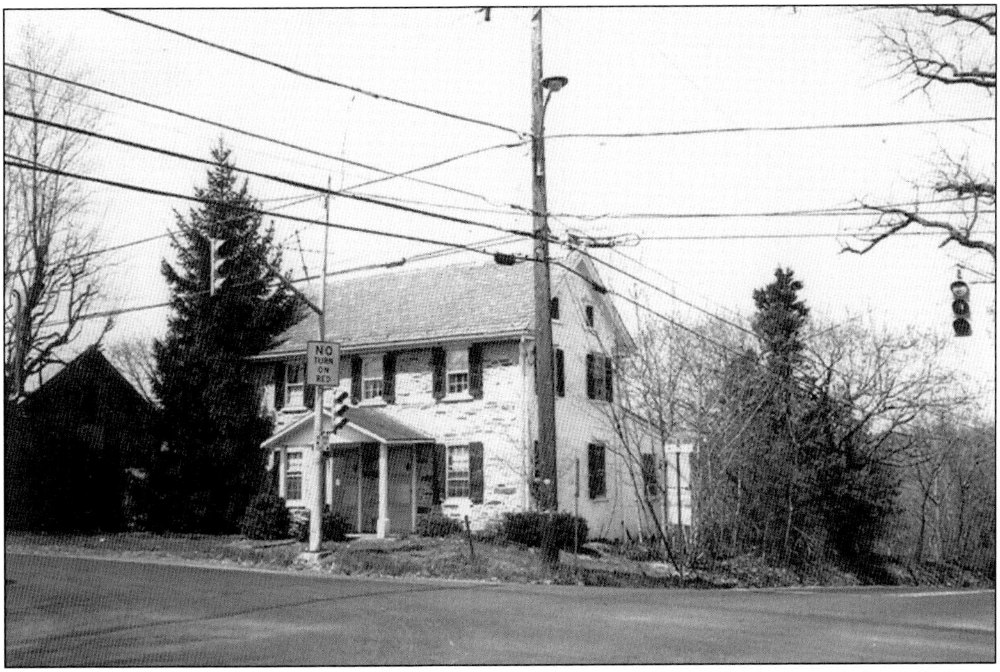

A later view shows that the wood siding was removed to show the natural stone. A frame barn to the left of the house was converted into living space when an addition was added, connecting the barn to the house. The stone walls of the barn are still visible, showing its original position.

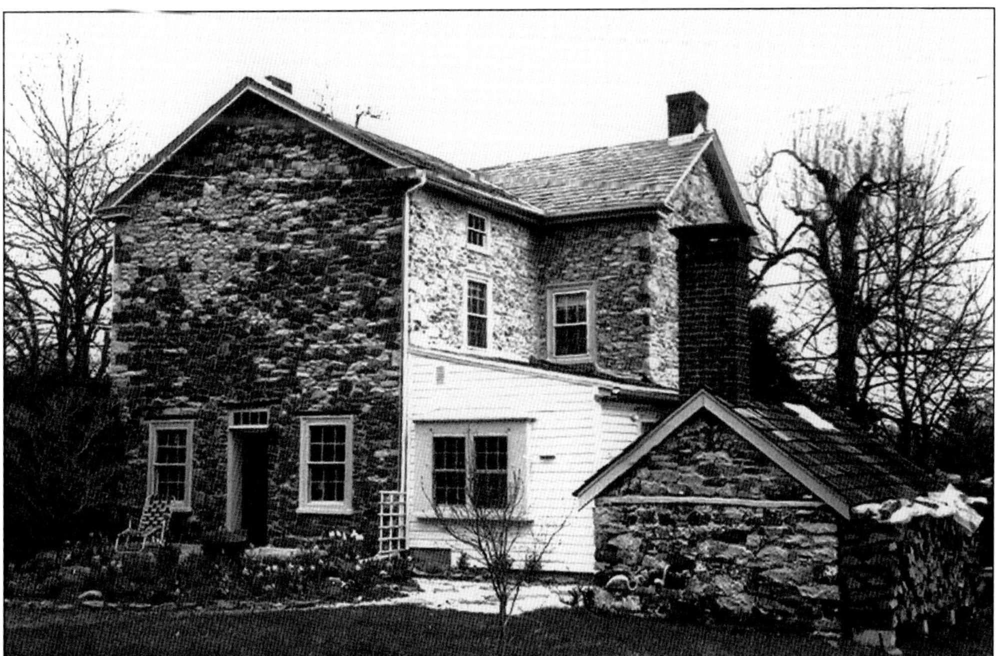

Built around 1820, this house, once owned by Jesse W. Shearer and the Kephart family, sits on the opposite corner of Lower State Road on the Warrington Township side of Bristol Road. Aside from the house, there are several outbuildings on the property. There is a large barn with several stalls and a smokehouse containing a firebox and a caldron.

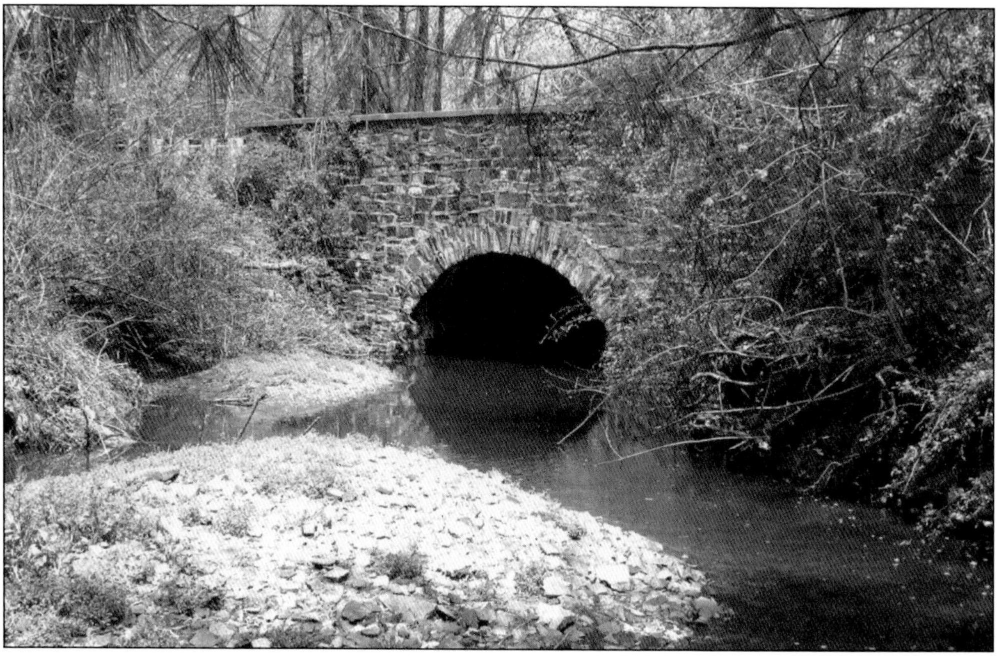

While most people are not even aware of its presence, this stone bridge is located on Bristol Road, on the border of Doylestown Township, just south of Lower State Road. It was built in 1900 and spans over the Mill Creek. This single-arch bridge, with a span of 15 feet, was made with local stone and replaced an earlier wooden structure.

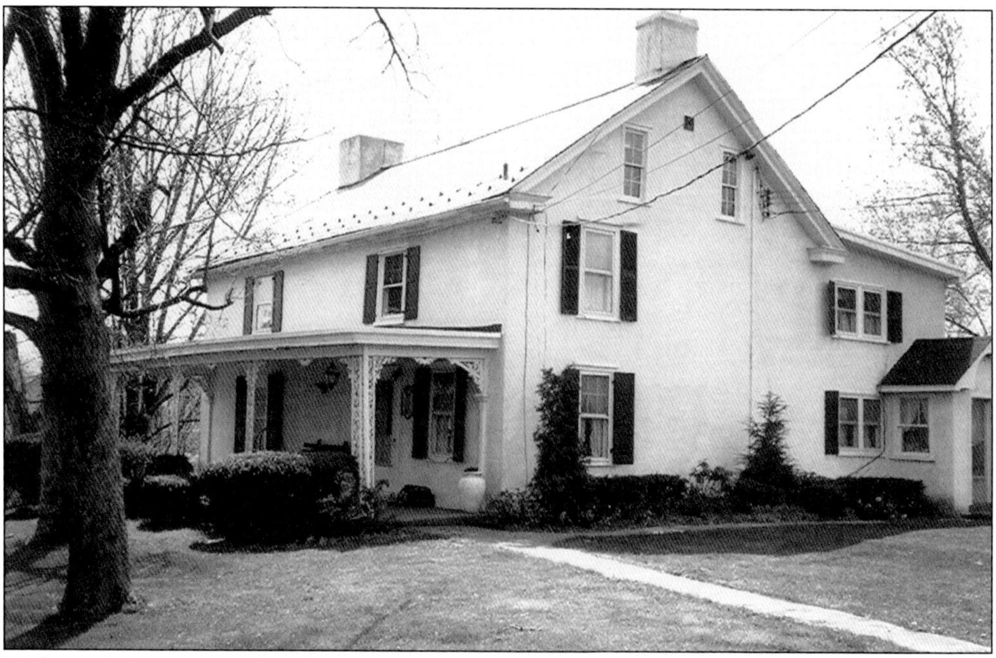

Mill Creek Farm, located on Bristol Road, currently consists of 10 acres. The farmhouse on the property was built in 1794, per a mounted iron fire mark. There is also a 3,000-square-foot barn, which was built in the mid-1800s on the property by subscription after the prior one constructed of logs burned to the ground in 1874.

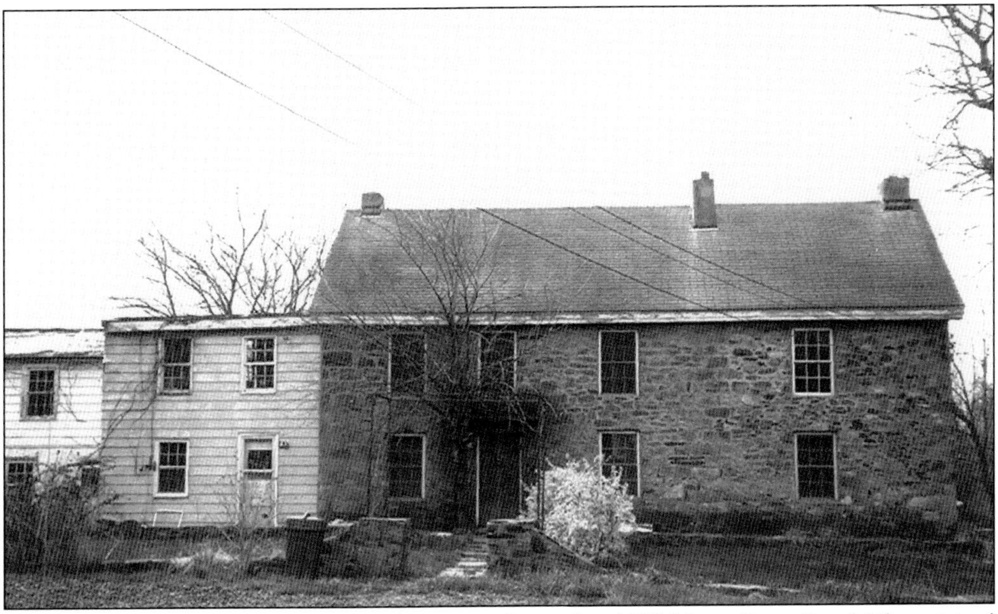

The J. Brinker and Horowitz farmstead was once located at 1225 Upper State Road. The original stone section, located in the center of the picture, was built around 1750. Several stone and frame additions were added throughout the years. The dwelling became eligible for the National Register of Historic Places in 1994. It was removed to make room for a housing development.

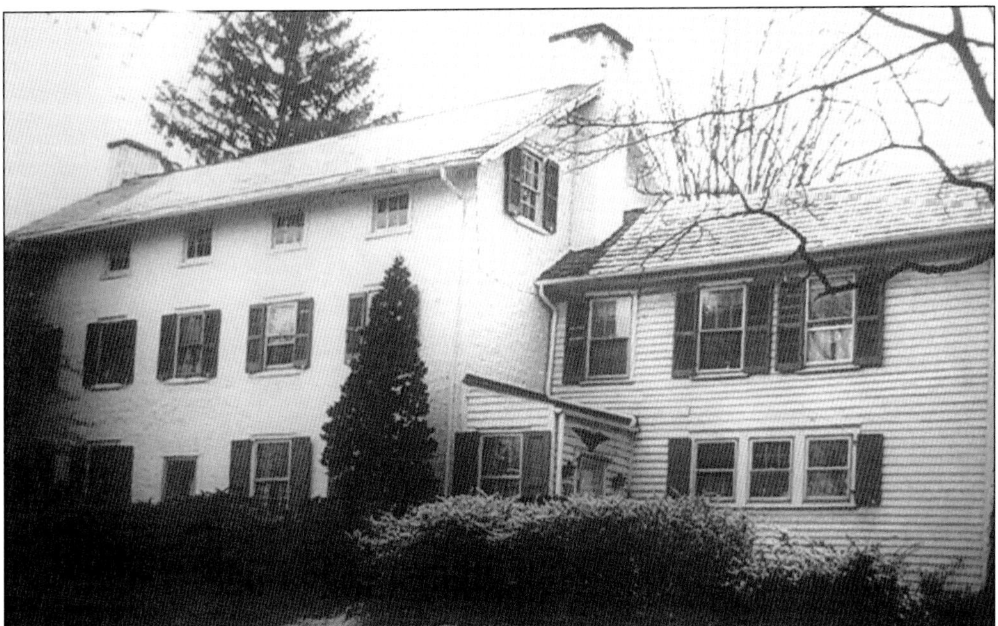

The Kenner farmstead, located at the corner of Upper State and Bristol Roads, was built around 1855. The 1798 tax records describe the house on the property as a one-story frame and log house measuring 30 feet by 26 feet. At that time, the property consisted of 100 acres. In 1855, the house was described as a substantial, modern, new stone home. The dwelling became eligible for the National Register of Historic Places in 1994.

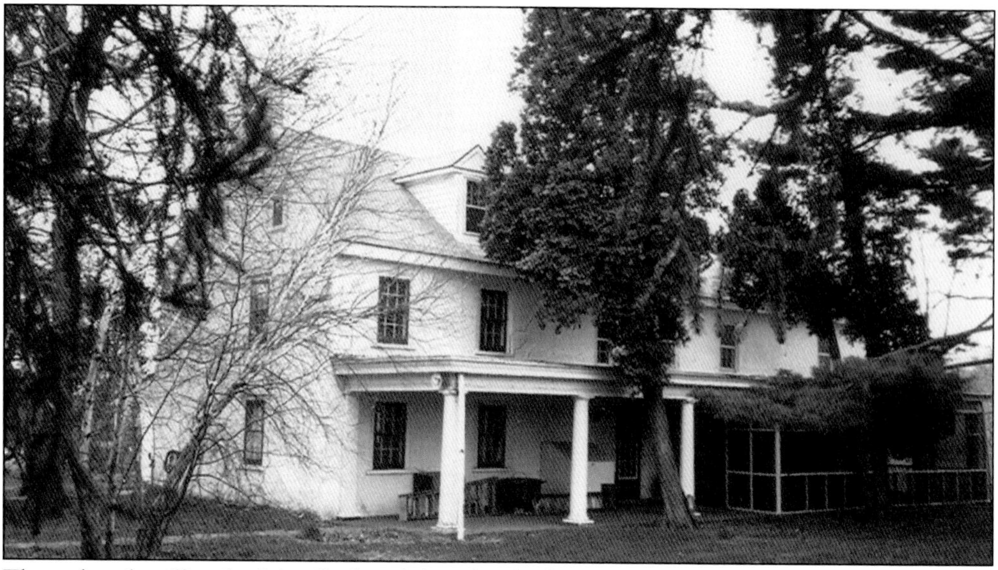

Through a sheriff's sale, John Rothrock bought the house and 62 acres back for $1,241 in July 1962. Rothrock named it Red Coat Farm, which translates to *rothrock* in German. The house was built in three sections. The first section was constructed of log. The property today consists of a little over three acres and includes a covered walkway to the smokehouse, garage, chicken coop, and a Swiss bank barn.

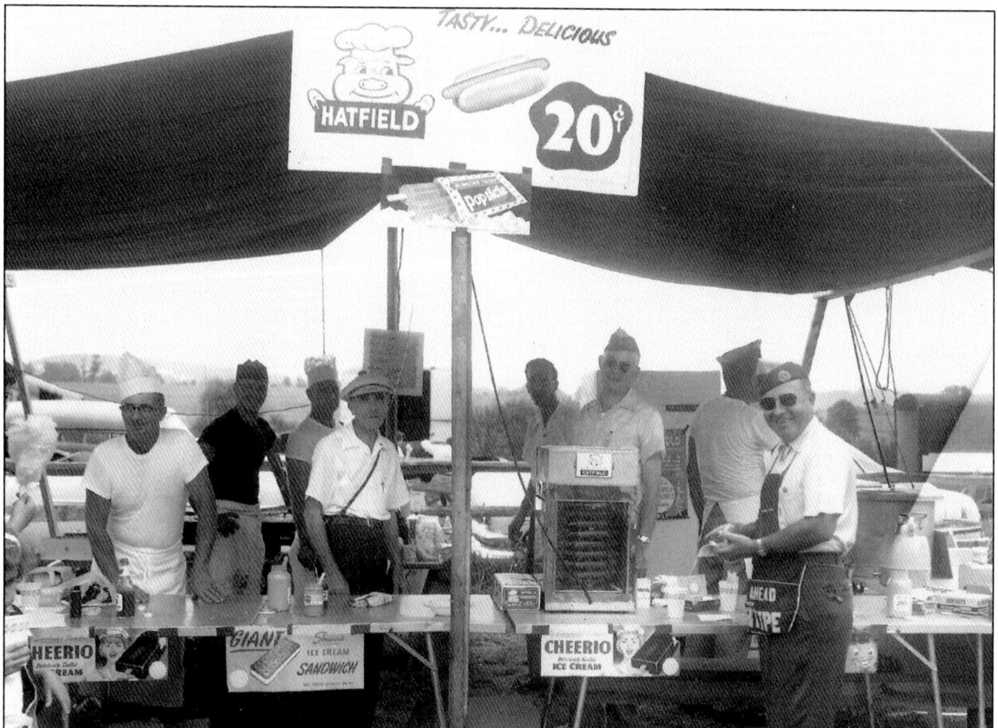

The Lions Club once held a popular annual "Horse and Pony Show." The first one-day show was held in August 1958 and eventually grew to a two-day event. In 1963, the shows were held at the Rothrock farm located on Pickertown Road. (Courtesy of the Warrington Lions Club.)

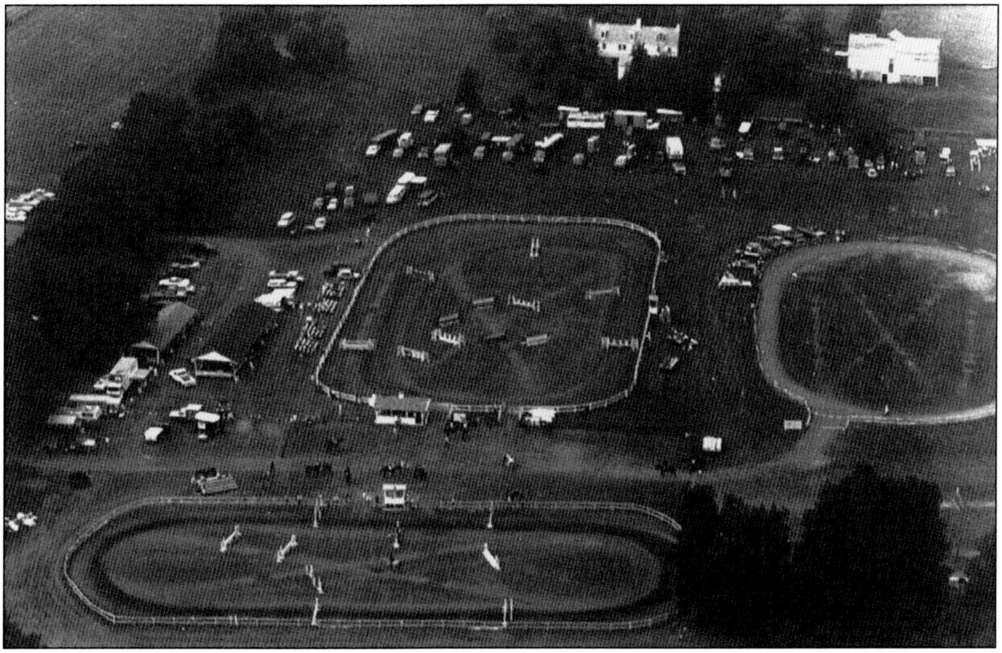

An aerial view of the Lions Club horse show, taken in 1965, shows the Rothrock house in the upper center portion. In October 1941, a group of men established the Warrington unit of Lions International. Primarily interested in the welfare of its community and its inhabitants, the group received its charter on December 7, 1941. (Courtesy of the Warrington Lions Club.)

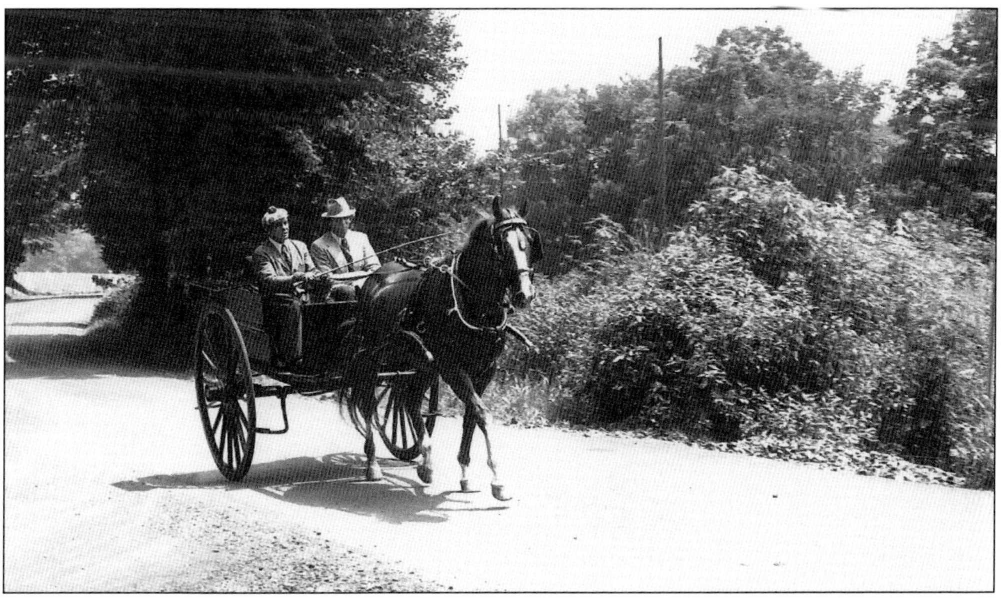

Pictured here is a horse and carriage on Pickertown Road on its way to a Lions Club Horse and Pony Show. These shows included classes such as showmanship, halter mare, walk trot, and barrel racing. In 1978, they started a three-day, class A show. These shows ended in July 1988 when the Rothrock property was sold for development. (Courtesy of the Warrington Lions Club.)

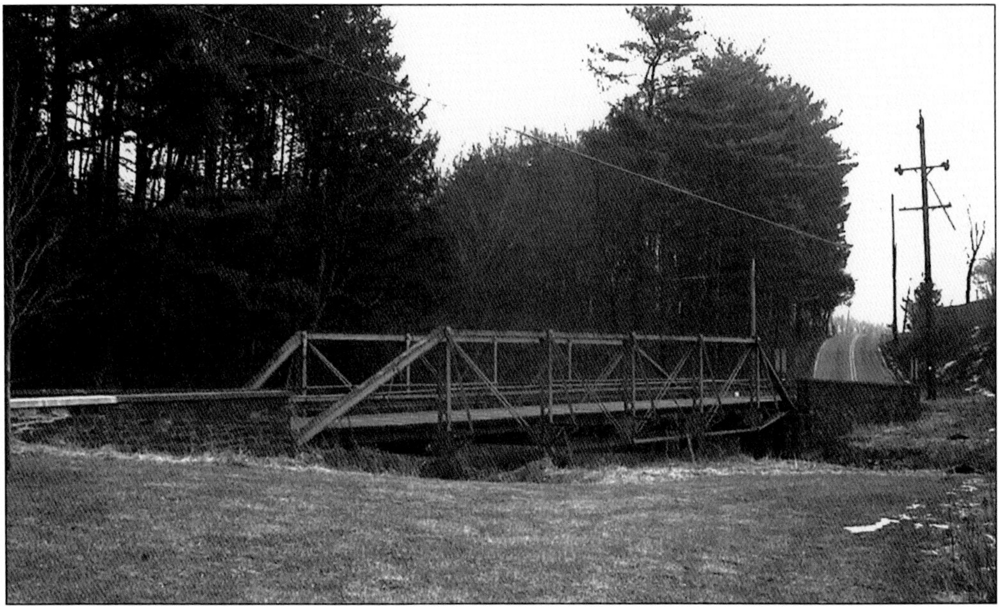

The Weisel Bridge (County Bridge 145), built in 1893, spans over the Mill Creek on Pickertown Road. It was originally built as a simple wooden footbridge in the early 1800s. It was a stone and iron structure, 80 feet long by 16 feet wide, with timber-plank decking. The bridge was eligible for listing on the National Register of Historic Places before being modified in 2005–2006.

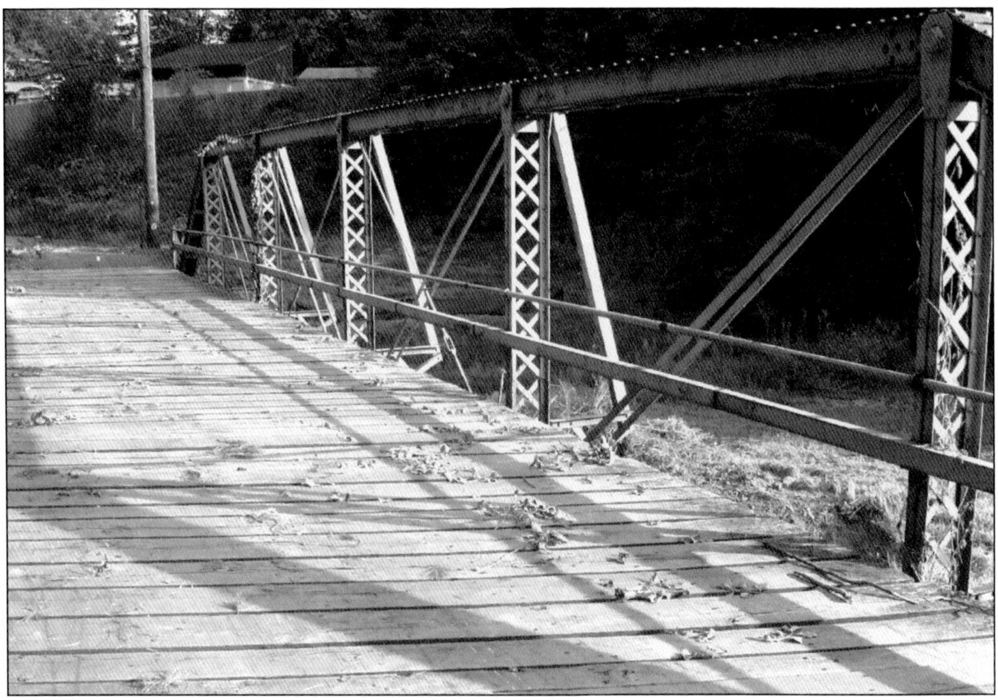

There are stories that in the early 20th century, boys on their way to and from the Mill Creek School would walk across the bridge via the tops of the iron trusses. It is known that at least one individual, Milton Masser, was unsuccessful in his trapeze walk and fell, but he did live to tell about it.

Five

Village Schools

From simple, handmade one-room schoolhouses to muiltimillion-dollar pillars of learning, schools within the township borders have grown and advanced with the times. Among the many historic buildings in Warrington Township, there are five that at one time served as public schools for the community. In the early years of the township, each village had its own school, containing grades one to eight. Four of the five are in active use today while plans are being made to utilize the fifth. In 1998, the township acquired the County Line Schoolhouse with an acre of land from the Cutler Group after it was purchased from the Schlecter family. The hope and mission of the Warrington Historical Society is to restore the structure back to a one-room schoolhouse.

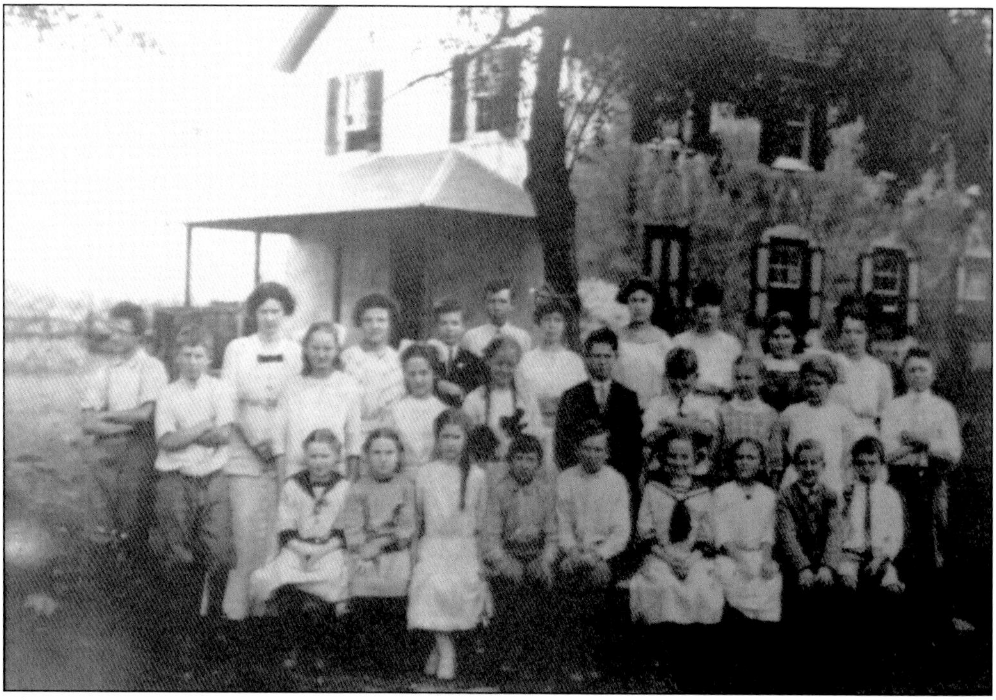

The Warrington Schoolhouse (also known as the Warringtonville School) was built in 1808 to replace a wood-framed schoolhouse that had been built in 1765. Located on Bristol Road, it was close to the center of Warrington Village. While in service, the school was closed due to events such as snow, heavy rain, typhoid epidemics, and harvest time. The schoolhouse has two floors.

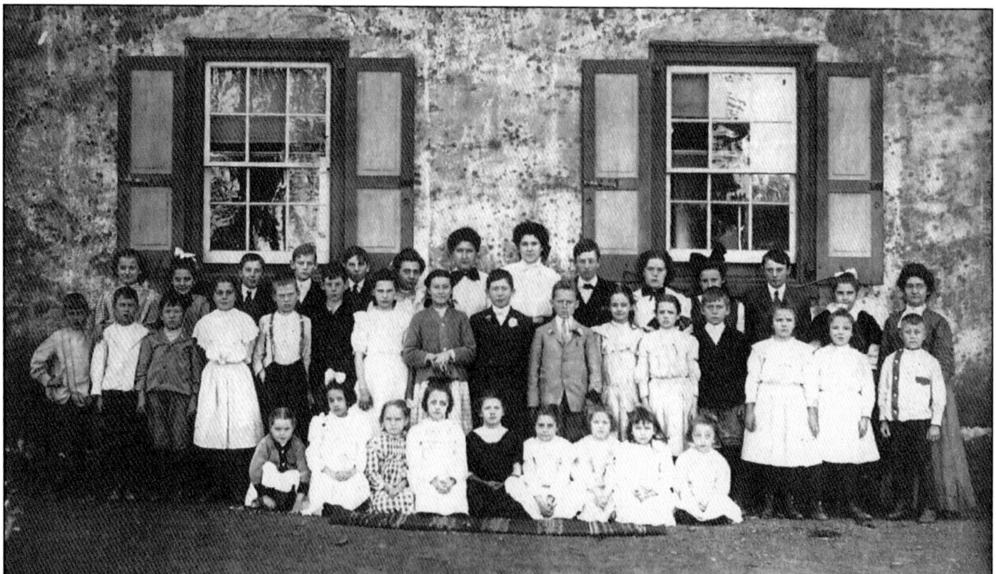

Grades one through four were taught on the first floor. Grades five through eight were taught on the second floor. Access to the second floor was gained via a narrow set of stairs to the right just as one entered the building. There were two stone outhouses on the property. Later a wooden porch with a metal roof was installed over the entire front of the schoolhouse.

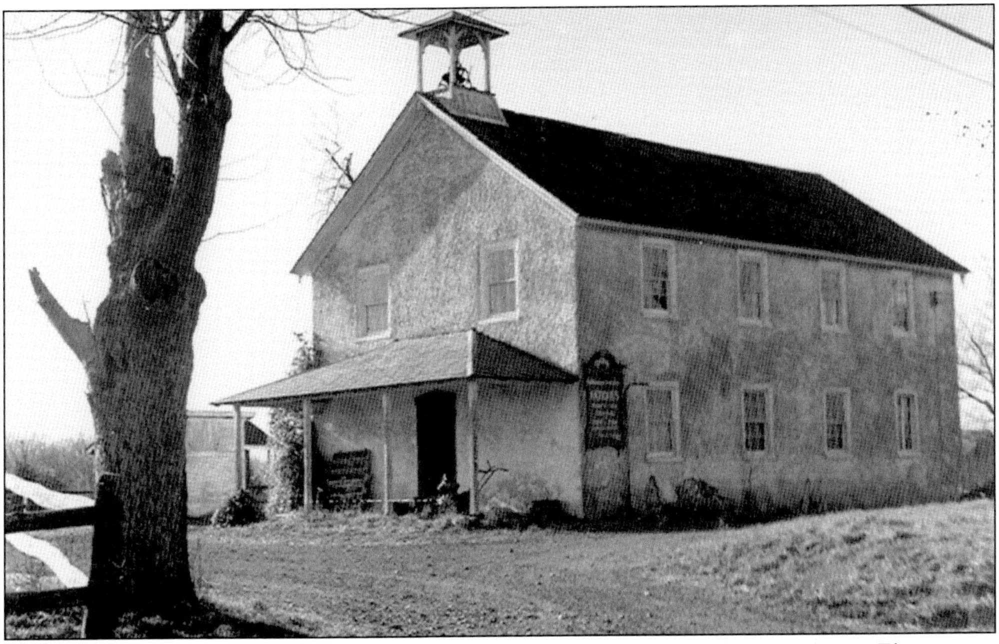

The school was in operation for 143 years until it closed in 1951 when the Warrington Elementary School opened its doors. When the building was opened as a place of business, the white pebble stucco was removed to expose the red stone exterior that is seen today. The school bell is still in its original position above the front door in the belfry.

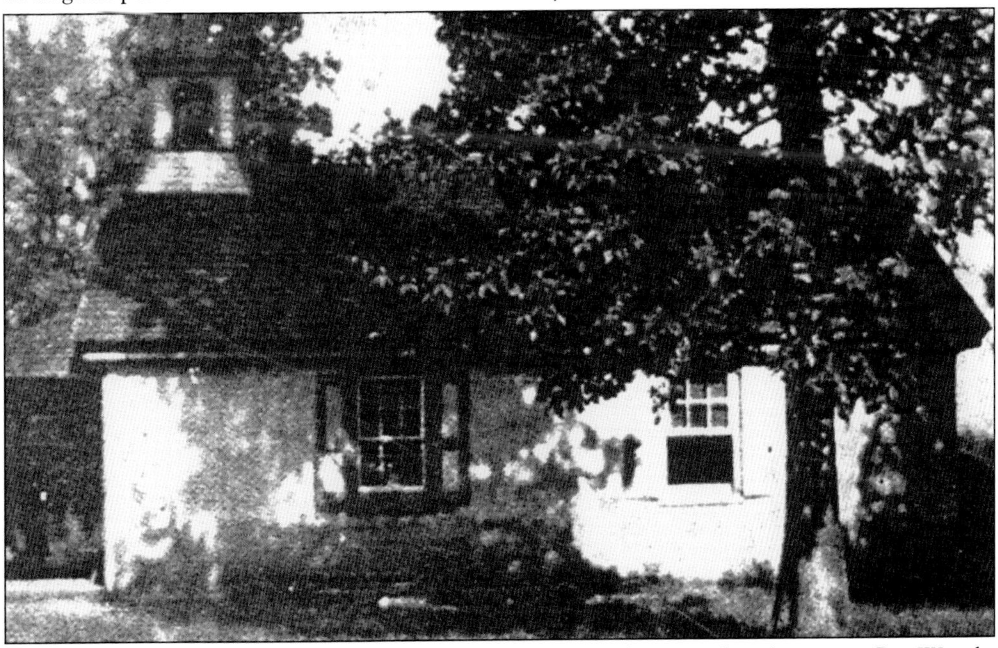

Known as the Grove School, due to its surroundings by what was then known as Big Woods, this school was owned and operated by the Mennonite Church. The first teacher recorded was John Haldeman in the winter of 1850. In 1858, Warrington took over operation of the school, renaming it the Mill Creek School. It was located in the Tradesville area, at the corner of Pickertown and Mill Creek Roads.

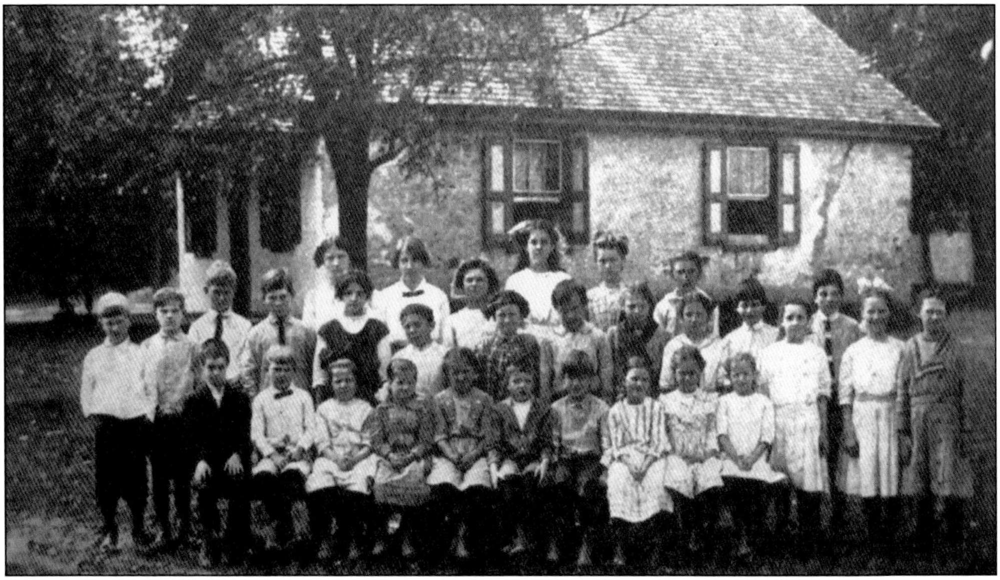

The second Mill Creek School was built in 1864 when the directors decided a new schoolhouse was needed to replace the old one; the trustees agreed to transfer the building and land by deed to the directors, reserving the right for people to hold religious meetings when school was not in session. James Cozens, a mason, and Joseph Garener, a carpenter, agreed to build the school at a cost of $1,290.

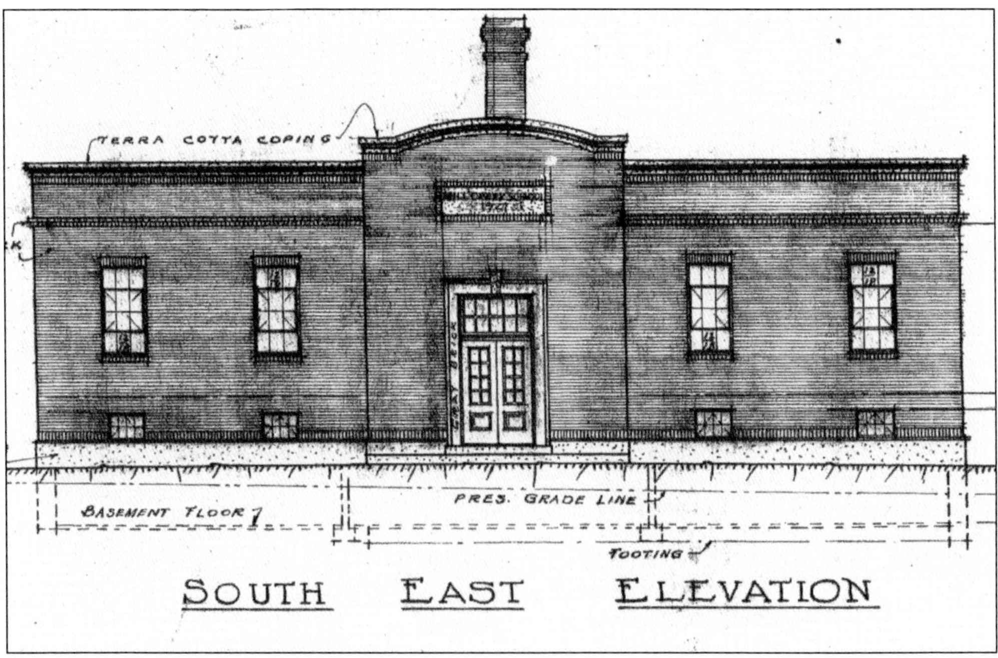

Water had to be carried from the home of Eli Clymer, which was located on what is now the parking lot of the Eureka Stone Quarry. Coal was shoveled to the stove by the students to heat the school in the winter months. In 1889, the north window was closed to make a receptacle for the school library. Flora McNair taught from 1920 to 1926, followed by her daughter, Frances McNair.

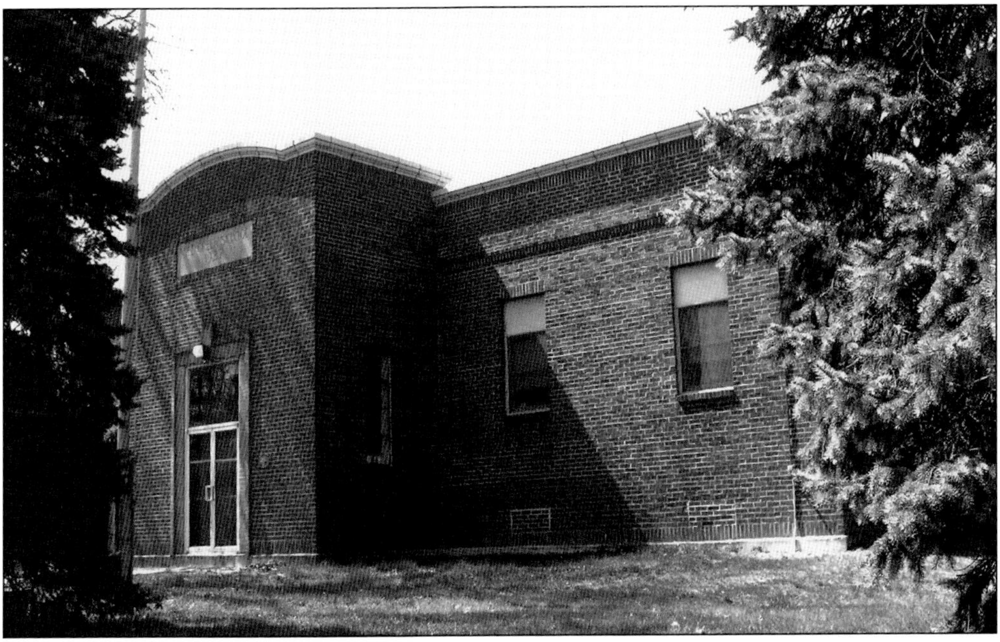

A petition was presented to consolidate Mill Creek and County Line Schools. The voters favored increasing the indebtedness to $20,000 in order to procure an additional acre of land to erect and equip a new schoolhouse, giving the children in the upper end of the township the same advantages as those in the lower part. The third Mill Creek School, designed by A. Oscar Martin, was built in 1927.

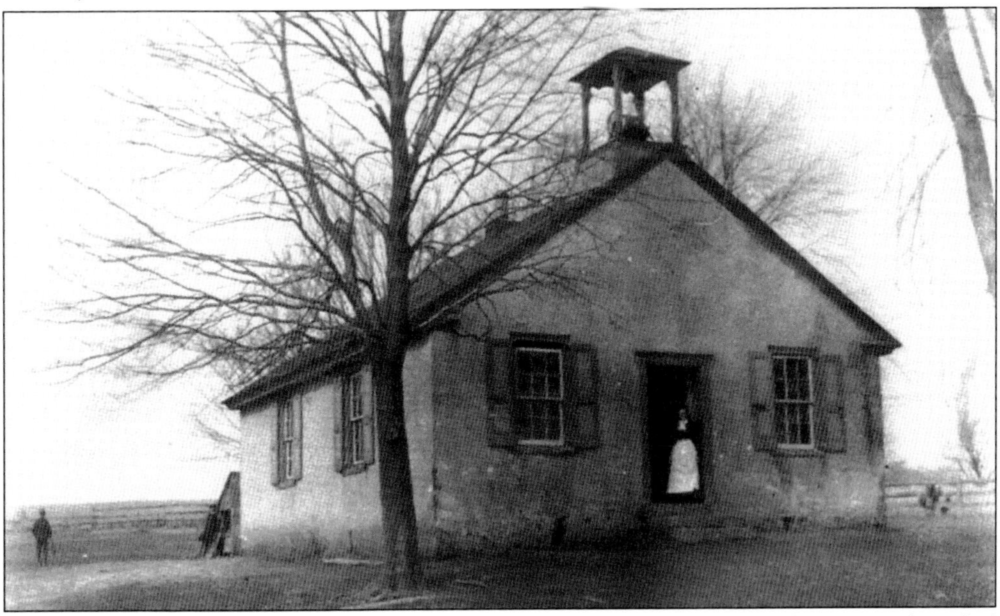

The County Line Schoolhouse is mentioned as early as 1751, when Ephraim Leech willed one acre of land at the southeast corner of his plantation joining County Line Road for a schoolhouse, forever. On Sunday afternoons, visiting ministers would hold religious services at the schoolhouse. In September 1840, meetings were held at this location to organize the German Reformed Church on Limekiln Pike. (Courtesy of Jane Henderson.)

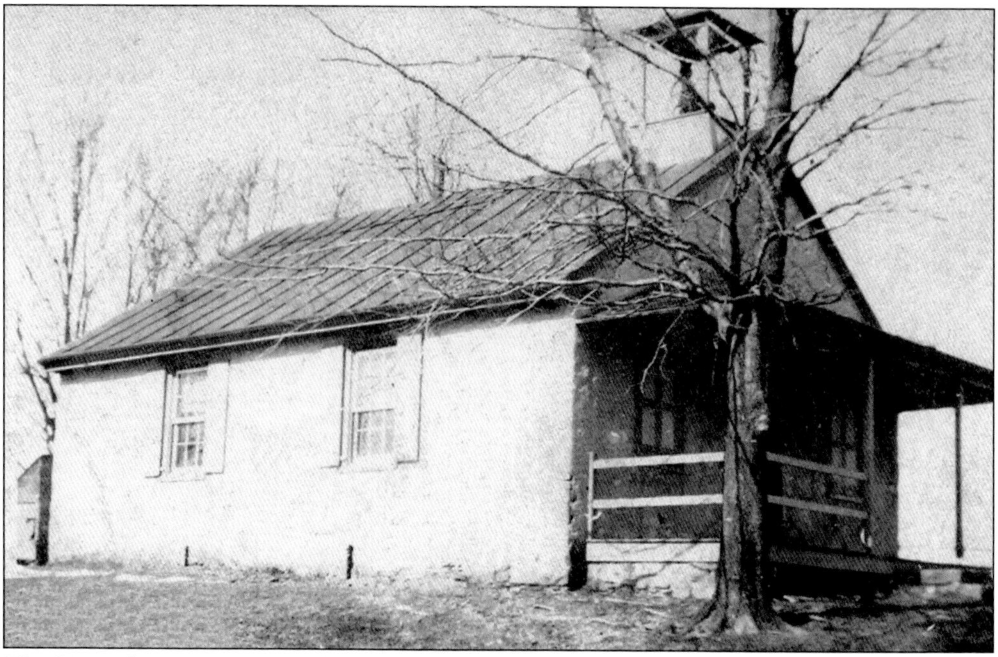

The Pennsylvania common school register for the County Line Schoolhouse has information about the demolition of the old schoolhouse and construction of a new schoolhouse. On June 5, 1857, Tilghman A. Hoover, the teacher at the County Line Schoolhouse, entered in the register, "Spent part of the afternoon cleaning the house. Board of Directors met at the house to make arrangement for the building of a new house."

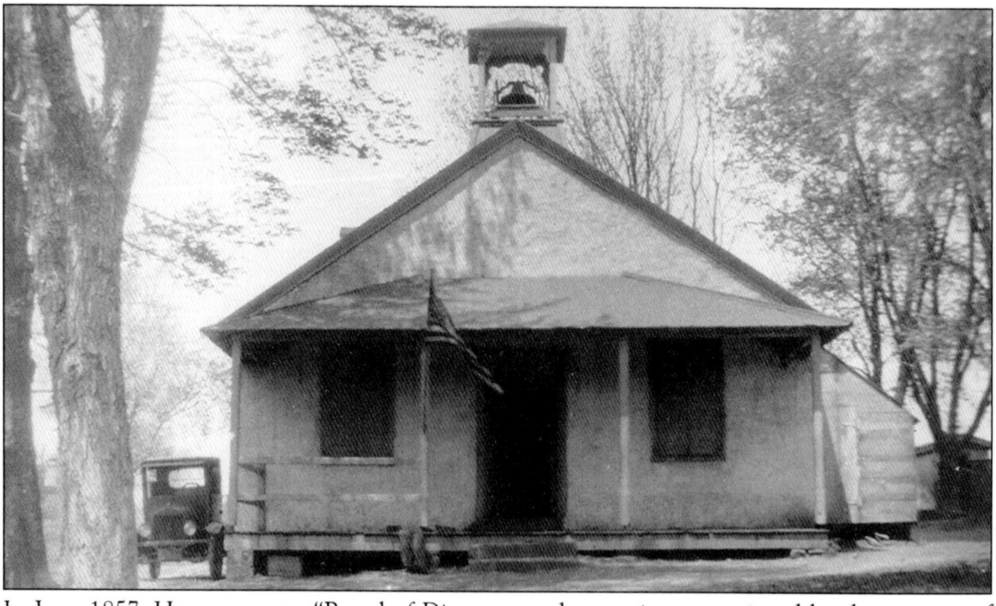

In June 1857, Hoover wrote, "Board of Directors and committee appointed by the patrons of the school met to prosecute the building of the new house." In October 1857, he wrote, "School closed on account of taking down house to build a new one." In February 1858, he wrote, "School recommenced the house partly finished having but one coat of mortar on the walls, the outside undashed." (Courtesy of Jane Henderson.)

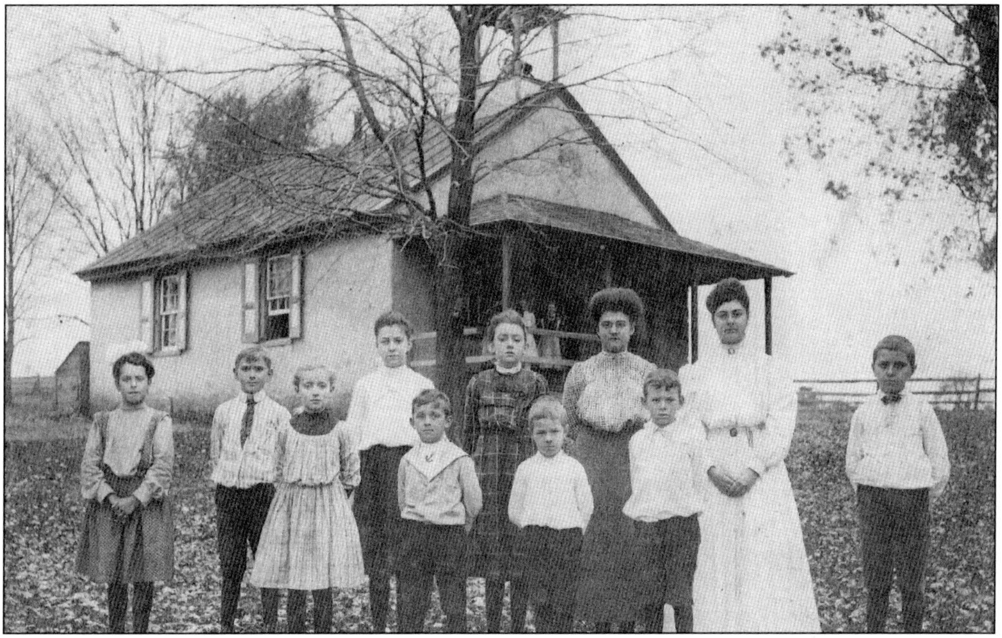

Seen here is the County Line Schoolhouse in 1907. Pictured here are, from left to right, Stella Kirk, Frank Steever, Estella Perry, Maria Hoover, Billie Kirk, Mae Kohler, Ethelbert Yost, Helen Creamer, Carl Kohler, teacher Mrs. Bertha (Pross) Swartley, and Merrill Yost. In the early 1900s, a red metal roof was placed over the original wood shingles (the locals would nickname the school "Red Top College"). (Courtesy of Jane Henderson.)

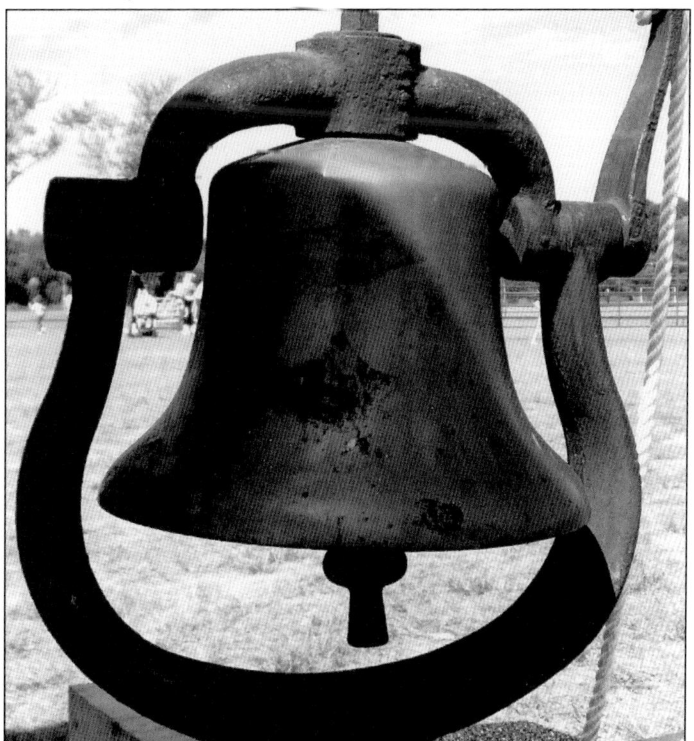

The building remained in operation until 1928, at which time it was sold to the Schlecter family and became a private residence. The belfry was removed, and the bell was loaned to the St. Joseph Church on Easton Road. The original bell, seen here, usually appears at Warrington Day festivities for children to ring. Future plans are for the bell to top the restored schoolhouse again.

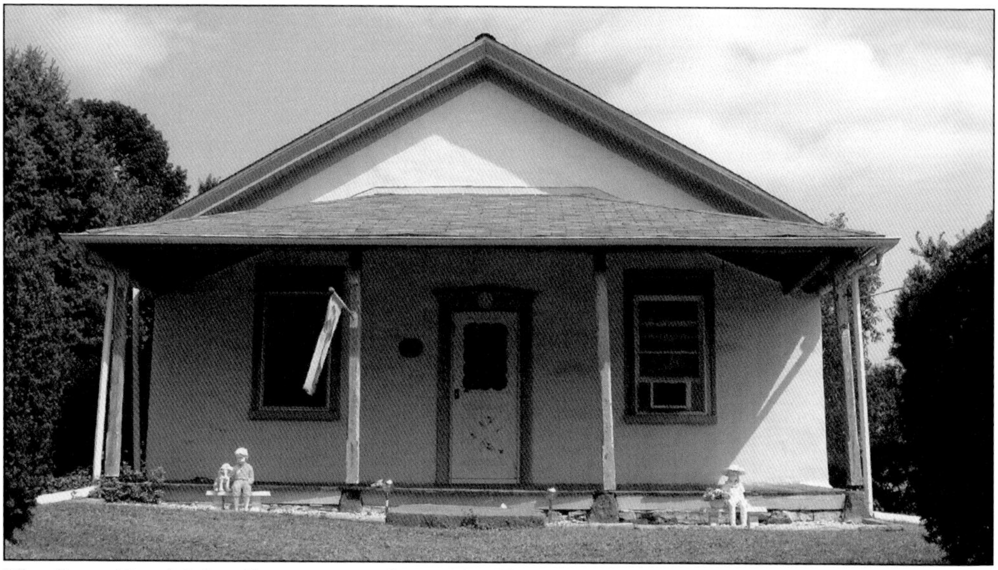

The Street Road Schoolhouse opened in 1864. There is very little information on this building. It is identical in style to the second Mill Creek and County Line Schoolhouses. The building at one time had a belfry with a bell. The school continued to operate until 1925, when the Neshaminy School down the street opened. The building was sold and has been a private residence ever since.

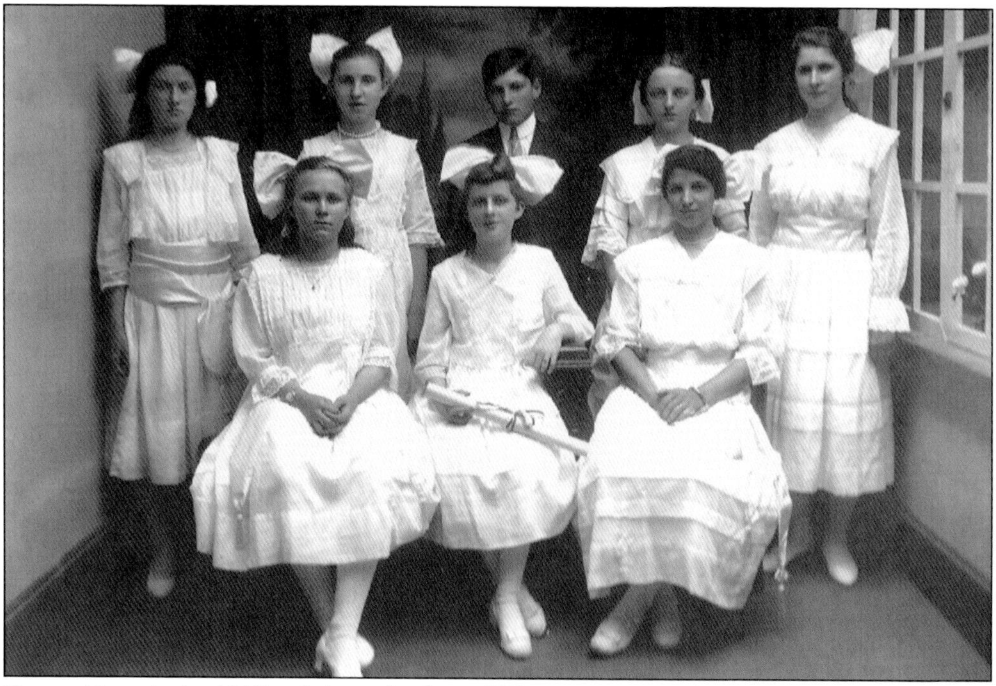

Pictured here is the 1917 eighth-grade class of Warrington Township School (which included the Warrington, County Line, Mill Creek, and Street Road Schoolhouses). Seen here are, from left to right, Dorthea Clymer, Eleanor Nash, and Florence Pleiss; (second row) Margaret McNair, Roberta Martin, Lawrence Kratz, Madesta Abbott, and Margaret Garges. (Courtesy of Jane Henderson.)

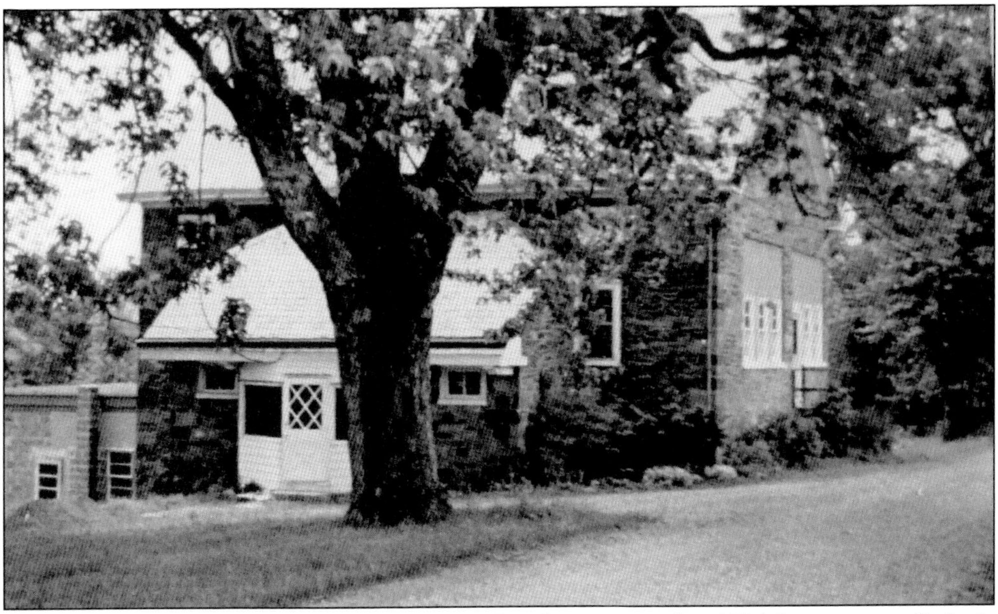

The Neshaminy School, located at 2040 Street Road, was opened in 1924. It was originally built in 1880 by the Paul Valley Dairyman's Association to be used as a creamery. Extensive work, at a cost of $12,000, designed by A. Oscar Martin, was done on the building to convert the creamery into a two-room elementary school. (Courtesy of Bux-Mont Unitarian Fellowship Church.)

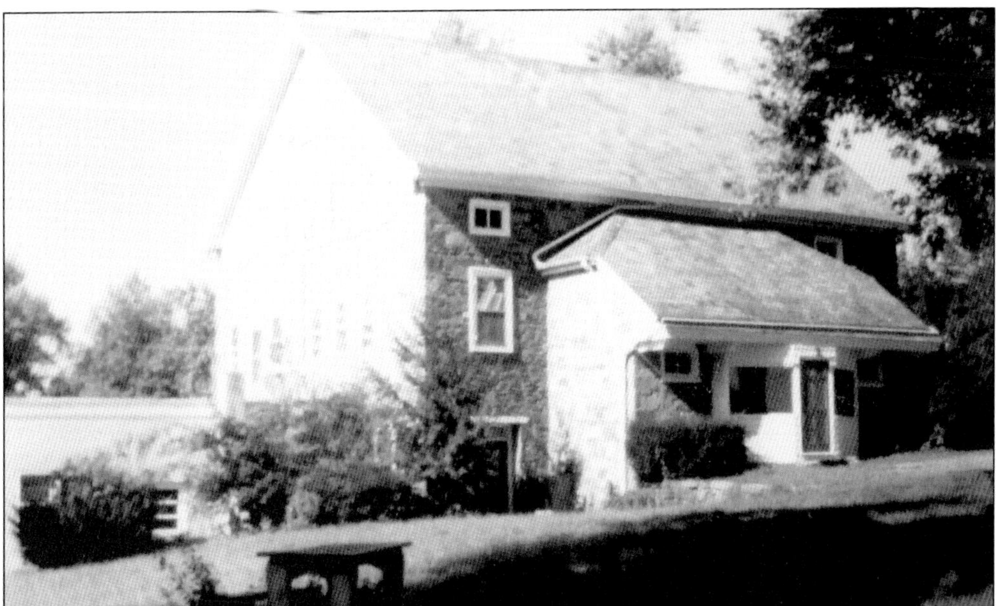

The school was complete with outside toilets, one for girls and one for boys, and a pump that often required priming. In the wintertime, the older boys carried coal from a ground-floor coal bin area to stoke the big black stoves in each classroom. Some also wore their ice skates to school so they could skate on the Neshaminy Creek at lunch. (Courtesy of Bux-Mont Unitarian Fellowship Church.)

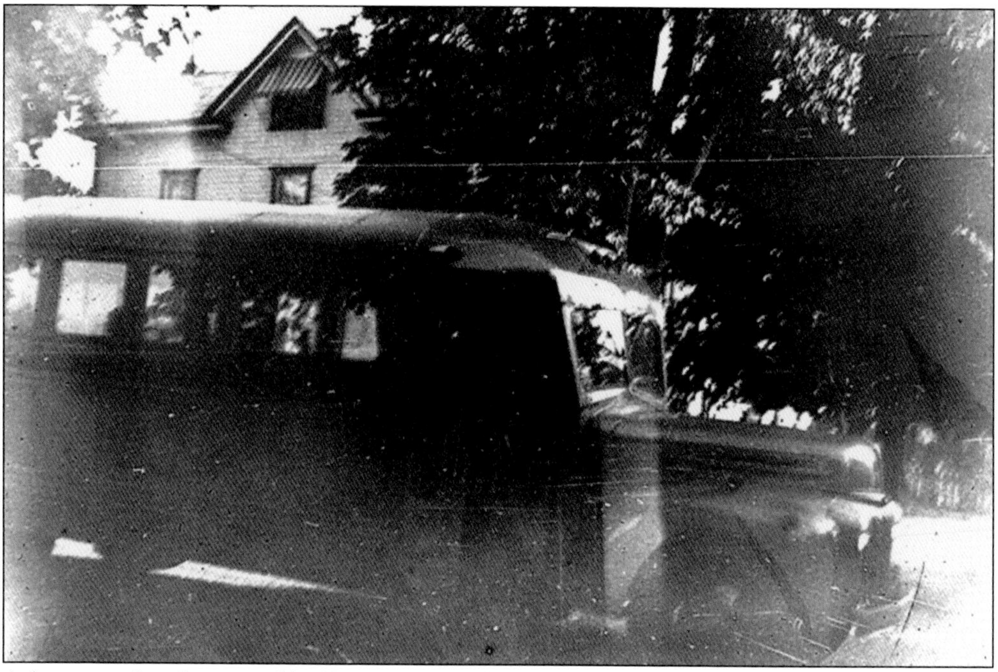

A bus owned and operated by Fritz Gross, and later Eugene Kratz, provided transportation for some children in a green converted truck with wooden benches lining the bed. In 1938, Kratz bought an actual yellow school bus to transport the children. Children who lived within two miles of the school of course walked. (Courtesy of Jeanne DeLong and Frank Ace.)

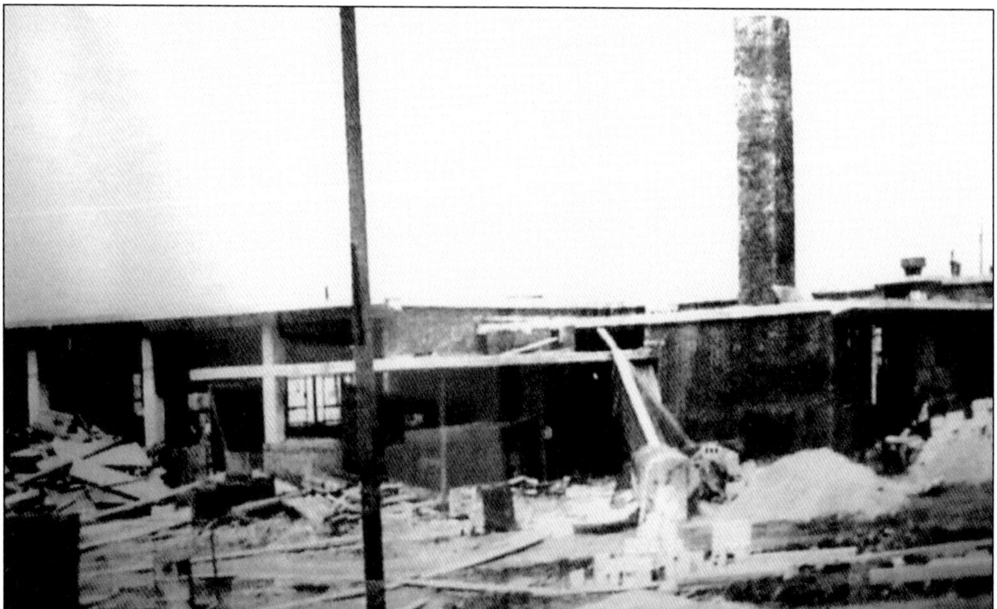

The Florence D. Titus Elementary School (originally named Warrington Elementary) was conceived in 1946 when it was announced at a Warrington Township Parent Teacher Association meeting that plans were being pushed by the board for construction of the school building located on Easton and Barness Roads. (Courtesy of Titus Elementary.)

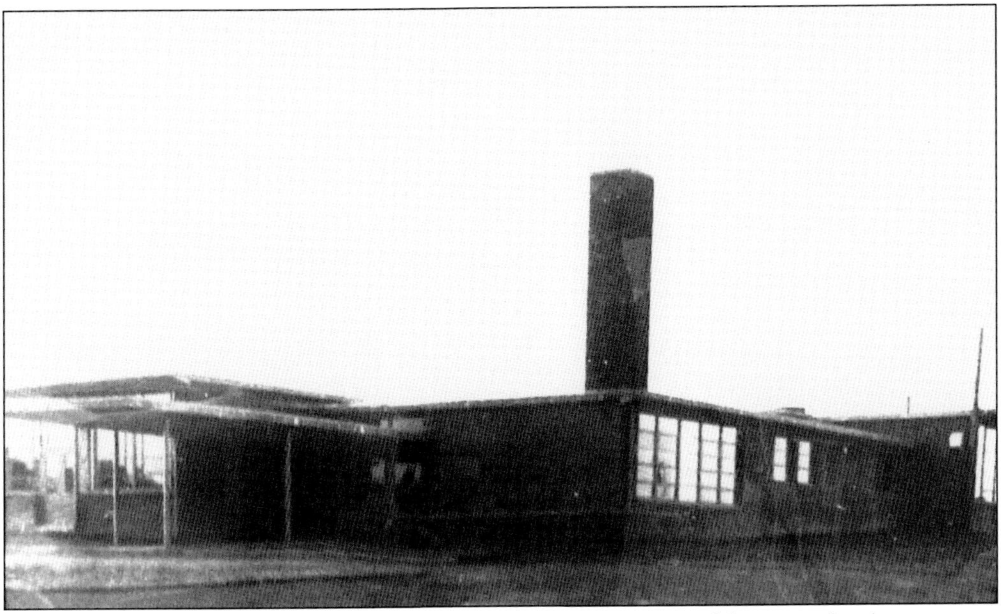

In 1949, the school board set plans in motion for the construction of the new school, a six-room building with a cafeteria. In 1951, the Warrington, Mill Creek, and Neshaminy Township schools closed when the new Warrington Elementary was opened. (Courtesy of Titus Elementary.)

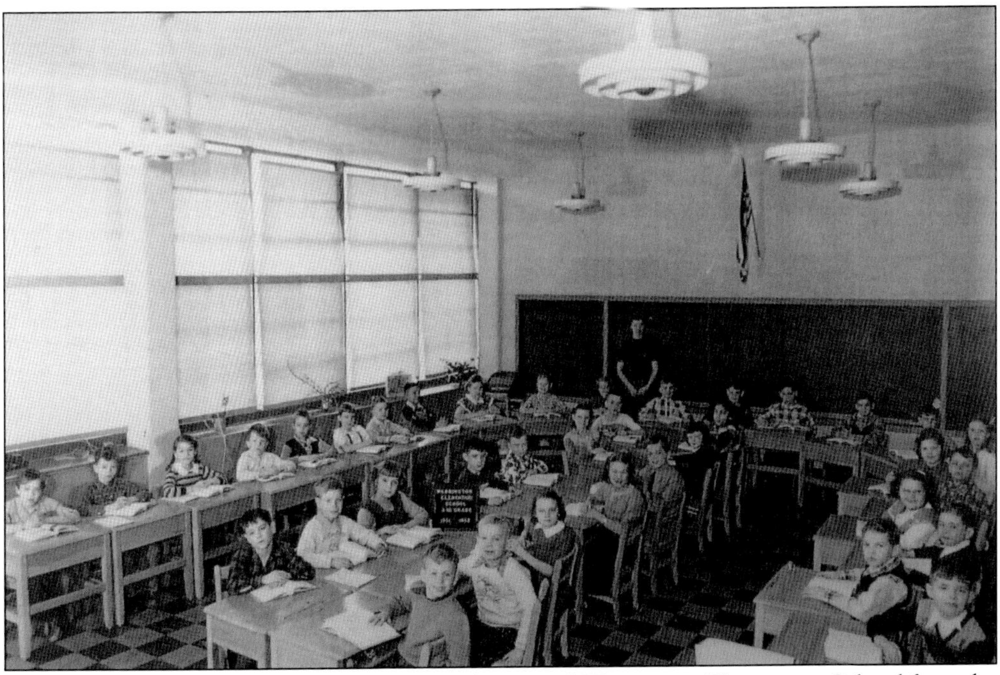

This third-grade class photograph of the newly opened Warrington Elementary School from the 1951–1952 school year shows the then modern room design and layout provided to the students and teacher. (Courtesy of Titus Elementary.)

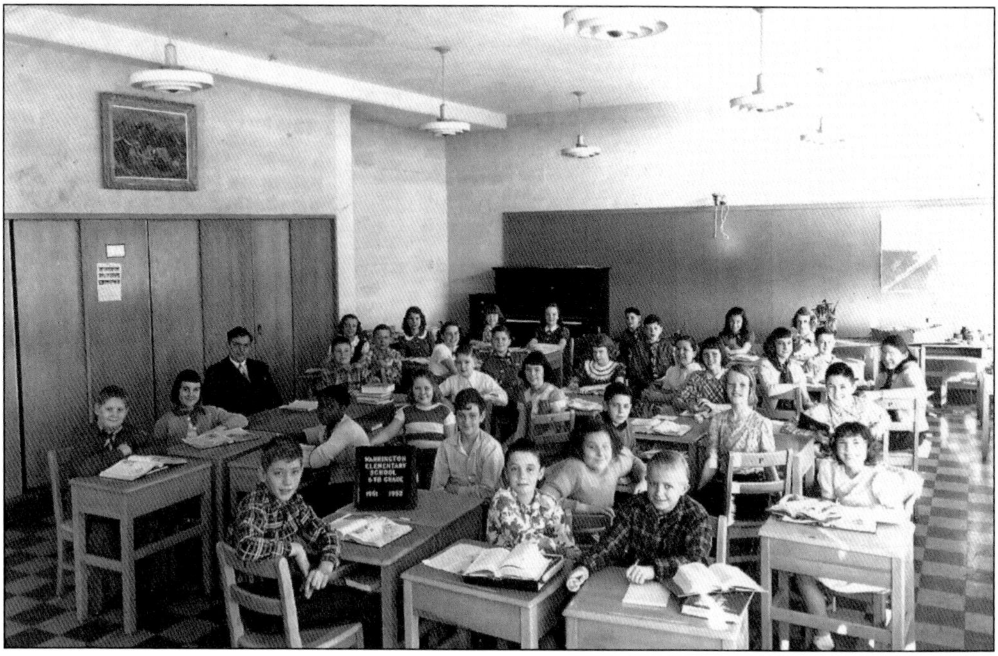

The sixth-grade class of the newly opened Warrington Elementary School, along with principal Max McComb, poses for a class photograph in the 1951–1952 school year. McComb reported the enrollment of 341 students at the new elementary school to the meeting of the Warrington School Board. (Courtesy of Dorothy Smith.)

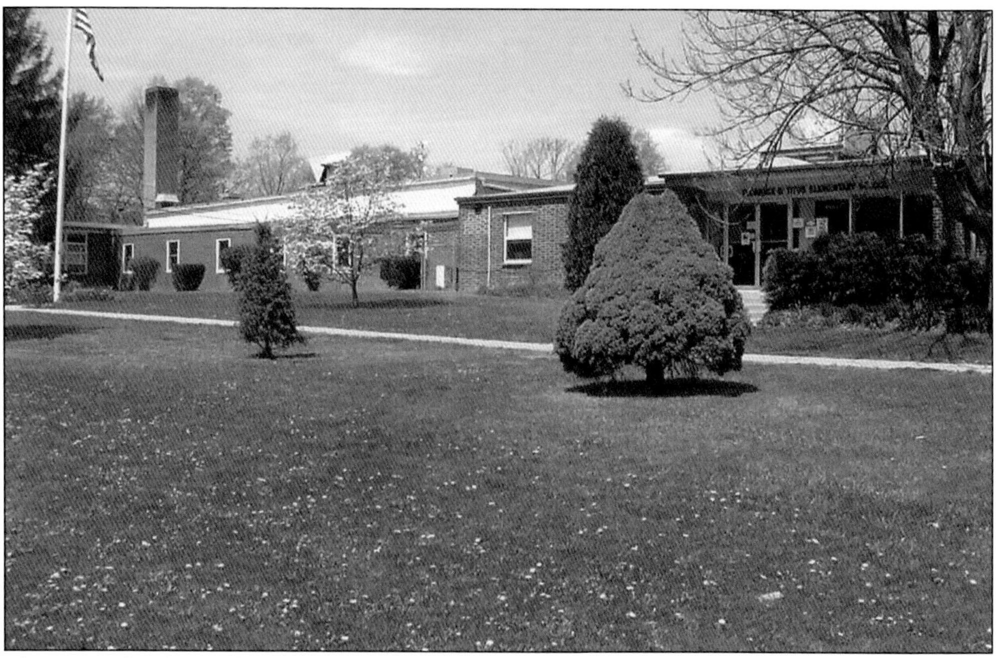

The new school was dedicated with praise to all involved, while mention was made that the school was designed so that another wing could be added when conditions warranted. In 1955, the first addition was constructed containing six additional classrooms, a corridor, storage, and an office. The building was renovated in 2004. (Courtesy of Titus Elementary.)

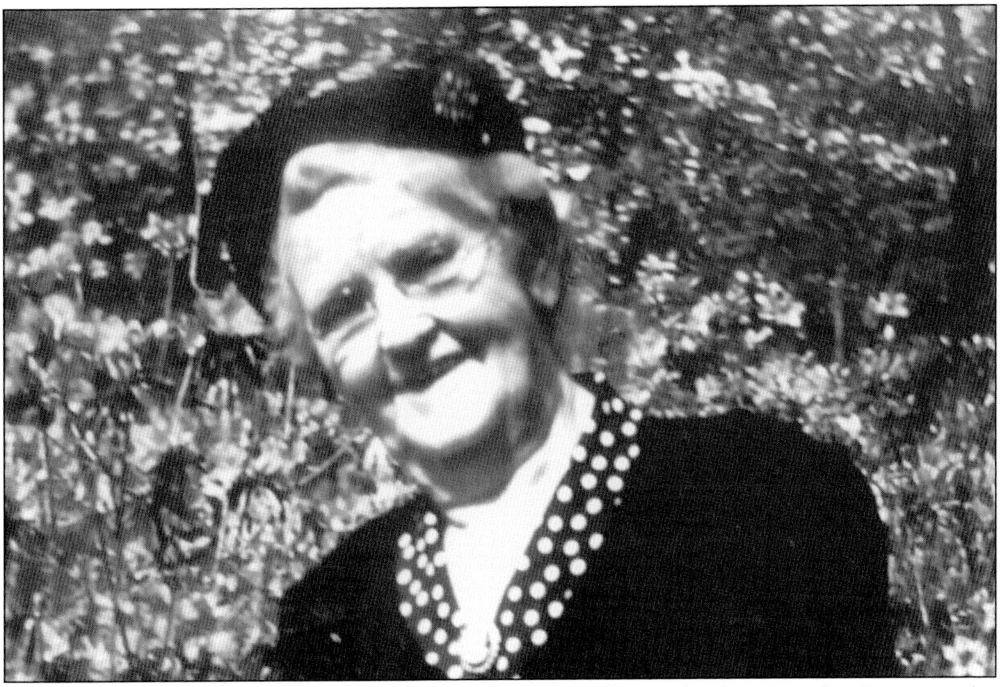

In 1965, when the elementary school was merged into the Bucks County school system, the school was renamed after a former president of the board of school directors and lifelong resident, Florence D. Titus (pictured here). (Courtesy of Titus Elementary.)

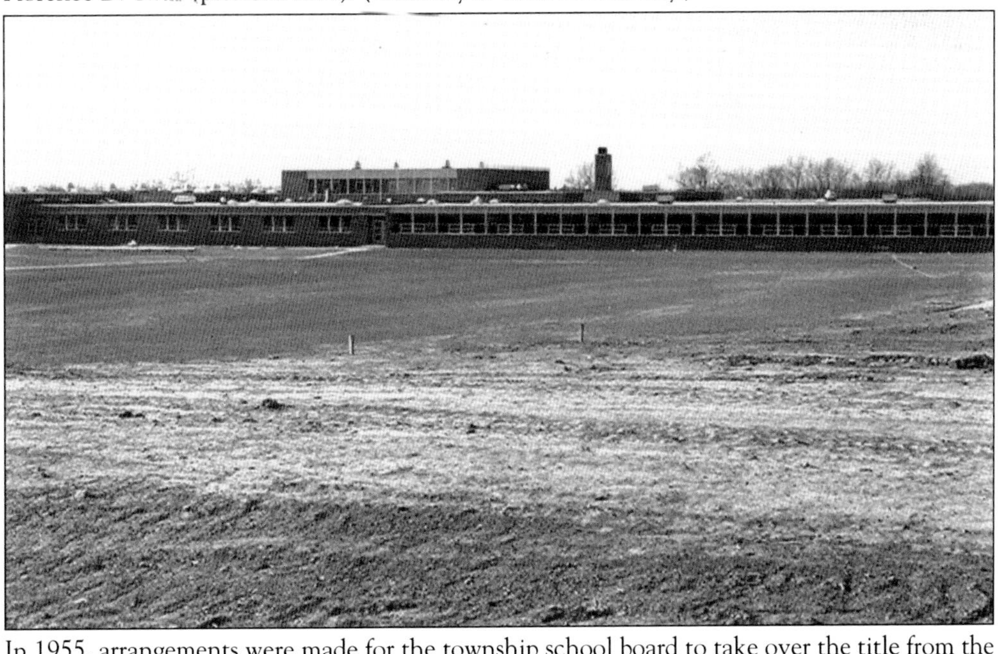

In 1955, arrangements were made for the township school board to take over the title from the Central Bucks Joint School Board for 33 acres on Stuckert Road. Built in 1961, it was originally to be named the Central Bucks Junior High School. Tamanend Junior High School opened in 1961. It was named after the Delaware Native American chief. This school would later be renamed Tamanend Middle School.

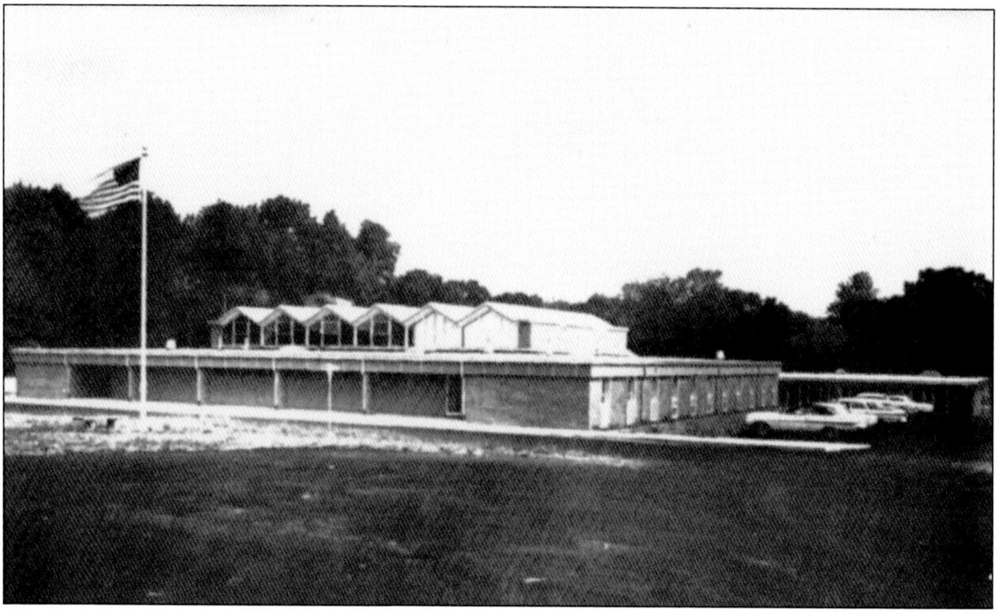

The second elementary school built in Warrington was opened in the Palomino Farms development and named after prominent resident John Barclay. The John Barclay Elementary School first opened its doors to students in September 1965. It was dedicated on October 10, 1965. The building was renovated in 2005. The school honors Barclay by celebrating his birthday on January 22. (Courtesy of Stuart Cohen.)

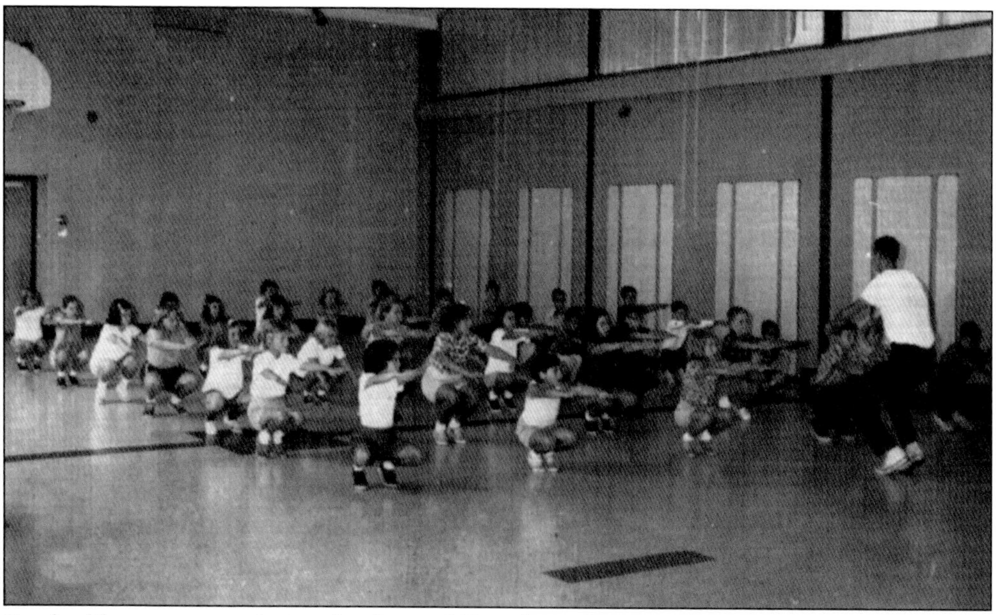

Barclay Elementary was designed to house 560 students. It originally consisted of 16 classrooms, an all-purpose room, kitchen, library, nurse's office, teacher's break room, and administrative suite. Each classroom was self-contained and included chalkboards, tackboards, a drinking fountain, a clock, an intercommunication system, a thermostat, and a teacher's wardrobe/storage closet. All these commodities cost the township $665,000. (Courtesy of Stuart Cohen.)

Six

Everyday Life

Warrington Township has always had a very active social calendar. There was always something to see and do. The Odd Fellows Lodge, Warrington Woman's Club, Warrington Junior Woman's Club, Lions Club, Criterion Club, Rotary Club, Jaycees, Warrington Garden Club, Ambulance Corps, Fire Department, Ladies Auxiliary, Republican Club, Democratic Club, Knights of Columbus, Father Joseph A. Gallen Council No. 5494, and local government appointments are just a few of the civic and service organizations that were or still are active in Warrington. These clubs and events such as Warrington Day have kept the residents within the township's borders a close-knit community even as it continued to grow and diversify.

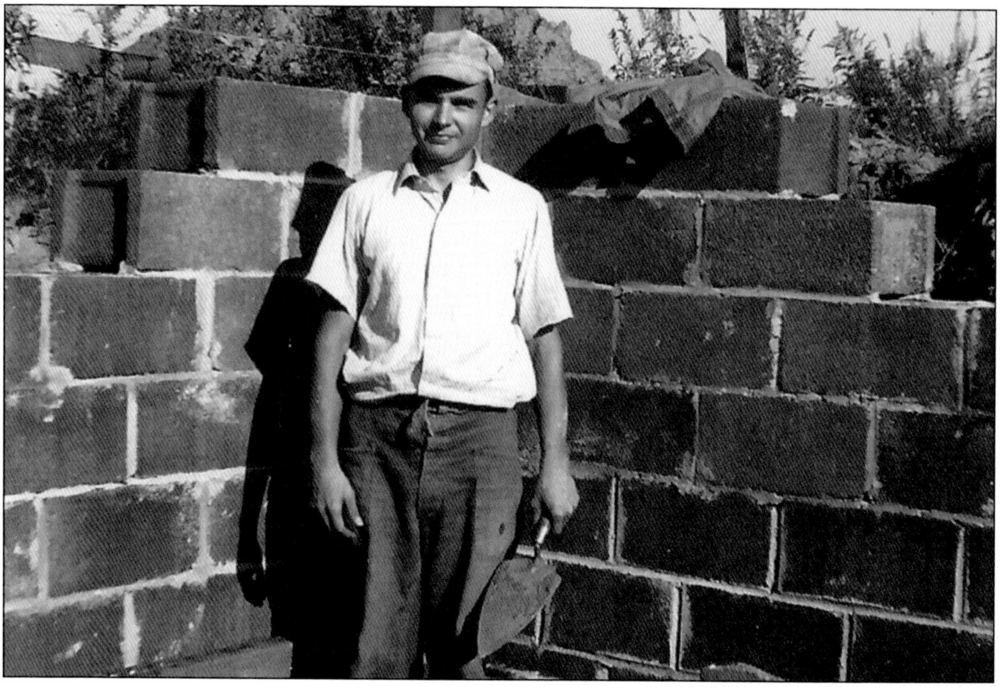

It was not uncommon for individuals to build their own homes to live in. After picking out a plot to purchase and plans to build by, one could have a piece of the American dream. Seen here in October 1952, Bill Grun builds his house from the ground up. (Courtesy of Bill Grun.)

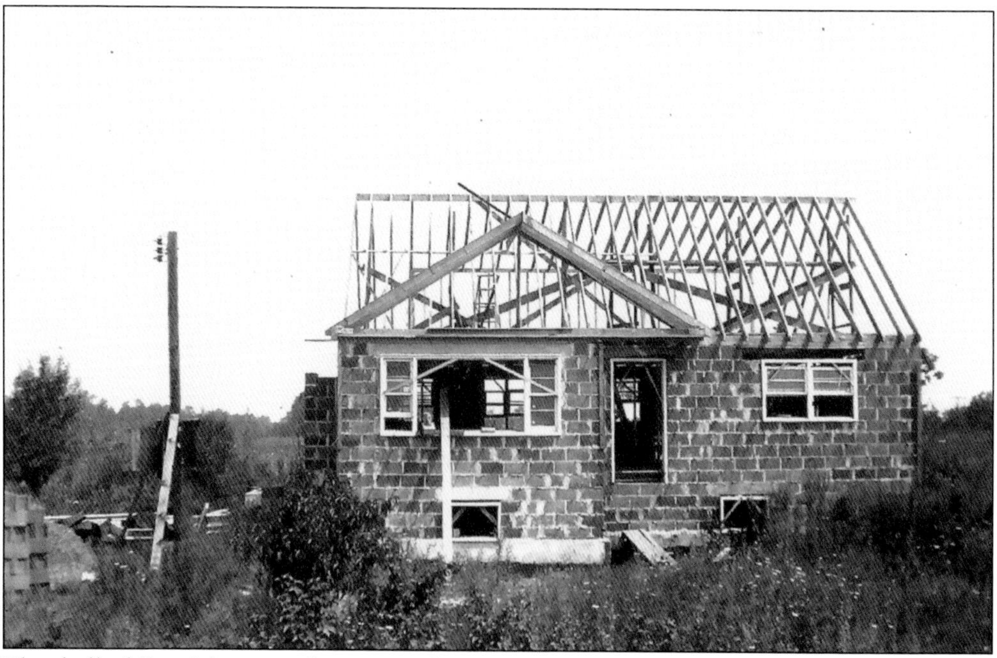

The shell of Grun's home is almost complete in August 1953. To this day, Grun still resides in the home located on Bristol Road, just west of Guinea Lane. Although he had a little help, he had his hands in all parts of his home's construction. (Courtesy of Bill Grun.)

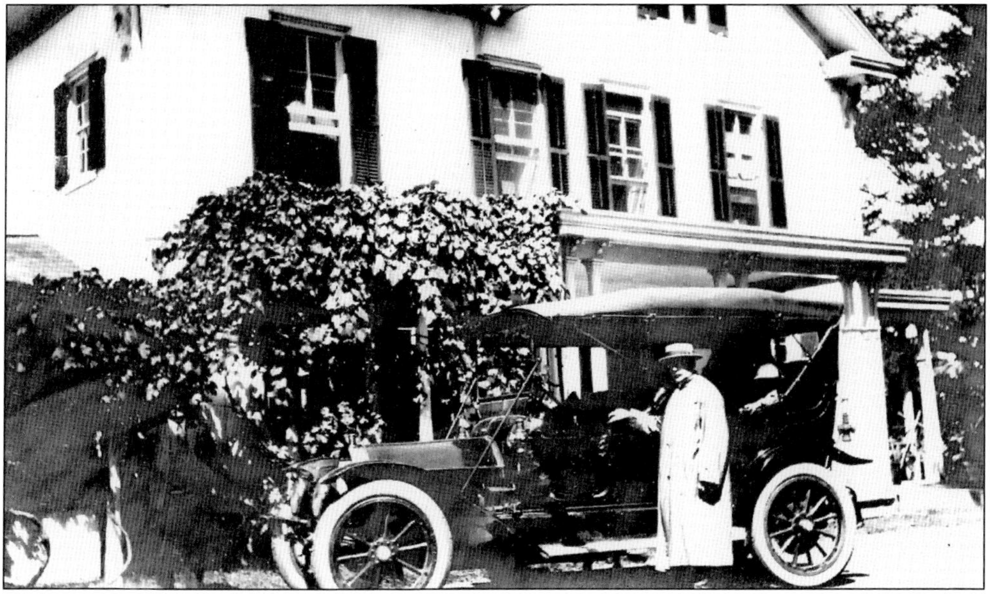

While getting ready to go out for a drive, William Penrose Sr. is seen here with his Pierce Arrow at 104 Easton Road. (Courtesy of Joseph Penrose Jr.)

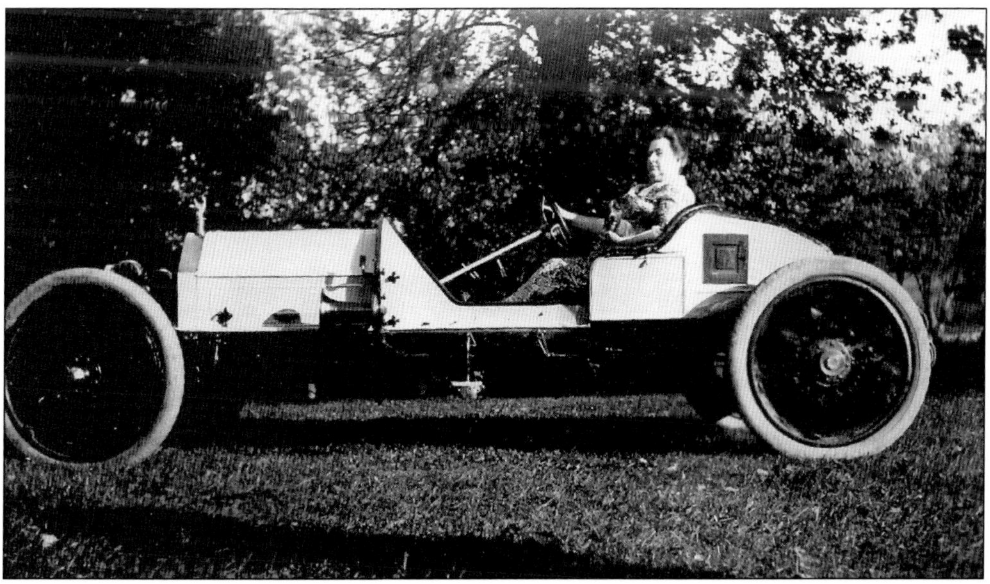

Anna Penrose poses with the family's 1910 Otto. In 1966, this Otto was recognized as being the longest continually owned car by a family in the area. The car was bought by William Penrose Jr. in 1910. Later his half brother, Joseph Penrose Sr., owned the car, then Joseph Penrose Jr. At the time of this writing, the car is still owned by the Penrose family. (Courtesy of Joseph Penrose Jr.)

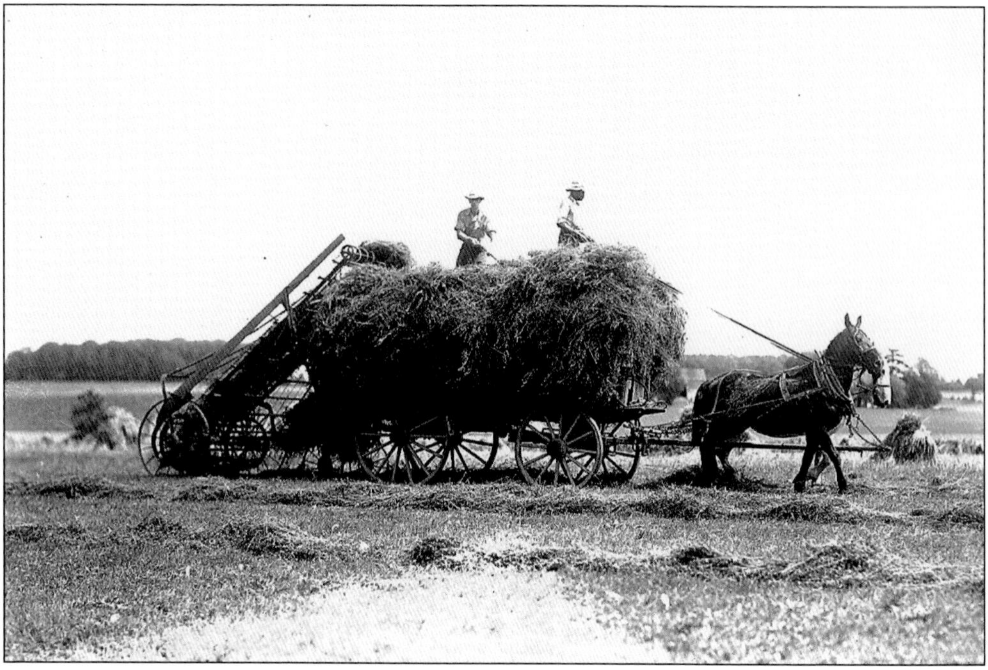

Joseph Penrose Sr. is pictured harvesting the farm's alfalfa crop. It was noted in 1941 that Native American relics, such as arrowheads, were found in these fields by Penrose as he seeded. (Courtesy of Joseph Penrose Jr.)

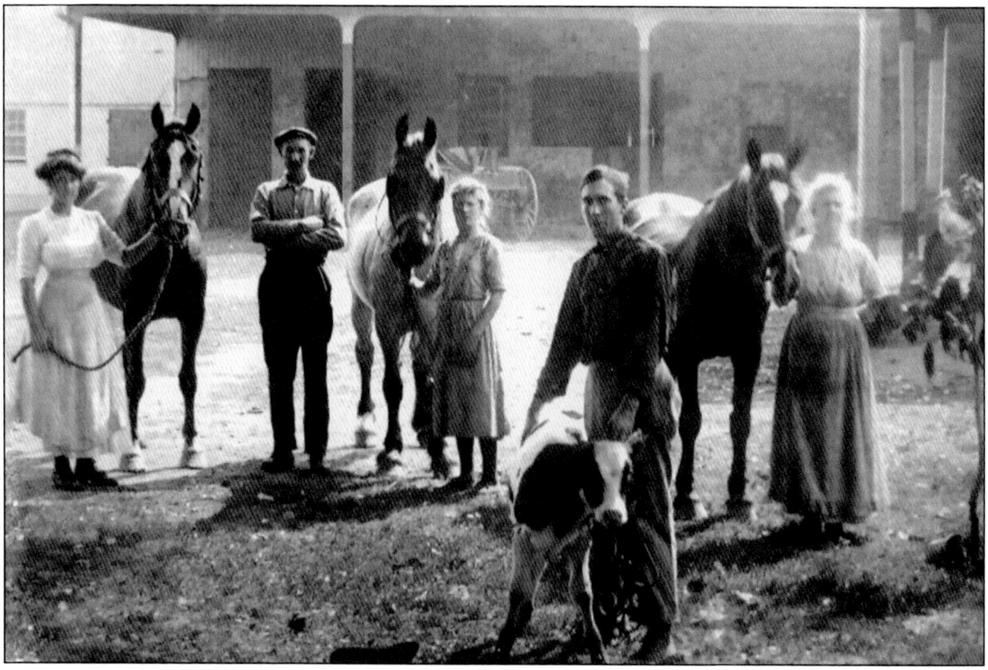

Animals are displayed for a photograph taken about 1895 on the Garges farm. Henry Garges tilled the fields and raised stock. He was particularly fond of horses and had some very valuable horses and cattle. He was also a market man who secured a large patronage in the Philadelphia markets. (Courtesy of the Garges family.)

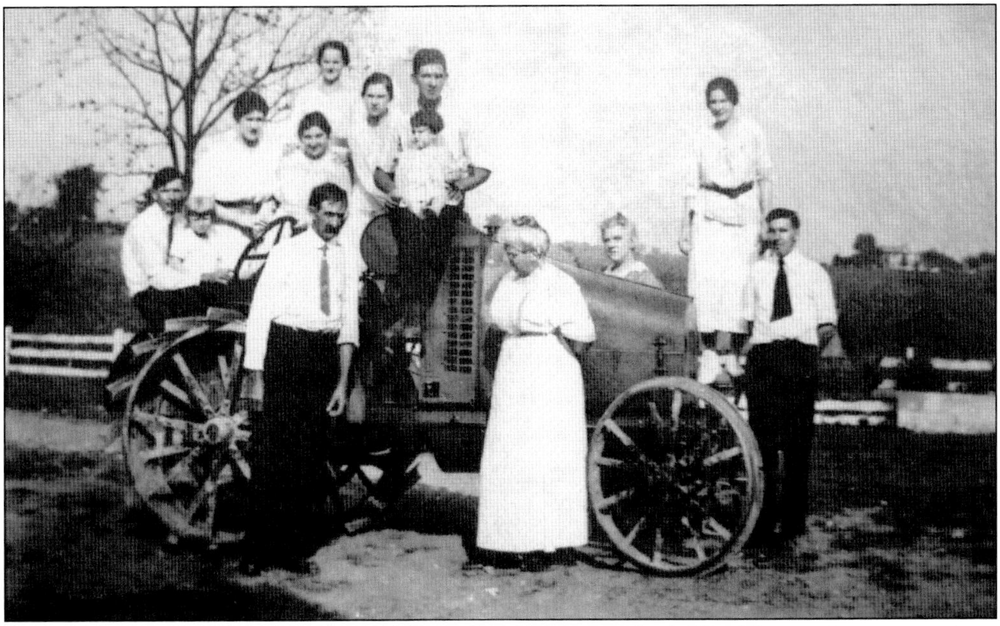

The Garges family poses with the workhorse farm tractor in the 1930s. Having the most modern equipment that worked was of the utmost importance as the Garges farmed their own large property, plus they rented the rights of usage from many others in the area. (Courtesy of the Garges family.)

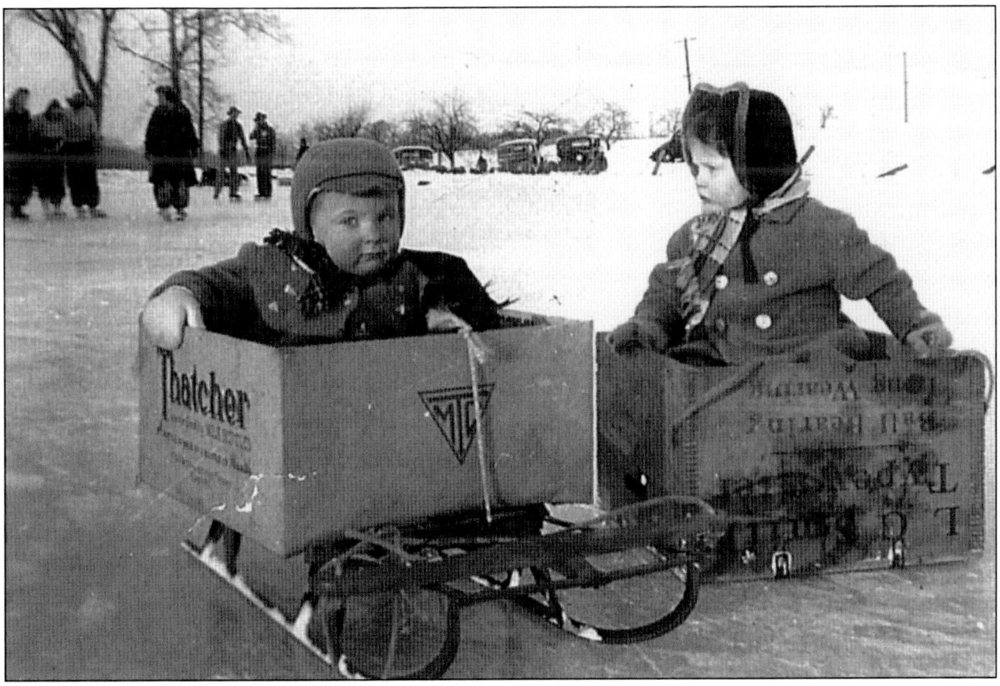

Bill and Ryda Garges, along with other residents, enjoy winter fun on the family farm in the 1940s. This working farm is known as Winding Brook Farm. The pond, which still exists, was a favorite place to fish and swim in the summer and ice-skate in the cold winter months. (Courtesy of the Garges family.)

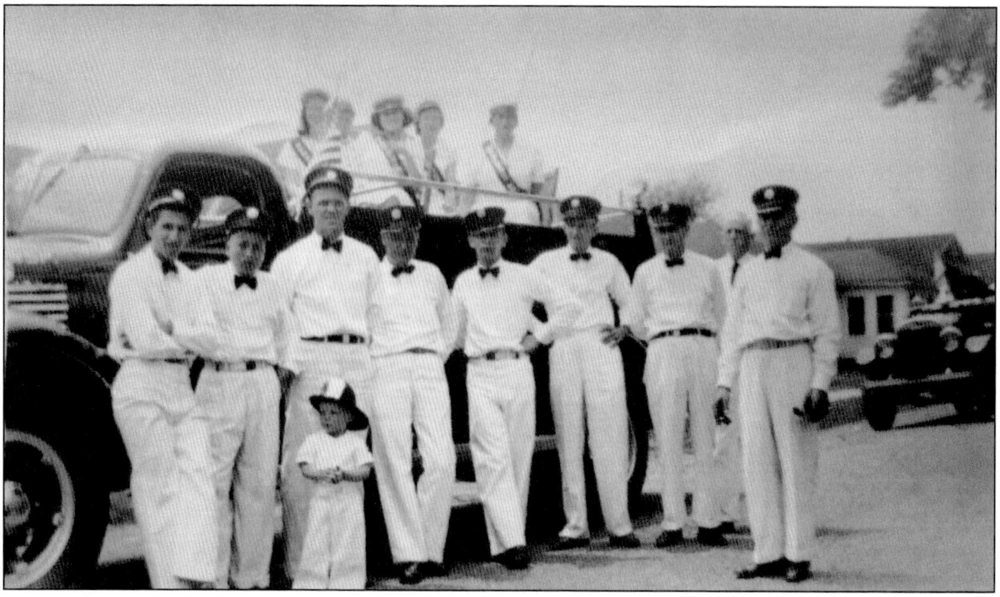

Pictured in the late 1940s, volunteers ready themselves on Kansas Road to march in a Warrington Day parade. Warrington Day, organized by Ethel Klein, was first held in 1938 at the Warrington Schoolhouse on Bristol Road. (Courtesy of Henry and Shirley Strawn.)

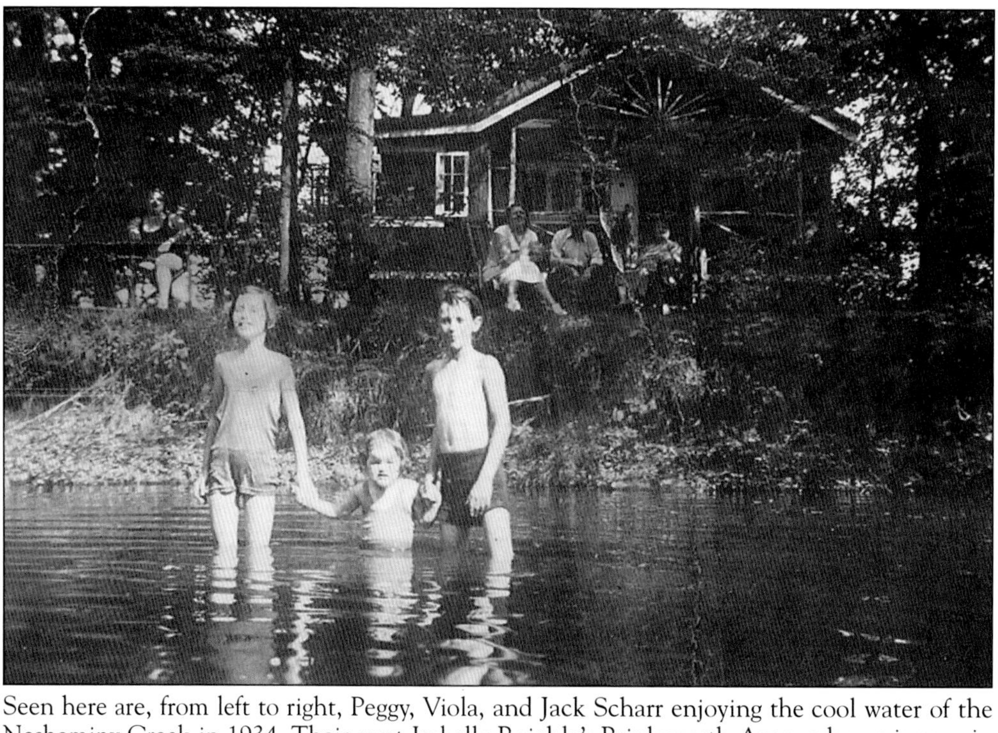

Seen here are, from left to right, Peggy, Viola, and Jack Scharr enjoying the cool water of the Neshaminy Creek in 1934. Their aunt Isabella Reichle's Brinksworth Avenue home is seen in the background. In winter months, ice-skating was a common recreation activity on the creek. It was a source of ice that would be harvested for sale to the public. (Courtesy of Ronald and Viola Scharr Lewis.)

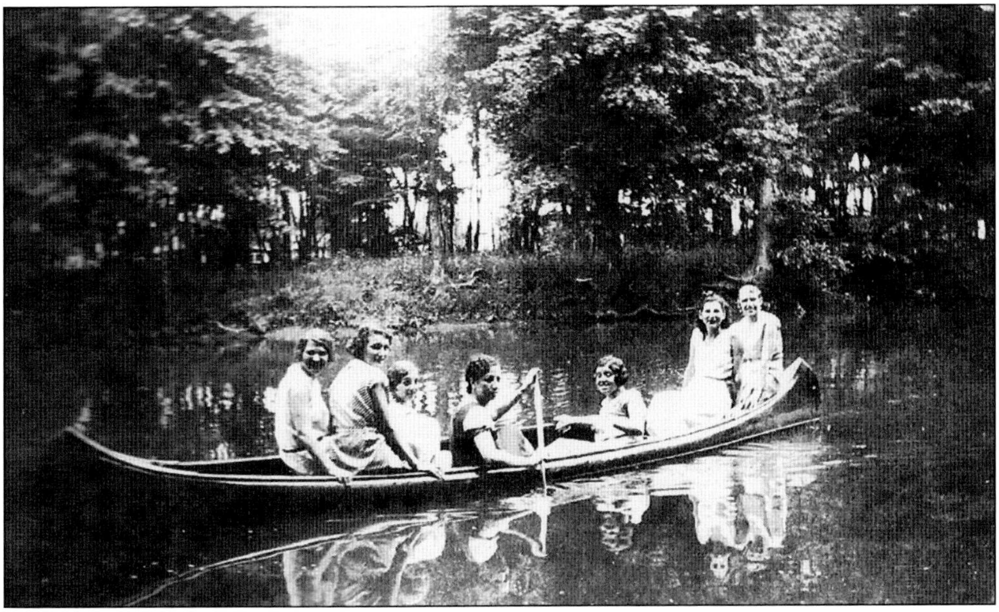

Although canoeing on Neshaminy Creek was usually carefree, on August 15, 1955, the creek showed how dangerous it could be. The township was flooded due to heavy rains from Hurricane Diane. A young woman drowned when the car in which she was riding was swept off Street Road by the raging waters. (Courtesy of Harrison Delano Jr.)

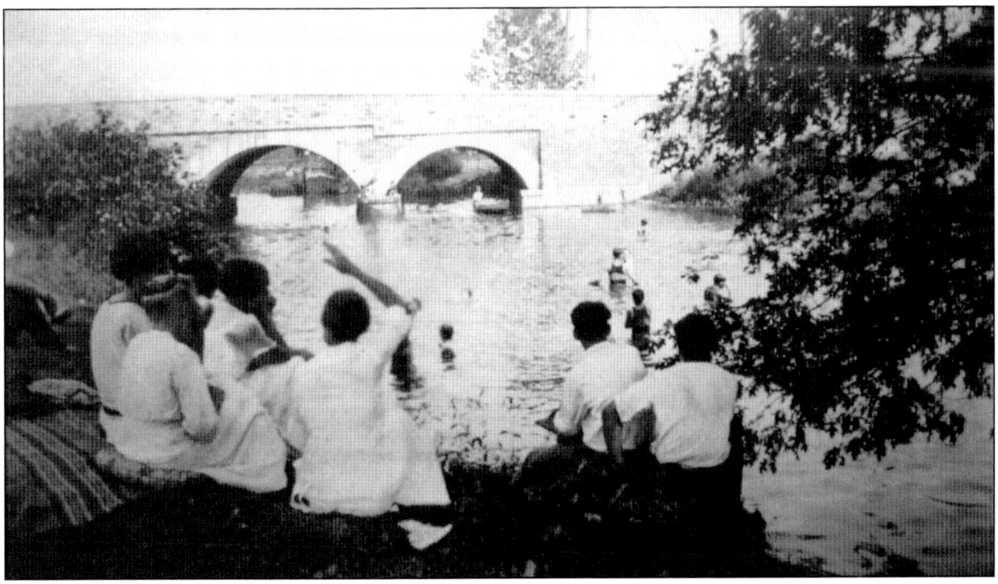

Along Easton and Street Roads, there are many bungalow-style homes. They were once used as summer residences for families from Philadelphia who longed for the peace and tranquility that was present along the Neshaminy Creek. Pictured above is summer play in the early 1930s with the Street Road two-arch bridge in the background. (Courtesy of Henry and Shirley Strawn.)

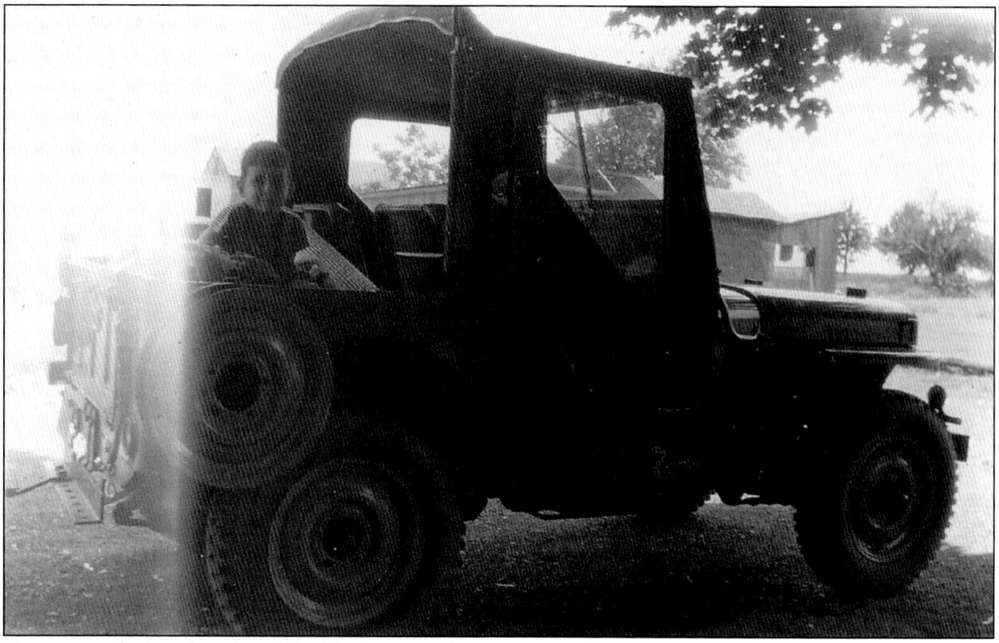

During and shortly after World War II, there was a shortage of farming equipment due to armament for the war. Farmers made use of the surplus of army-issued Willys jeeps that were available to maintain their fields. Pictured here is Frank Ace in the new family farm apparatus. (Courtesy of Jeanne DeLong and Frank Ace.)

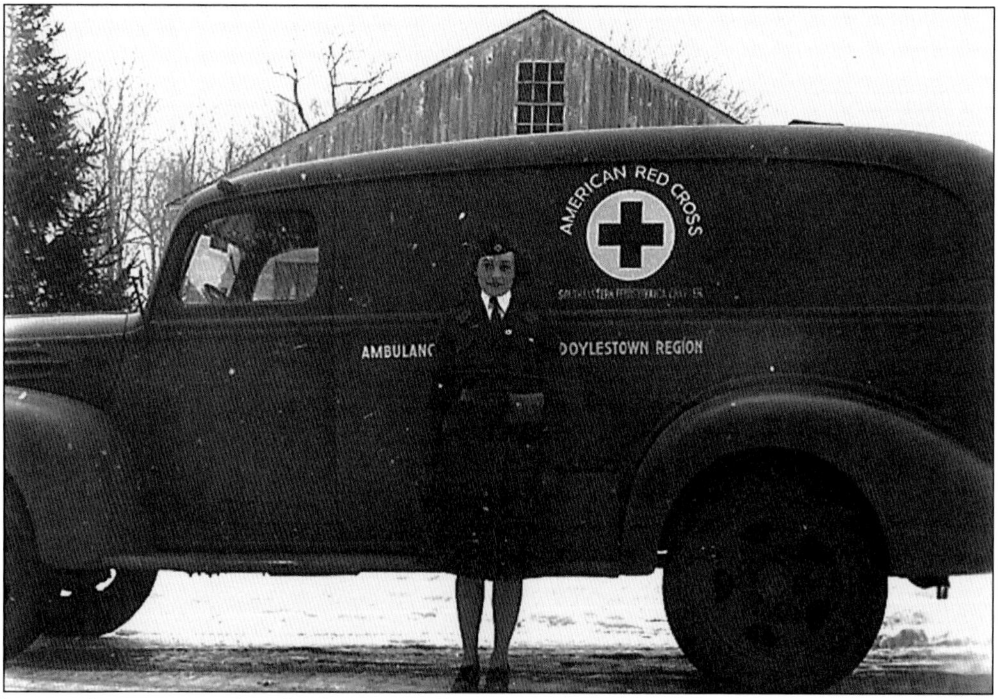

Jeanne Ace is pictured in the driveway of her residence on Folly Road with an American Red Cross ambulance in 1943. She drove wounded servicemen to area hospitals as needed during World War II. (Courtesy of Jeanne DeLong and Frank Ace.)

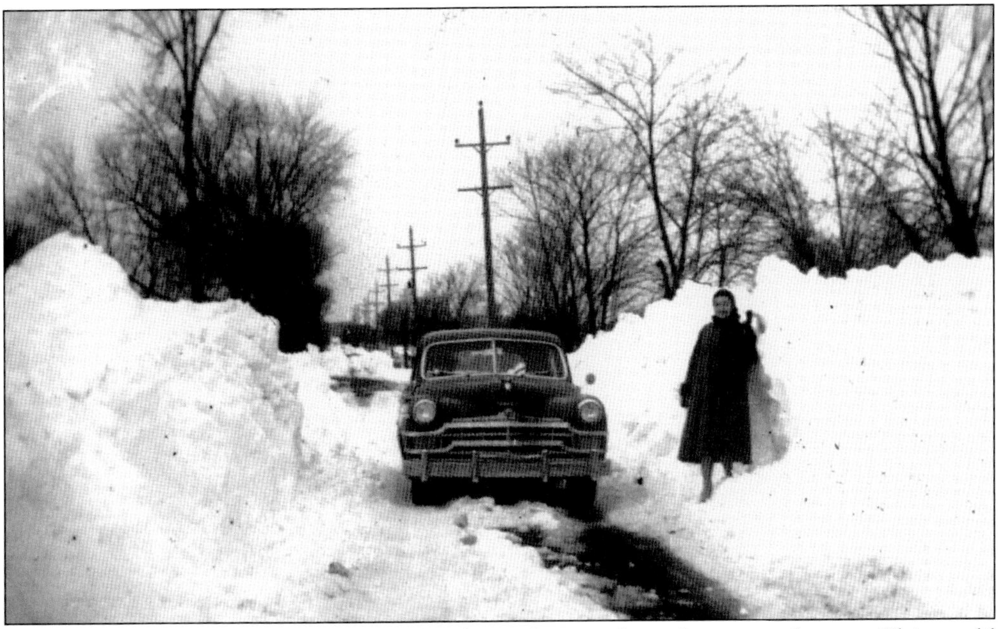

Heavy snowfall on February 7 and 8, 1958, dropped over a foot of snow on the area. This would be the first of many storms that would hit the region hard, leaving two to three feet on the ground when the snow finally ceased to fall. Taken on February 14, this picture shows Jeanne Ace DeLong on a plowed Folly Road. (Courtesy of Jeanne DeLong and Frank Ace.)

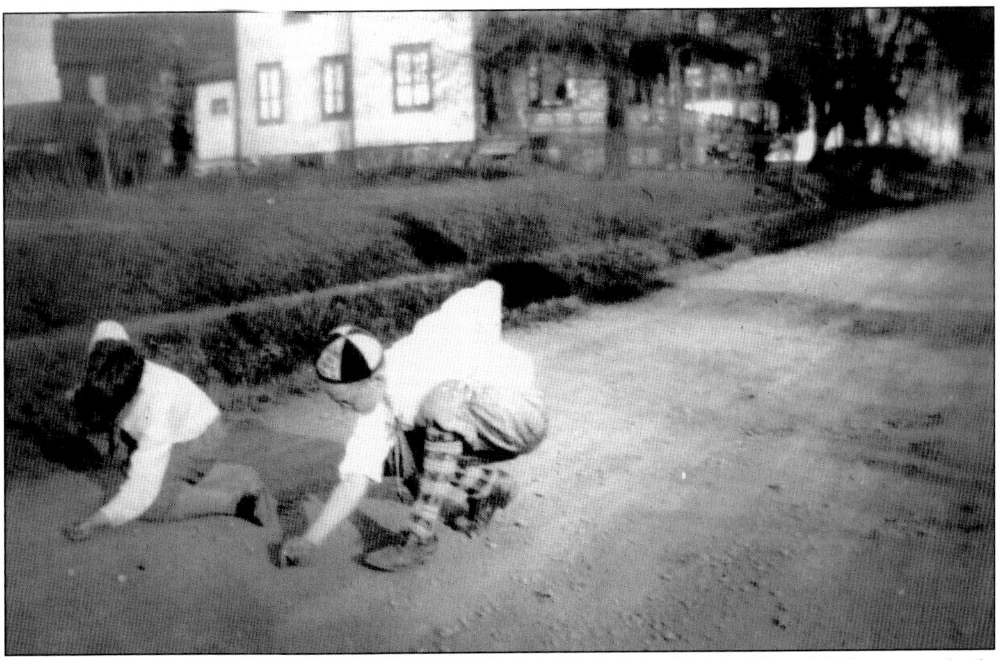

Here children are playing marbles on Bristol Road just west of Easton Road. There was little danger of them getting hit by a car, as a half dozen cars passing in an hour would have been considered a lot of traffic. In the background is the double house behind the family's general store. Both structures were owned by the Holbert family. (Courtesy of Judy Holbert Paterson.)

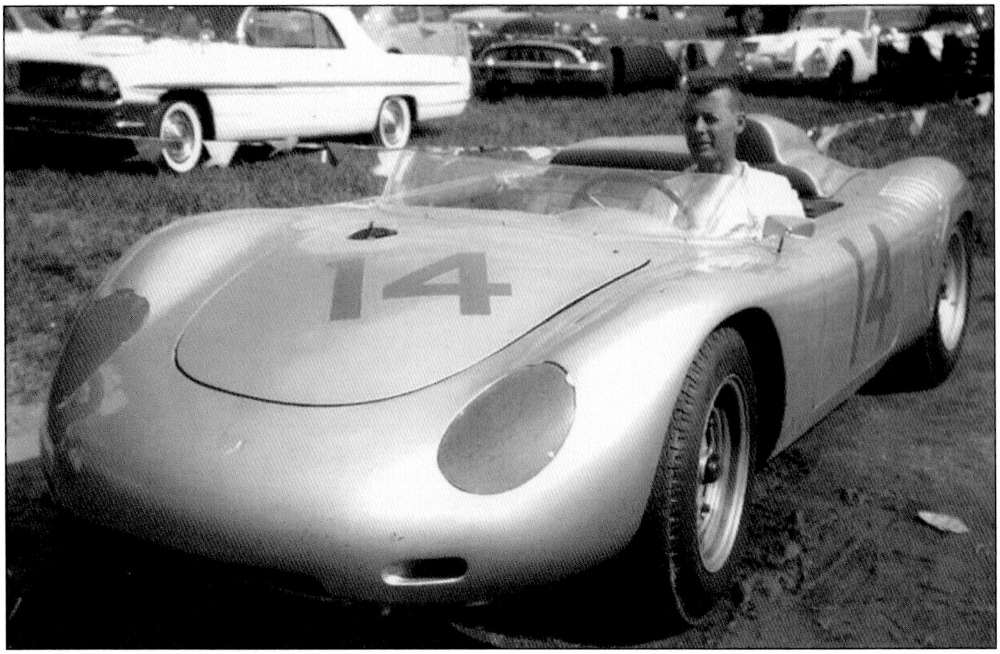

In 1953, Bob Holbert started racing in an MG and then switched to Porsches in 1957. His subsequent racing activities in Porsche's RS-550 and RSK led to four Sports Car Club of America (SCCA) national championships and a podium finish at Le Mans. He later became a Shelby Cobra team factory driver, winning the first United States Road Racing Championship title in 1963. (Courtesy of Bill Reynolds and www.virhistory.com.)

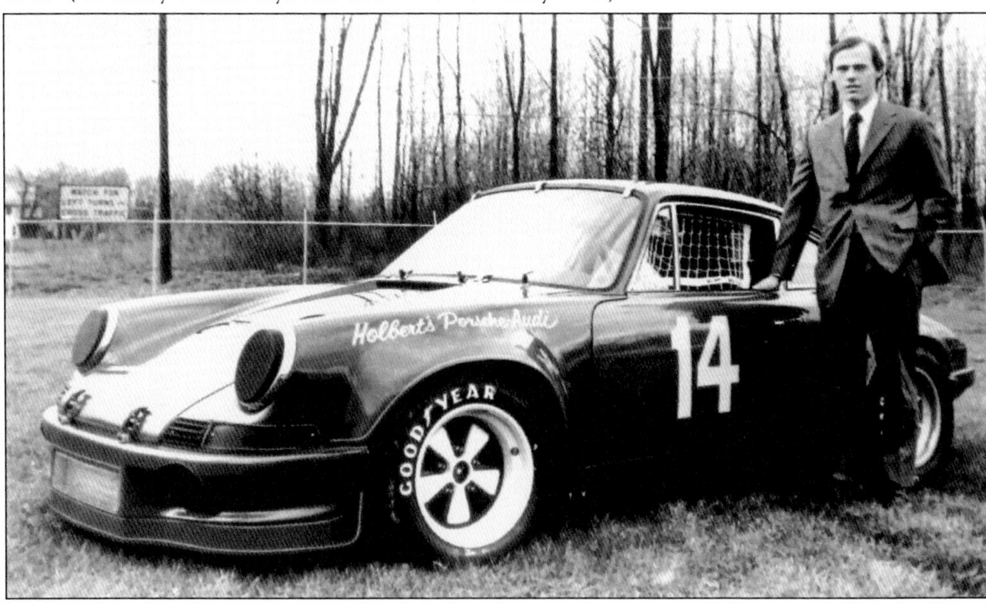

Al Holbert earned his first of five International Motor Sports Association (IMSA) championships in 1976. In 1983, he won both the IMSA GT and Can-Am titles, the 24 Hours of Le Mans three times and the Rolex 24 at Daytona twice. He competed in 19 NASCAR races in the late 1970s and raced at the Indianapolis 500 in 1984, where he started 16th and finished 4th. (Courtesy of Holbert Porsche of Warrington.)

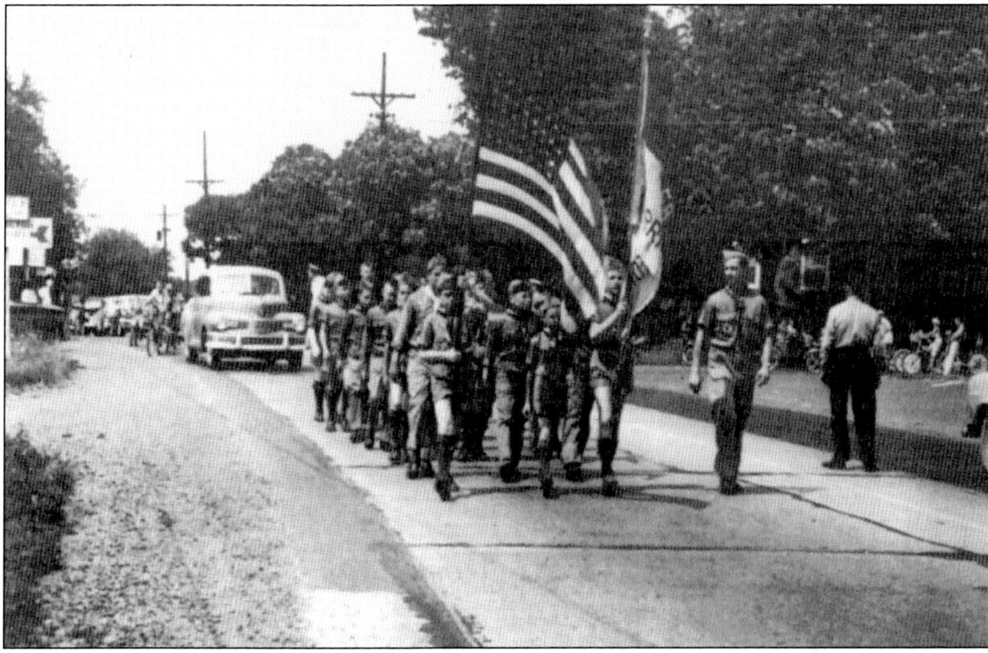

Scouts with Troop 58 and scoutmaster George Gee march down Easton Road in 1955. It was not long ago that Easton Road was used as a parade route for patriotic holidays and Warrington Days. Usually the southbound traffic would be diverted to share the northbound lanes so parades could march with reasonable safety.

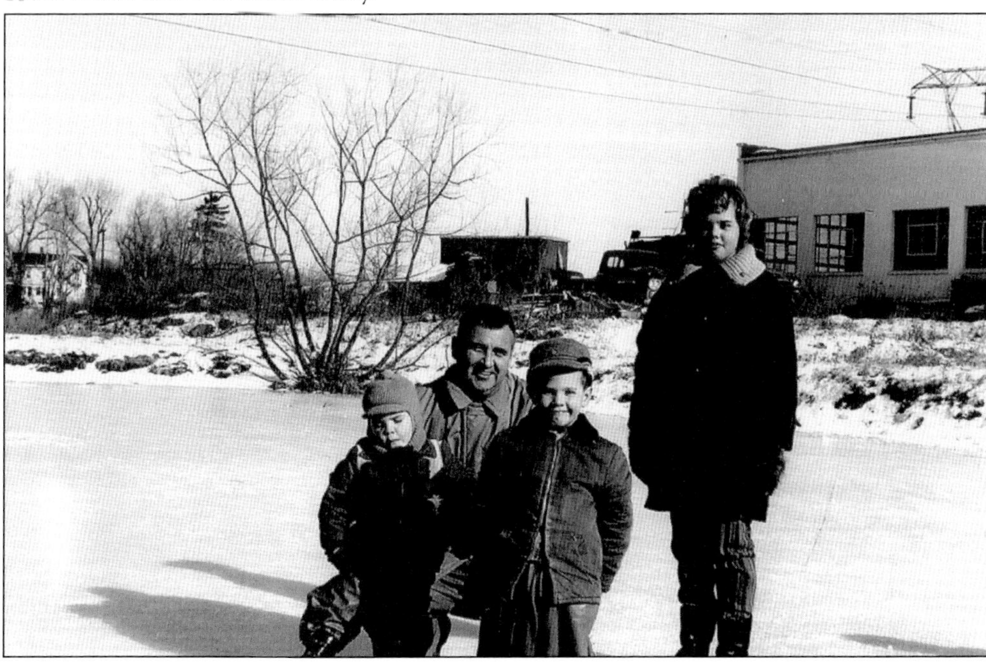

In the days before township parks, residents had plenty of outlets for recreational activities. Pictured above are members of the Doyle family ice-skating on the "pond" behind Joe Esso's Garage on Easton Road. The garage later became Malcom's Garage and Auto Repair and is currently vacant. (Courtesy of Janet Doyle.)

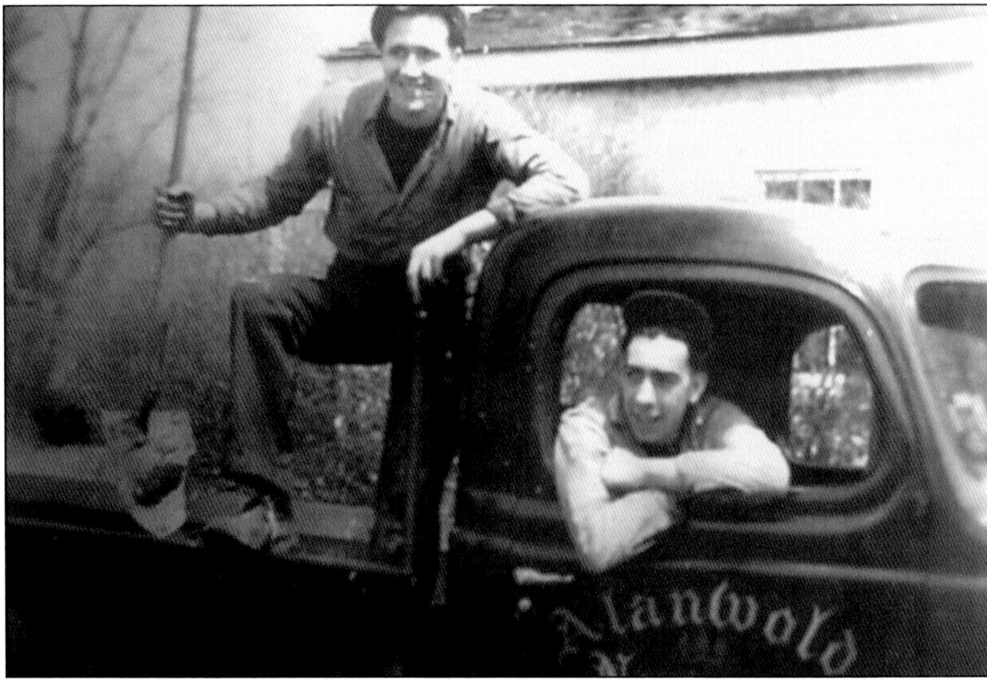

The Henkels ran a nursery from 2708 Street Road. Today this location is in the middle of the Woodlawns Development. Many local young men were employed by them, transplanting the shrubs on many "Main Line" estates. They grew many rare plants and until recent years had one of the largest dawn redwood trees in Pennsylvania. Seen here is one of the work trucks. (Courtesy of Joseph and Marjorie Simons.)

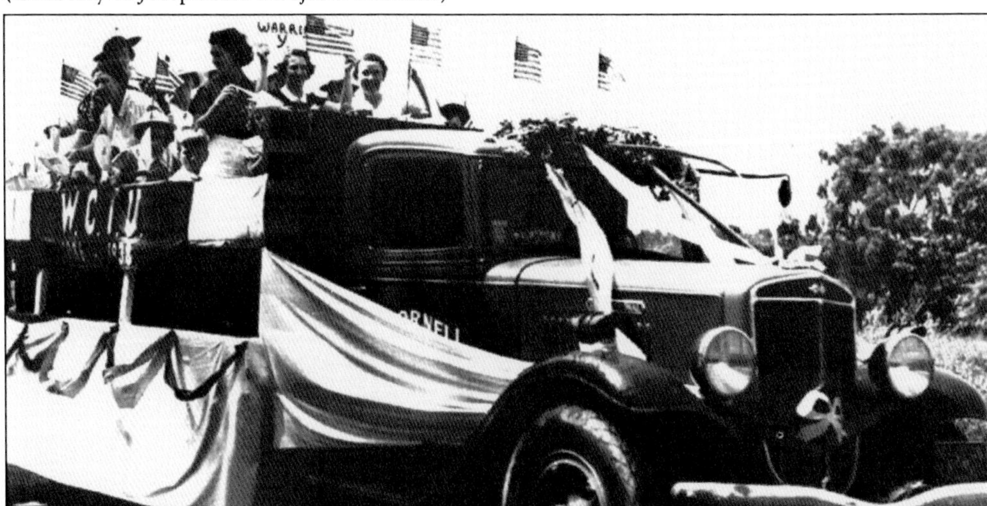

Pictured here is a Cornell farm truck with individuals from the Women's Christian Temperance Union (WCTU) in the 1938 Warrington Day parade. The WCTU was organized by women who were concerned about the problems alcohol was causing their families and society. The members chose total abstinence from all alcohol as their lifestyle. Members advanced their cause by entering liquor-selling establishments and singing, praying, and urging keepers to stop selling alcohol.

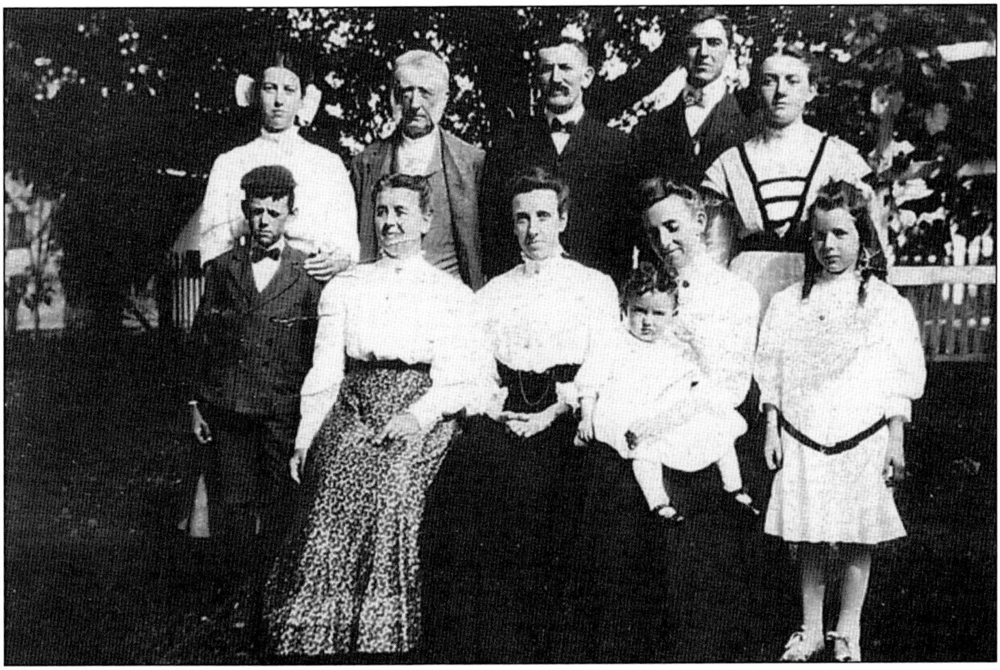

Residents of Eureka pose for a group photograph around 1902. They are, from left to right, (first row) Carl Kohler, Emma Weir, Clemmie Hoover, Jennie Kohler with baby Jane, and Frances Hoover; (second row) Maria Hoover, Jim Weir, William Kohler, Dowell Hoover, and Mae Kohler. (Courtesy of Jane Henderson.)

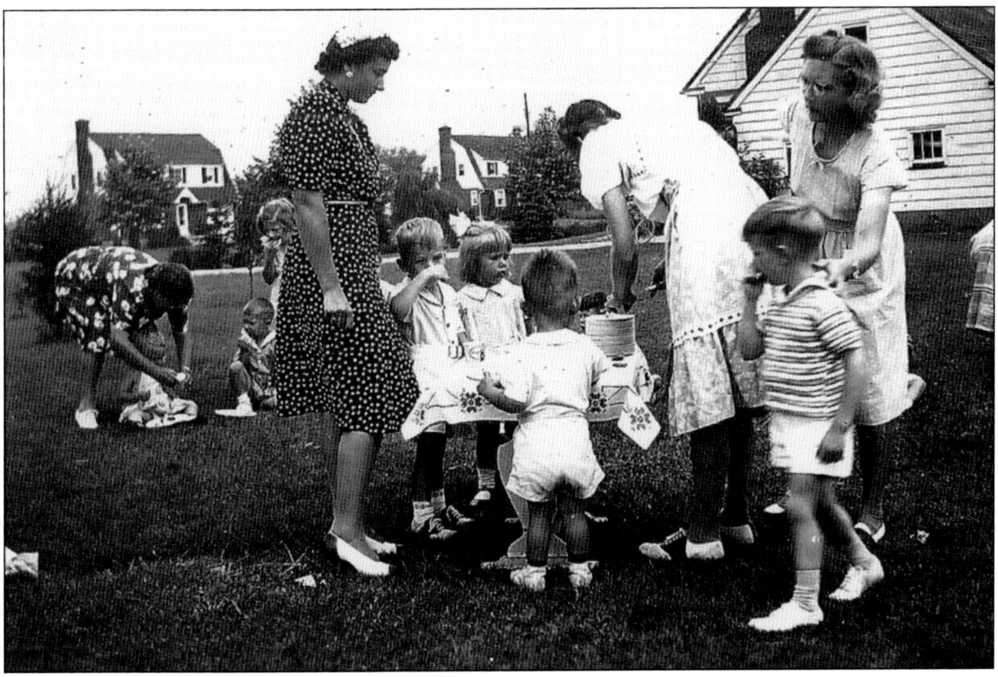

Seen here is a typical Warrington child's birthday celebration on School Lane. These were good times and memorable events in the late 1940s. (Courtesy of Jeanne DeLong and Frank Ace.)

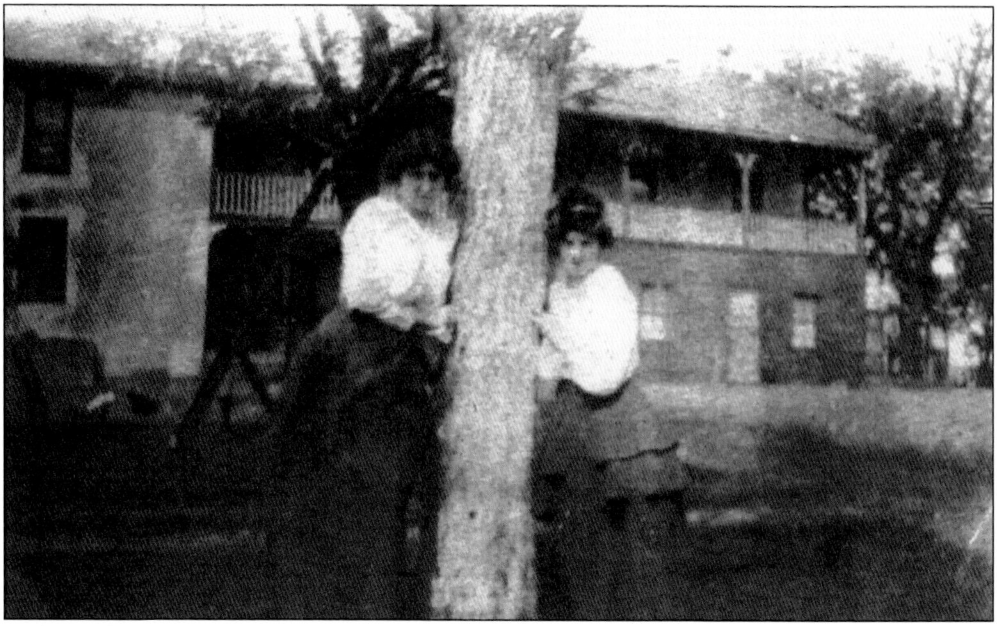

Early residents of Warrington pose for a picture. The Warrington Inn, located at the corner of Bristol and Easton Roads, can be seen in the background before the many additions were added to it. The inn at the time was described as "a substantial, convenient two-story stone hotel, with kitchen attached, with fifteen rooms and double piazza on each front." Since 2006, the inn has been known as Villa Barolo.

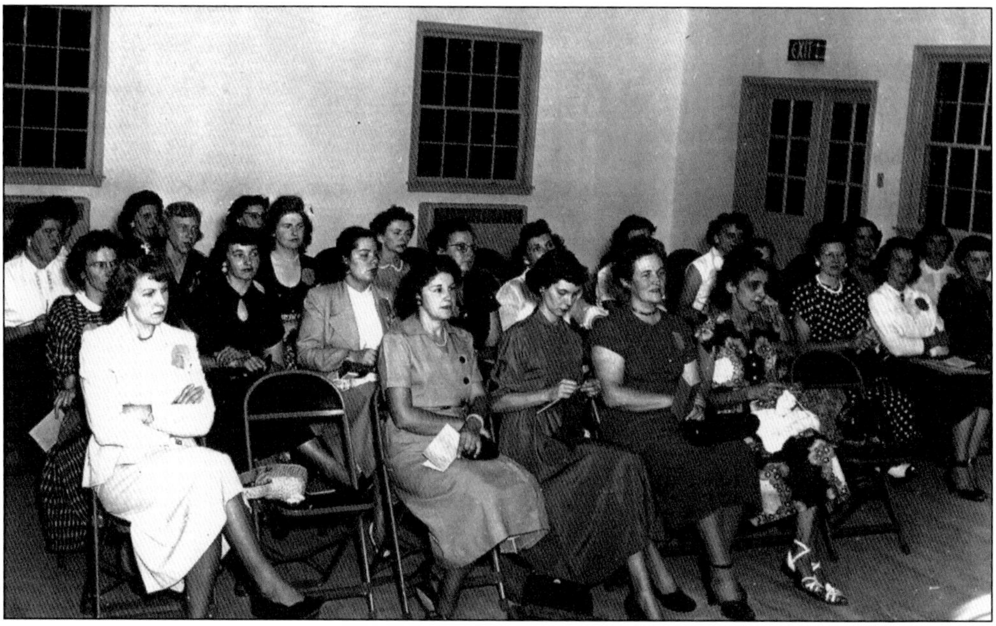

Warrington Junior Woman's Club members gather in the community building in 1951. The club formed in 1934 and disbanded in 1964 after many years of valuable community service. It was a branch of the Warrington Woman's Club, which was formed in 1915 by 13 women who met on the upper floor of the Warrington Schoolhouse. The original name was the Warrington Welfare Association, and annual dues were 50¢.

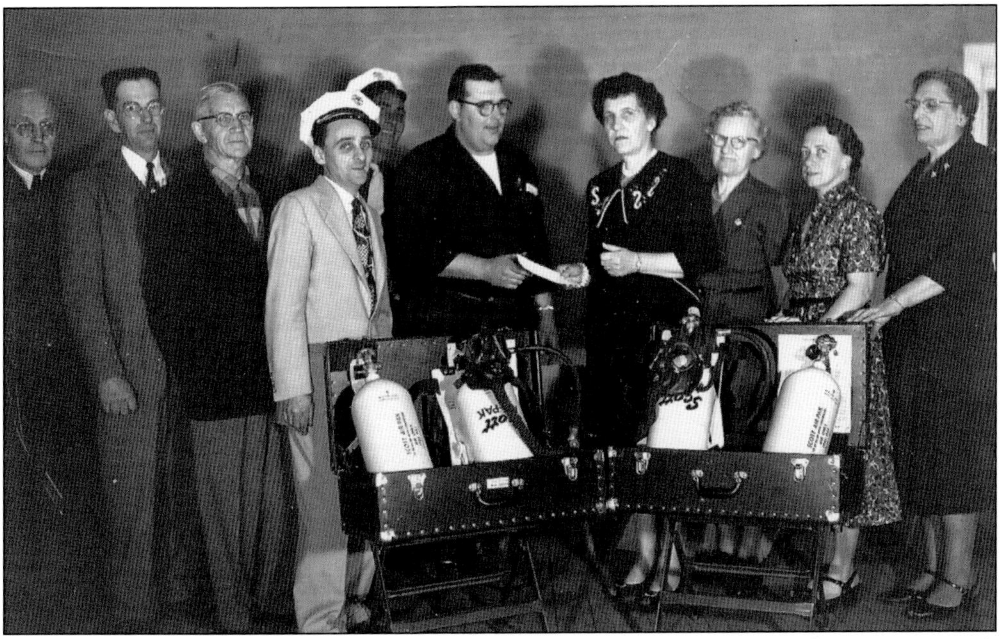

On April 13, 1955, the Ladies Auxiliary (which formed in 1925) presented the firemen with Scott-Packs. Pictured here are, from left to right, David Worthington, Joseph Penrose, Irvin MacNair, Joseph Gallen, Harry Kaslik, James Gilbert, Isabelle Bentley, Lenola Emerson, Bertha Yowell, and Anna Murray. (Courtesy of Betty Feriod.)

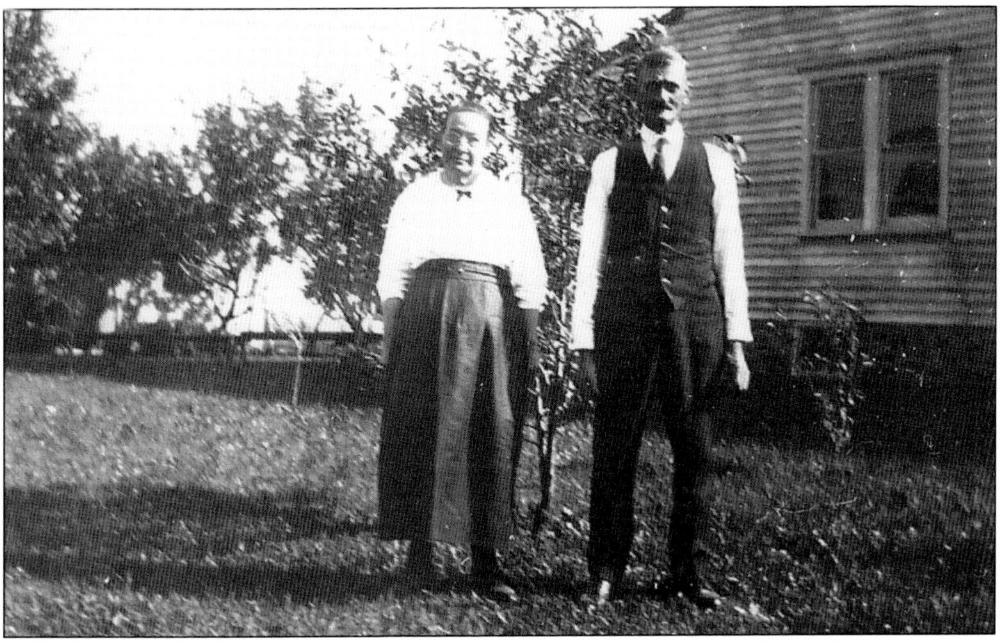

Martha "Maddie" and her husband, Warren Lewis, are seen here in 1913, standing next to the home Warren built on Easton Road. This house was demolished in 2008. Their sons, Elmer and Ellis, raised their families in Warrington. Ellis's son and grandson are still Warrington residents. Maddie was born in a house across Easton Road that was razed for a town house development. (Courtesy of Ronald and Viola Lewis.)

Bibliography

Battle, J. D. *The History of Bucks County*. Philadelphia: A. Warner and Company, 1887.

Capone, Delores Deabler. *From Wilderness to Bustling Community, A History of Warrington Township*. Warrington: Warrington Township, 1976.

———. *Warrington Chronicles: 1784–1984*. Warrington: Warrington Township, 1984.

Davis, William Watts Hart. *The History of Bucks County Pennsylvania.* 2nd ed. Doylestown, Pennsylvania: Lewis Publishing Company, 1905.

Frackenthal, Dr. B. F., Jr. *John Barclay-Biographical.* Riegelsville, Pennsylvania: Bucks County Historical Society, 1938.

Historical Booklet of the Pleasantville Evangelical and Reform Church. Warrington: 1940.

Hopkins, Thomas Cramer. *The Building Materials of Pennsylvania.* Harrisburg, Pennsylvania: C. M. Busch, 1897.

Hough, Mary Paul Hallowell. *Hallowell-Paul Family History 1552–1924*. Philadelphia: H. Ferris, 1924.

MacReynolds, George. *Place Names of Bucks County*. Doylestown, Pennsylvania: Bucks County Historical Society, 1942.

McNair, Frances. *History of Mill Creek School*. Warrington: Warrington Township, 1928.

Pennsylvania common school register for the County Line School, Warrington Township, 1857–1858.

Penrose, Joseph, Sr., Anne Miller, and Bertha Yowell. *Warrington Township Fire Department History 50th Anniversary*. Warrington: Warrington Township, 1974.

Proud, Robert. *Proud's History of Pennsylvania.* Philadelphia: Zachariah Paulson, 1798.

Rezer, Wilma Brown. *The History of 140 Easton Road*. Warrington: 1979.

Turner, Rev. D. K. *The Little Neshaminy*. Hartsville, Pennsylvania: Bucks County Historical Society, June 20, 1897.

Weisel, Samuel. Notebook, 1828–1916. Private collection.

WARRINGTON HISTORICAL SOCIETY

The Warrington Township Historic Commission was established by the board of supervisors on February 24, 1998. Five members were appointed to the commission, which held its first meeting on October 5, 1999. Eventually the commission added two additional appointments, bringing the total number of members to seven. The members of the Warrington Historic Commission formed the Warrington Historical Society in June 2007. It was created to have an independent organization that was tax exempt to help with the solicitation of contributions and grants. The mission of the society is to locate, acquire, preserve, and exhibit any and all articles, documents, photographs, papers, artifacts, and other items of historic, cultural, and educational value that pertain to Warrington Township; to develop educational materials for use with schools/public and promote recognition of the history and development of Warrington Township; and to restore and maintain 10 Folly Road /County Line Road Schoolhouse for use as headquarters/ museum/storage of the society. This book is the initial project of the society and will hopefully be the first of many successful endeavors that help the society reach its goals. Anyone possessing an interest in preserving the history of Warrington Township and supporting the mission of the society may become a member. The society can be contacted at P. O. Box 706, Warrington, Pennsylvania 18976, or by e-mail at WarringtonHistoricalSociety@gmail.com.